Alasdair MacIntyre

The contribution to contemporary philosophy of Alasdair MacIntyre is incontestably enormous. His writings on ethics, political philosophy, the philosophy of religion, the philosophy of the social sciences, and the history of philosophy have established him as one of the philosophical giants of the last fifty years. His best-known book, *After Virtue* (1981), spurred the profound revival of virtue ethics. Moreover, MacIntyre, unlike so many of his contemporaries, has exerted a deep influence beyond the bounds of academic philosophy.

This volume focuses on the major themes of MacIntyre's work, with critical expositions of MacIntyre's views on the history of philosophy, the role of tradition in philosophical inquiry, the philosophy of the social sciences, moral philosophy, political theory, and his critique of the assumptions and institutions of modernity.

Written by a distinguished roster of philosophers, this volume will have an unusually wide appeal outside philosophy to students in the social sciences, law, theology, and political theory.

Mark C. Murphy is Associate Professor of Philosophy at Georgetown University.

Contemporary Philosophy in Focus

Contemporary Philosophy in Focus offers a series of introductory volumes to many of the dominant philosophical thinkers of the current age. Each volume consists of newly commissioned essays that cover major contributions of a preeminent philosopher in a systematic and accessible manner. Comparable in scope and rationale to the highly successful series **Cambridge Companions to Philosophy**, the volumes do not presuppose that readers are already intimately familiar with the details of each philosopher's work. They thus combine exposition and critical analysis in a manner that will appeal to both students of philosophy and professionals as well as students across the humanities and social sciences.

PUBLISHED VOLUMES:

Stanley Cavell edited by Richard Eldridge
Donald Davidson edited by Kirk Ludwig
Daniel Dennett edited by Andrew Brook and Don Ross
Thomas Kuhn edited by Tom Nickles
Robert Nozick edited by David Schmidtz

FORTHCOMING VOLUMES:

Paul Churchland edited by Brian Keeley
Ronald Dworkin edited by Arthur Ripstein
Jerry Fodor edited by Tim Crane
David Lewis edited by Theodore Sides and Dean Zimmermann
Hilary Putnam edited by Yemima Ben-Menahem
Richard Rorty edited by Charles Guignon and David Hiley
John Searle edited by Barry Smith
Charles Taylor edited by Ruth Abbey
Bernard Williams edited by Alan Thomas

Alasdair MacIntyre

Edited by

MARK C. MURPHY
Georgetown University

CAMBRIDGE
UNIVERSITY PRESS

PUBLISHED BY THE PRESS SYNDICATE OF THE UNIVERSITY OF CAMBRIDGE
The Pitt Building, Trumpington Street, Cambridge, United Kingdom

CAMBRIDGE UNIVERSITY PRESS
The Edinburgh Building, Cambridge CB2 2RU, UK
40 West 20th Street, New York, NY 10011-4211, USA
477 Williamstown Road, Port Melbourne, VIC 3207, Australia
Ruiz de Alarcón 13, 28014 Madrid, Spain
Dock House, The Waterfront, Cape Town 8001, South Africa

http://www.cambridge.org

First published 2003

Printed in the United States of America

Typefaces Janson Text Roman 10/13 pt. *and* ITC Officina Sans *System* LaTeX 2ε [TB]

A catalog record for this book is available from the British Library.

Library of Congress Cataloging in Publication data

Alasdair MacIntyre / edited by Mark C. Murphy.
p. cm. – (Contemporary philosophy in focus)
Includes bibliographical references and index.
ISBN 0-521-79042-5 – ISBN 0-521-79381-5 (pbk.)
1. MacIntyre, Alasdair C. I. Murphy, Mark C. II. Series.
B1647.M124 A43 2003
192 – dc21 2002035081

ISBN 0 521 79042 5 hardback
ISBN 0 521 79381 5 paperback

For Jane and Tom Ryan

Contents

	List of Contributors	*page* xi
	Introduction MARK C. MURPHY	1
1	MacIntyre on History and Philosophy GORDON GRAHAM	10
2	Tradition in the Recent Work of Alasdair MacIntyre JEAN PORTER	38
3	MacIntyre in the Province of the Philosophy of the Social Sciences STEPHEN P. TURNER	70
4	Modern(ist) Moral Philosophy and MacIntyrean Critique J. L. A. GARCIA	94
5	MacIntyre and Contemporary Moral Philosophy DAVID SOLOMON	114
6	MacIntyre's Political Philosophy MARK C. MURPHY	152
7	MacIntyre's Critique of Modernity TERRY PINKARD	176
	Bibliography	201
	Index	221

Contributors

J. L. A. GARCIA is Professor of Philosophy at Boston College. His work spans metaethics, normative ethics, and applied ethics, and he also writes on philosophical sociology. Among his papers are "Double Effect," *Encyclopedia of Bioethics*, ed. Warren Reich, second edition (1995); "The New Critique of Anti-Consequentialist Moral Theory," *Philosophical Studies* 71 (1993); "The *Tunsollen*, the *Seinsollen*, and the *Soseinsollen*," *American Philosophical Quarterly* 23 (1986); and "Goods and Evils," *Philosophy and Phenomenological Research* 47 (1987). He is currently at work on *The Heart of Racism*, a book of essays.

GORDON GRAHAM is Regius Professor of Moral Philosophy at the University of Aberdeen, a Fellow of the Royal Society of Edinburgh, and editor of the *Journal of Scottish Philosophy*. He has published extensively in aesthetics, ethics, applied philosophy, and the philosophy of history. His most recent books are *The Shape of the Past: A Philosophical Approach to History* (1997), *Philosophy of the Arts*, second edition (2000), *Evil and Christian Ethics* (Cambridge University Press, 2001), and *Genes: A Philosophical Inquiry* (2002).

MARK C. MURPHY is Associate Professor of Philosophy at Georgetown University. He writes on ethics, political philosophy, the philosophy of law, the philosophy of religion, and the moral and political theory of Thomas Hobbes. He is the author of *Natural Law and Practical Rationality* (Cambridge University Press, 2001) and *An Essay on Divine Authority* (2002).

TERRY PINKARD is Professor of Philosophy at Northwestern University. His research interests cover German philosophy as well as political philosophy and the philosophy of law. He is the author of *Hegel's Phenomenology: The Sociality of Reason* (Cambridge University Press, 1994), *Hegel: A Biography* (Cambridge University Press, 2000), and *German Philosophy 1760–1860: The Legacy of Idealism* (Cambridge University Press, 2002).

JEAN PORTER is John A. O'Brien Professor of Theology at the University of Notre Dame. Working primarily in moral theology, she is the author of numerous articles as well as of *Natural and Divine Law: Reclaiming the Tradition for Christian Ethics* (1999), *Moral Action and Christian Ethics* (Cambridge University Press, 1995), and *The Recovery of Virtue: The Relevance of Aquinas for Christian Ethics* (1990).

DAVID SOLOMON is Associate Professor and H. P. and W. B. White Director of the Center for Ethics and Culture at the University of Notre Dame. His work focuses on normative and applied ethics. Among his papers are "Internal Objections to Virtue Ethics," *Midwest Studies in Philosophy* 13 (1988), and "Moral Realism and the Amoralist," *Midwest Studies in Philosophy* 12 (1987). He is currently working on a book on the revival of virtue ethics in contemporary moral philosophy.

STEPHEN P. TURNER is Graduate Research Professor and Chair of Philosophy at the University of South Florida. He has written extensively on the philosophy of social science and the history of social science, including several books on Max Weber. He edited *The Cambridge Companion to Weber* and recently coedited, with Paul Roth, the *Blackwell Guide to the Philosophy of Social Science*. His most recent books are *Brains/Practices/Relativism: Social Theory after Cognitive Science* (2002) and *Liberal Democracy 3.0: Civil Society in an Age of Expertise* (2002).

Alasdair MacIntyre

Introduction

MARK C. MURPHY

In a 1991 interview, Alasdair MacIntyre summarized the history of his own philosophical work as follows:

> My life as an academic philosopher falls into three parts. The twenty-two years from 1949, when I became a graduate student of philosophy at Manchester University, until 1971 were a period, as it now appears retrospectively, of heterogeneous, badly organized, sometimes fragmented and often frustrating and messy enquiries, from which nonetheless in the end I learned a lot. From 1971, shortly after I emigrated to the United States, until 1977 was an interim period of sometimes painfully self-critical reflection.... From 1977 onwards I have been engaged in a single project to which *After Virtue* [1981], *Whose Justice? Which Rationality?* [1988], and *Three Rival Versions of Moral Enquiry* [1990] are central. (MacIntyre 1991a, pp. 268–269)

The seven chapters that follow deal, for the most part,[1] with aspects of MacIntyre's mature position, the theses that have emerged from the "single project" – I will call this, for shorthand, the "*After Virtue* project" – to which *After Virtue*, *Whose Justice? Which Rationality?*, *Three Rival Versions of Moral Enquiry*, and (since that interview) *Dependent Rational Animals* (1999) have contributed. My aim in this Introduction is to provide, albeit sketchily, some context for the emergence of MacIntyre's mature view. I want to say something, that is, about the pre-1971 inquiries that he labels "fragmented." It is true that MacIntyre's writings during this period are remarkably diverse in the topics treated, in the styles employed, and in the fora in which they appeared. One does not find the singleness of purpose and the coherence of thought that mark his later work. But there is nonetheless a set of concerns and commitments exhibited in these writings that makes intelligible the trajectory of MacIntyre's work to and beyond *After Virtue*.

1. SOCIAL CRITICISM, IDEOLOGY, AND PHILOSOPHY

The direction of MacIntyre's early work is made intelligible by his search for an adequate standpoint from which to engage in large-scale social criticism, his conviction that Marxism was the most promising standpoint on offer, and his view that available formulations of Marxist doctrine were nonetheless ultimately inadequate to this task.

MacIntyre's intellectual work has always been at the service of social criticism. (This is true not only of his early writings, but also of the work belonging to the *After Virtue* project. The notion that the MacIntyre of the *After Virtue* project is some sort of social and political conservative is given the lie by the extent to which his later work emphasizes the ways in which virtue theory and natural law ethics are countercultural and indeed revolutionary: see, e.g., "*Sophrosune*: How a Virtue Can Become Socially Disruptive" [MacIntyre 1988c] and "Natural Law as Subversive: The Case of Aquinas" [1996a]. See also Knight 1996.) The social criticism to which MacIntyre aspired, though, was not a piecemeal affair but rather a systematic inquiry into the defectiveness of modern social, cultural, economic, and political institutions. To engage in such systematic critique requires a standpoint from which to carry out such criticism. MacIntyre shows himself in his early work to be preoccupied with major ideologies – Marxism, psychoanalysis, and Christianity are at the center of his focus – that claim to be able to diagnose the ills of modernity and to point the way to a cure.

"Ideology" is employed by many writers in a merely pejorative fashion. (This is no doubt in part a manifestation of the conviction that we have moved beyond the need for ideology – a conviction which, as MacIntyre has argued, seems all too clearly to be itself an ideology; see MacIntyre 1971b, p. 5.) But ideologies as MacIntyre understood them offer the promise of affording a standpoint for large-scale social criticism. Ideologies, MacIntyre wrote, have three central features. First, they ascribe properties to the world beyond simply those knowable by empirical investigation. Second, they concern both fact and value, offering an account both of the way the world is and how it ought to be; they offer a particular picture of the relationship between these factual and evaluative domains. And third, ideologies make themselves manifest in such a way that they define the social lives of their adherents (MacIntyre 1971a, pp. 5–7).[2] It is true that ideologies can isolate themselves from philosophical and sociological challenge so that they become barren, contentless. But in offering a systematic picture of the world, one that can unite the factual and evaluative realms and can be entrenched in the social lives of its adherents, an adequate ideology is in the vicinity of what one who seeks to engage in wholesale social criticism should be looking for.

The standpoint in terms of which MacIntyre's early work is articulated is a Marxist one. He was at one time a member of the Communist Party (though he left the Party prior to Khruschev's revelations about the moral horrors of the Stalinist regime) and continued to be active in socialist causes (Knight 1998, p. 2). But MacIntyre's commitment to Marxism coexisted with deep uneasiness about its ultimate adequacy. Marxism, MacIntyre wrote, has been refuted a number of times; its staying power can be due only to its capacity to articulate truths that are not articulable in other ideological frameworks (*Marxism and Christianity*, pp. 117–118). What MacIntyre had in mind, I take it, was Marxism's account of the distorting effects on human life and human relationships produced by the economic and political institutions of modern capitalism:

> When man as a worker becomes himself a commodity, he is fundamentally alienated, estranged from himself. Under the form of labour, man sees himself as a commodity, as an object. Hence as labour he objectifies, externalises his own existence. A consequence of this is that life becomes not something which he enjoys as part of his essential humanity. . . .
>
> [T]o be human is to be estranged. But when man is a being divided against himself, able to envision himself as a commodity, he breaks the community of man with man. (*Marxism: An Interpretation*, p. 50)

It is because MacIntyre took Marxism to be fundamentally right on these points that he had an allegiance to that viewpoint. In fact, MacIntyre's allegiance to this view of the destructive character of the institutions of capitalism, including the modern bureaucratic state, has remained entirely unaltered to the present day; it is, MacIntyre has acknowledged, one of the few points on which he has not held different views at different points in his academic career (see MacIntyre 1994b, pp. 35, 44). Still, MacIntyre was unable to ally himself with any of the formulations of Marxist thought available to him: neither Stalinist "scientific socialism" nor the humanist alternatives to Stalinism popular within the British New Left were ultimately sustainable.[3]

The facing of a choice between these understandings of Marxism was not, by any means, an unfamiliar experience for Marxists. Marxists had faced such a stark choice at least since the formulations of scientific Marxism by Karl Kautsky and of revisionist, humanistic Marxism by Eduard Bernstein (see Kautsky 1906 [1914] and Bernstein 1899 [1993]; for a helpful discussion of these views, see Hudelson 1990, pp. 3–28). Scientific Marxism emphasizes the notion of Marxism as social science, as articulating laws of social, political, and economic development and transformation that indicate the inevitable path through capitalism and eventually to socialism. Humanistic Marxism, on the other hand, emphasizes the moral element of Marxism, offering a critical account of the moral failures of capitalist society, of the morally imperative character of socialism, and of the morally appropriate means to transform capitalist modes of life into socialist modes of life. Scientific Marxism, one might say, is the Marxism of 'is'; humanistic Marxism is the Marxism of 'ought'.

MacIntyre's early writings take both of these modes of Marxist theorizing as targets. Understood as an inevitabilist account of the development of social forms, scientific Marxism faces, on MacIntyre's view, two insuperable difficulties. First, to take the content of Marxism to be simply a set of social scientific laws is to make Marxism into no more than a tool for those in power to manipulate social change, an instruction manual for how the masses can be manipulated by those in power. It is precisely this understanding of Marxism that is central to Stalinist socialism, in which the state's role was one of adjusting the levers and pushing the buttons that could ultimately bring about universal socialism. Because that perspective was entirely value-free, there were no ways of adjusting the levers and pushing the buttons that could be morally called into question. If there were no more to Marxism than an account of correlations between historical, social, economic, and political states of affairs, then purges, mass killings, and show trials – if employed as a part of those conditions that ultimately bring about universal socialism – could not be criticized from a Marxist standpoint. Thus one fundamental criticism leveled by MacIntyre against the scientific Marxist standpoint was that it was *morally empty* (MacIntyre 1958, p. 32). The other criticism leveled by MacIntyre against this standpoint was that it was, to put it bluntly, false: there are no social scientific laws available to be discovered that would enable the would-be central planner to adjust the levers to bring about the downfall of capitalism and the rise of socialism. Features of human agency preclude the possibility of adequately formulating any such laws (see *Marxism and Christianity*, pp. 82–86; *After Virtue*, pp. 88–102). Scientific Marxism is not only morally empty, it is *scientifically* empty.

It is not surprising, then, that MacIntyre would express admiration for those Marxists who rejected Stalinist socialism on moral grounds. One might also expect MacIntyre to side with the humanistic Marxists; indeed, one recent chronicler of the development of MacIntyre's views has asserted that MacIntyre is clearly in this camp (McMylor 1994, p. 12). But while it is true that MacIntyre's commitment to Marxism came on account of its capacity to bring into the open the deformities in social relations prevalent in capitalist societies, even early on MacIntyre expressed little confidence that a standpoint could be found from which Stalinist horrors could be criticized and the moral content of Marxism vindicated. Bernstein, writing at the end of the nineteenth century, shows no signs of worry concerning the vindication of the moral content of Marxism; perhaps this is because of his confidence in a generally Kantian philosophical view that persons are never to be treated as mere means but always as ends-in-themselves. MacIntyre, writing in the mid-twentieth century, has no such confidence.

It is not at all surprising that MacIntyre would lack confidence on this score. In the 1950's, the dominant theoretical viewpoints in Anglo-American moral philosophy were versions of emotivism and prescriptivism, according to which moral judgment consists simply in (respectively) expression of emotion (e.g., "rigged trials are wrong" means something like "rigged trials – boo!") or articulation of preference (e.g., "rigged trials are wrong" means something like "let rigged trials not take place"). What MacIntyre cannot see is how, given these understandings of moral judgment, we are to account for the *authority* purported in moral approval and condemnation. When the humanist Marxist condemns the techniques of Stalinist socialism, what is the authority wielded in that condemnation? If all that is going on in such criticism is the critic's reaffirmation of his or her disapproval of the Stalinist's techniques, why on earth should anyone listen to him or her? (*Marxism and Christianity*, pp. 124–127; see also *After Virtue*, p. 68.) The moral critic of Stalinism, wrote MacIntyre, is "often a figure of genuine pathos" (MacIntyre 1958, p. 31). MacIntyre in his early work is just such a figure.

2. IS THERE A PATH OUT OF THE "MORAL WILDERNESS"?

MacIntyre confronted the Stalinist and the Stalinist's moral critic, the humanist, in a two-part essay written for the *New Reasoner*[4] in 1958 entitled "Notes from the Moral Wilderness." In it he diagnoses the difficulties in the humanist's position as rooted in the humanist's acceptance of the autonomy of moral principle, that is, that the province of the moral stands independently of and in contrast to the province of natural, social, and historical facts. By cutting the domain of moral judgment off from the domains of history, sociology, economics, and anthropology, the moral critic of Stalinism cuts him- or herself off from any argumentative route to his or her moral conclusions (see also *Marxism and Christianity*, p. 124). All that remains is arbitrary choice – I approve of these values, I prefer this way of life to that one. But this isolation renders moral criticism ineffective and moral evaluation unintelligible. Such an understanding of morality allows the Stalinist to play the choice game as well: "If [the moral critic of Stalinism] chooses his values in the spirit of *Hier steh' ich, ich kann nicht anders*, is it not equally open to [the Stalinist] to do the same?" (MacIntyre 1958, p. 35) Morality thus cut off from other realms of judgment and inquiry becomes "like primitive taboos, imperatives which we just happen to utter. It is to turn 'ought' into a kind of nervous cough with which we accompany what we hope will be the more impressive of our pronouncements" (MacIntyre 1959b, p. 42).[5]

Both the scientific socialist and the humanist, in their own ways, sever the connection between the factual and the evaluative, and thus preclude the possibility of social criticism from an authoritative moral standpoint. The scientific socialist does so by treating the realm of moral judgment as illusory or merely epiphenomenal; the humanist does so by stripping it of its authority. What is needed is a middle way – a way to connect morality tightly enough to history, sociology, psychology, and other domains to preclude it from being a matter of mere preference or choice, but not so tightly that *what ought to be* becomes simply *what is guaranteed to be*. MacIntyre suggests that this middle way can be achieved by connecting ethics with what we might call *authentic* human desire, desire that is not warped or distorted (MacIntyre 1959b, pp. 46–47). Thus morality is grounded in the 'is' of desire, but is not subsumed by it, for he allows that it is authentic desire, not desire that is deformed, that is the standard for moral judgment. The trick is to explain what the Marxist critique of capitalist society presupposes: that we can explain in a non-question-begging way why it is that certain forms of social life distort desire, and precisely how they do so. What is needed, MacIntyre writes, is a "concept of human nature, a concept which has to be the centre of any discussion of moral theory" (MacIntyre 1959b, p. 45). In providing such an account, we will have to be mindful of the extent to which human nature is historically conditioned, and we will have to be mindful that the ethics that we endorse can be institutionalized. As MacIntyre reminds us from his very early work onward, there is no morality for rational beings as such; there is only morality for human beings, as practiced at some time, in some social setting.

Any adequate ethic, then, would have to be historically situated. But MacIntyre realized – in part as a result of an early attempt to write an adequate history of ethics, his 1966 *A Short History of Ethics* (MacIntyre

1991d, p. 260) – that to make the historical condition of human beings a part of the substance of an ethical view is inadequate. It would be, to say the least, paradoxical to hold that the norms of conduct, the virtues and rules that govern the life of a good person, are historically conditioned and exist only as concretely realized in social life, but also to hold that the criteria of rational justification by which we show that this is the correct view of morality are entirely ahistorical and exist apart from the practices of any community of inquiry. History, if it is to enter ethics at the level of substantive moral theory, must also enter at the metalevel, the level at which substantive theories of morality are justified. Such appeals to history characteristically bring with them worries that such a view will fall into a soggy relativism. It would hardly be a victory for MacIntyre's alternative route in moral theory if that route were justified only according to a theory of rational inquiry that is itself not superior to any of the various theories of rational inquiry that might reject that route.

The path out of the moral wilderness is the formulation of an ethics of human nature – where human nature is not merely a biological nature but also an historical and social nature – and the formulation of an historical, but not relativistic, account of rationality in inquiry. Only accounts such as these would make possible authoritative political and social criticism. The vindication of such a substantive moral outlook, and of a theory of rationality in inquiry that would sustain that outlook, are the central tasks of the *After Virtue* project.[6]

3. THE *AFTER VIRTUE* PROJECT

The conclusions tentatively reached by MacIntyre in his early writings concern both what the substance of an adequate morality would be like and what a conception of rationality needed to show the superiority of this substantial morality would have to be like. The chapters in this volume explain how these tentative conclusions reached in MacIntyre's early work have been developed and connected to each other in MacIntyre's mature position. Gordon Graham ("MacIntyre on History and Philosophy") considers MacIntyre's views on the relationship between history and philosophy, views that culminate in MacIntyre's notion of a tradition of inquiry. Jean Porter ("Tradition in the Recent Work of Alasdair MacIntyre") takes up this notion of tradition in greater detail, analyzing its development over the various works that constitute the *After Virtue* project. Stephen Turner writes on MacIntyre's contributions to the philosophy of social science

("MacIntyre in the Province of the Philosophy of the Social Sciences"), contributions that inform (and are informed by) MacIntyre's views on rationality, morality, and politics. J. L. A. Garcia and David Solomon present a picture of the negative and positive (respectively) sides of MacIntyre's substantive moral theory: Garcia's chapter ("Modern(ist) Moral Philosophy and MacIntyrean Critique") lays out MacIntyre's criticisms of modern moral philosophy, while Solomon's ("MacIntyre and Contemporary Moral Philosophy") shows how that critique developed into MacIntyre's own distinctive version of Aristotelian ethics. I ("MacIntyre's Political Philosophy") discuss MacIntyre's views on political philosophy, focusing on MacIntyre's preoccupation with the modern state. Terry Pinkard ("MacIntyre's Critique of Modernity") concludes the collection by considering MacIntyre's criticisms of the assumptions and institutions of modernity, trying to make clear the ways in which MacIntyre is, and is not, himself a modern. A selected bibliography of MacIntyre's books and most important papers follows.

Notes

1. The exception is Chapter 3, which deals with MacIntyre's views on the philosophy of social science. While MacIntyre has continued to write in this area, his main positions were developed along the way to, and play a central role in, *After Virtue*.
2. It seems to me that the notion of "tradition," which plays such a central role in the *After Virtue* project (see Chapter 2), is a recognizable successor concept to "ideology."
3. For a discussion of the extent to which the British New Left had its origins in Khruschev's revelations concerning the horrors of the Stalin regime, see Chun 1993, pp. 1–4.
4. The *New Reasoner* was an independent journal of socialist thought, founded by E. P. Thompson – an ex-Communist party member – in order to provide a forum in which more adequate debate and criticism of socialist principles and policy could take place. It was published from 1957 to 1959, at which point it merged with another journal, *Universities and Left Review*, to form the *New Left Review*.
5. The comparison of the institutions of morality to the institutions of taboo is a theme to which MacIntyre has returned over and over again in his career: see, for examples, the 1981 *After Virtue*, pp. 110–113, and the 1990 *Three Rival Versions*, pp. 182–186.
6. It is worth reemphasizing that in carrying this inquiry forward, MacIntyre did not take himself to be introducing elements into Marxism that were entirely foreign to it, but rather to be working through the problematic internal to Marxism. In criticizing contemporary Marxist philosophy on account of its intellectual stagnation,

MacIntyre lays out what he takes to be the central tasks facing philosophers who have allegiance to a Marxist viewpoint:

> Marx was intimately concerned with two problems that necessarily arise for everyone who engages seriously in philosophy. He was concerned with the perspective of ultimate belief, with the problems which engage the philosophy of religion; and he was concerned with the question of how the philosopher should relate himself to his philosophy and the sense in which philosophy can or cannot affect one's ultimate views and commitments. (MacIntyre 1956, p. 370)

While the bulk of MacIntyre's work early in his career is concerned with rival ideologies, and in particular their relevance for social criticism, he also did a fair bit of work squarely in the philosophy of religion: he co-edited (with Antony Flew) *New Essays in Philosophical Theology* and wrote papers on immortality (1955c), visions (1955d), the logical status of religious belief (1957b), atheism (*Atheism*, pp. 1–55), and other topics in the philosophy of religion. This book does not contain a chapter on MacIntyre's philosophical theology because it has not been a focus of much of his work during the *After Virtue* project. (But see 1986c and 1994a.)

1 MacIntyre on History and Philosophy

GORDON GRAHAM

In *An Autobiography*, R. G. Collingwood writes:

> The Oxford philosophical tradition insisted upon a fine training in philosophical scholarship. Under the reign of 'realism' this tradition certainly survived but it weakened year by year. When I myself examined in the middle 1920's I found that very few candidates showed any first hand knowledge of any authors about whom they wrote.... This decline in philosophical history was openly encouraged by the 'realists'; it was one of their most respected leaders who, expressly on the ground that the 'history' of philosophy was a subject without philosophical interest, procured the abolition of the paper so entitled in the school of Philosophy, Politics and Economics.
>
> During the war ... I set myself to reconsider this 'realist' attitude towards the history of philosophy. Was it really true, I asked myself, that the problems of philosophy were, even in the loosest sense of that word, eternal? Was it really true that different philosophies were different attempts to answer the same questions? I soon discovered that it was not true; it was merely a vulgar error, consequent on a kind of historical myopia which, deceived by superficial resemblances, failed to detect profound differences. (Collingwood 1938, pp. 60–61)

For Collingwood to convince those locked in this historical myopia otherwise, however, was not an easy matter, because of the readiness with which they argued in a circle.

> It was like having a nightmare about a man who got it into his head that trireme was the Greek for 'steamer', and when it was pointed out to him that descriptions of triremes in Greek writers were at any rate not very good descriptions of steamers, replied triumphantly, 'That is just what I say. These Greek philosophers (or, 'these modern philosophers', according to which side he was on in the good old controversy between the Ancients and the Moderns) 'were terribly muddle-headed, and their theory of steamers is all wrong'. (Collingwood 1938, p. 64)

Almost exactly the same charge that Collingwood here levels against the Oxford realists of the 1920s and 1930s was repeated forty years later by Alasdair MacIntyre, and also against Oxford philosophy, this time in its linguistic rather than its realist incarnation. The opening of MacIntyre's *A Short History of Ethics* (1966) is strikingly similar in sentiment to Collingwood.

> Moral philosophy is often written as though the history of the subject were only of secondary and incidental importance. This attitude seems to be the outcome of a belief that moral concepts can be examined and understood apart from their history. Some philosophers have even written as if moral concepts were a timeless, limited, unchanging, determinate species of concept, necessarily having the same features throughout their history, so that there is a part of language waiting to be philosophically investigated which deserves the title "the language of morals" (with a definite article and a singular noun). . . . In fact, of course, moral concepts change . . . and it would be a fatal mistake to write as if, in the history of moral philosophy, there had been one single task of analyzing the concept of, for example, justice, to the performance of which Plato, Hobbes, and Bentham all set themselves. (*Short History*, pp. 1–2)

MacIntyre himself notes (in *After Virtue*) that the relation between history and philosophy informed his approach to the subject from the start.

> A central theme of much of [my] earlier work (*Secularization and Moral Change*, 1967; *Against the Self-Images of the Age*, 1971) was that we have to learn from history and anthropology of the variety of moral practices, beliefs and conceptual schemes. The notion that the moral philosopher can study the concepts of morality merely by reflecting, Oxford armchair style, on what he or she and those around him or her say or do is barren. (*After Virtue*, p. ix)

Omitted from the first of these quotations is an intervening passage of equal importance:

> In fact moral concepts change as social life changes. I deliberately do not write "because social life changes" for this might suggest that social life is one thing, morality another, and that there is merely an external, contingent causal relation between them. This is obviously false. Moral concepts are embodied in and are partially constitutive of forms of social life. (*Short History*, p. 1)

No less important, for my purposes, is a subsequent remark:

> The complexity [of the relationship between social life and moral concepts] is increased because philosophical inquiry itself plays a part in changing moral concepts. It is not that we have a straightforward history of moral concepts and then a separate and secondary history of philosophical comment. For to analyze a concept philosophically may often be to assist in its transformation. . . . The moral concepts which are available for analysis to the philosophers of one age may sometimes be what they are partly because of the discussions by philosophers of a previous age. [Moreover,] A history which takes this point seriously, which is concerned with the role of philosophy in relation to actual conduct, cannot be philosophically neutral. (*Short History*, pp. 2–3)

These quotations make plain that, as one commentator remarks, "[o]vercoming the double barrenness of detached philosophy and mindless history has been an . . . aim promoted by MacIntyre throughout his career" (Wokler 1994, p. 168). Yet, as it seems to me, it is not altogether clear how the historical and the philosophical are interconnected. There are at least three important, and importantly different, contentions about the relation between history and philosophy embedded in these remarks. The first is that moral philosophy cannot ignore the course of social history if it is to pursue its own ends satisfactorily. The second is that philosophical inquiry and the exploration of ideas can affect the way social history goes. And the third, a rather deeper contention to my mind, is that the adequacy of philosophical thought is itself a product of history.

There is no doubt that together these three contentions provide both the foundation and the distinguishing mark of a philosophical program pursued with remarkable consistency over four decades or more. The question is how, and whether, they can be made to cohere. In this essay I propose to explore each of these three contentions as they are elaborated by MacIntyre in his major works, concluding with a brief discussion of the new turn his thought has taken in his most recent book, *Dependent Rational Animals*.

At the outset, though, it is important to add two caveats. First, such a relatively simple scheme of analysis is unlikely to do full justice to the rich complexity of his thought and writing; second, my concern is not to pass judgment on the success or failure of MacIntyre's whole project, but merely to examine the conceptual relations between the historical and the philosophical that it may be taken to imply.

An important illustration of the first of these contentions – that moral philosophy cannot ignore the course of social history if it is to pursue its own ends satisfactorily – is to be found in the "disquieting suggestion" with which *After Virtue* opens. The second – that philosophical inquiry and the exploration of ideas can affect the trajectory of social history – makes one of its most striking appearances in MacIntyre's account, in *Whose Justice? Which Rationality?*, of the place of philosophy in the social order of eighteenth century Scotland. And the third – that the adequacy of philosophical thought is itself a product of history – comes to prominence, as one might expect, in exploring the relative merits of *Three Rival Versions of Moral Enquiry*, and in the defense of the concept of an intellectual tradition that is to be found there.

1. SOCIAL HISTORY AND THE LANGUAGE OF MORALS

After Virtue famously begins with an analogy:

> Imagine that the natural sciences were to suffer the effects of a catastrophe. A series of environmental disasters are blamed by the general public on the scientists. Widespread riots occur, laboratories are burnt down, physicists are lynched, books and instruments are destroyed. Finally a Know-Nothing political movement takes power and successfully abolishes science teaching in schools and universities, imprisoning and executing the remaining scientists. Later still there is a reaction against this destructive movement and enlightened people seek to revive science, although they have largely forgotten what it was. But all that they possess are fragments: a knowledge of the experiments detached from any knowledge of the theoretical context which gave them significance. . . . None the less all these fragments are re-embodied in a set of practices which go under the revived names of physics, chemistry and biology. Adults argue with each other about the respective merits of relativity theory and phlogiston theory, although they possess only a very partial knowledge of each. Children learn by heart the surviving portions of the periodic table and recite as incantations some of the theorems of Euclid. Nobody, or almost nobody, realizes that what they are doing is not natural science in any proper sense at all. For everything that they do and say conforms to certain canons of consistency and coherence and those contexts which would be needed to make sense of what they are doing have been lost, perhaps irretrievably.
>
> In such a culture men would use expressions such as 'neutrino', 'mass', 'specific gravity', 'atomic weight' in systematic and often interrelated ways which would resemble in lesser or greater degrees the ways in which such expressions had been used in earlier times before scientific knowledge had

> been so largely lost. But many of the beliefs presupposed by the use of these expressions would have been lost and there would appear to be an element of arbitrariness and even of choice in their application which would appear very surprising to us.... Subjectivist theories of science would abound and would be criticized by those who held that the notion of truth embodied in what they took to be science was incompatible with subjectivism.
>
> This imaginary world [w]e may describe ... as a world in which the language of natural science ... continues to be used but is in a grave state of disorder. We may notice that if in this imaginary world analytical philosophy were to flourish, it would never reveal the fact of this disorder. For the techniques of analytical philosophy are essentially descriptive of the language of the present....
>
> Nor again would phenomenology or existentialism be able to discern anything wrong.... A Husserl or a Merleau-Ponty would be as deceived as a Strawson or a Quine.
>
> What is the point of constructing this imaginary world inhabited by fictitious pseudo-scientists and real, genuine philosophy? The hypothesis I wish to advance is that in the actual world which we inhabit the language of morality is in the same state of grave disorder.... What we possess, if this view is true, are the fragments of a conceptual scheme.... We possess indeed the simulacra of morality, we continue to use many of the key expressions. But we have – very largely, if not entirely – lost our comprehension, both theoretical and practical, of morality. (*After Virtue*, pp. 1–2)

Science, of course, is not in this condition; there has been no catastrophe of this sort in its history. But morality is. What we think of as 'morality' today is no more than the dislocated remains of a once coherent and socially embedded set of practices. According to MacIntyre, the resulting character rather than the originating cause of this moral fragmentation is moral individualism – the ascription of complete moral autonomy to the mind and/or conscience of the individual, and the relegation of the properly political to the social coordination of felt desires (what economists call "preferences") and the conflicting opinions of self-contained individuals.

So deep is its impoverishment that liberal individualism goes as far as to make a positive virtue out of this conception of moral and political life. In other words, it represents individual autonomy and the politics of public choice as the consummation of humankind's search for freedom and enlightenment. But in fact, or so MacIntyre contends, the reality is that such autonomy amounts to a moral vacuum, a condition in which the legislative sovereignty of individual moral agents means that the crucial distinction between "good" and "believed to be good" disappears. In this way modern "morality" is deprived of any rational foundation, as knowledge would be if there were no distinction between "true" and "believed to be true." In short, there is nothing upon which our beliefs about "the good" can be based. The whole system of ideas rests upon a radical distinction between "fact" and "value" whose implication is that, in contrast to the realm of real "facts" and rational "means," there is nothing to temper the wildest flights of the moral imagination. Indeed, precisely because this is so, the "democratized self has no necessary social content and no necessary social identity, [and] can then be anything, can assume any role or take any point of view, because it *is* in and for itself nothing" (*After Virtue*, p. 32).

However, and more important yet for present purposes, despite its vacuity modern "morality" is not without its articulation, its accompanying philosophy. One version of this is to be found in the existentialism of Sartre, another in the sociology of Erving Goffman. But both are, upon analysis, essentially varieties of emotivism. It is in the widespread contemporary subscription to emotivism – "the doctrine that all evaluative judgments are nothing but expressions of preferences, expressions of attitude or feeling, insofar as they are moral or evaluative in character" (*After Virtue*, pp. 11–12) – that we find the distillation of our modern malaise. According to emotivism the function of moral terms is not to *describe* the things and people they are employed to evaluate, but rather to express and evince the subjective feelings of approval and disapproval that are prompted by those things. On this account moral judgments are criterionless; any one is as good (or as bad) as any other. But if so, then the much vaunted moral freedom of the individual is not so much freedom as emptiness; in the language of John Locke, license has replaced liberty. Since we can assert and affirm what we will, there is no point in asserting this rather than that, and hence no point in asserting anything at all.

One further feature of emotivism must be recorded before its peculiar, and defective, character is properly understood.

> A moral philosophy – and emotivism is no exception – characteristically presupposes a sociology. For every moral philosophy offers explicitly or implicitly at least a partial conceptual analysis of the relationship of an agent to his or her reasons, motives, intentions and actions, and in so doing generally presupposes some claim that these concepts are embodied or at least can be in the real social world. . . . Thus it would generally be a decisive refutation of a moral philosophy to show that moral agency on its own account of the matter could never be socially embodied; and it also follows that we have not yet fully understood the claims of any moral philosophy

> until we have spelled out what its social embodiment would be. . . . [B]ut at least since Moore the dominant narrow conception of moral philosophy has ensured that the moral philosophers could ignore this task; as notably do the philosophical proponents of emotivism. (*After Virtue*, p. 23)

In brief, modern morality is a fragmentary residue of the moral world that preceded it, and if it appears to accord with, even be endorsed by, philosophical emotivism, this is only because emotivism has singularly failed to seek, let alone engage with, the historical-cum-sociological understanding that any adequate moral philosophy requires.

This is, I think, a reasonably accurate account of the picture MacIntyre paints in the first three chapters of *After Virtue*. Yet, as I shall suggest, it is one not wholly in accord with what follows in the remainder of the book. Understanding the element of dissonance, in fact, gives us an important insight into the real relation that MacIntyre sees between history and philosophy, and reveals the internal dialectic that continues to work itself out in subsequent volumes.

Let us return to the analogy with science. The imaginary hypothesis is that at some point in the past a social and political catastrophe befell the activity of science, such that those who later attempted to recover the elements of scientific understanding were destined to fail, and at the same time were unable to know of their failure. The new generation of would-be scientists is in "a world in which the language of natural science . . . continues to be used but is in a grave state of disorder." Furthermore, "if in this imaginary world analytical philosophy were to flourish, it would never reveal the fact of this disorder. For the techniques of analytical philosophy are essentially descriptive of the language of the present."

This imaginary story of the state of science is unquestionably compelling, but it is not altogether easy to see how the analogy is to be applied to contemporary morality. Nor is it easy to see quite how it fits with what MacIntyre says about emotivism. To begin with we may reasonably ask: What are the moral equivalents of widespread riots, factories being burned down, books destroyed, physicists lynched? What is the counterpart to the Know-Nothing political movement? And when did all this happen? And where?

If MacIntyre is right, the present state of morality and the present state of moral philosophy can only be understood by an appeal to history. He has much more to say about this history, a topic to be returned to shortly. But in subsequent pages he records no social and political episodes of the type that mark his imaginary history of science and that have hitherto gone unnoticed. Of course, it is only an analogy, but the observation of this dissimilarity, as it seems to me, is not altogether idle. Are we to suppose that there has been a moral catastrophe of equally striking proportions, or not? And if there has been, by what events has it been marked? However, for present purposes the importance of making this observation lies rather in its highlighting of this fact: MacIntyre's general conception is one in which historical investigation uncovers philosophical inadequacy; the scientific analogy for its part suggests that the history in question is, so to speak, a *material* one, one of riots, lynchings, political movements and so on. Indeed, on the strength of this analogy, it would not be wholly mistaken, but indeed quite understandable, to construe MacIntyre's account of emotivism and (following the last quotation) analytical philosophy more broadly as something like the Marxist account of ideology: Such philosophy reflects and confirms the self-images of the age, but cannot reveal their deficiencies, however critical its own self-image may be.

> The derivation of political, juridical and ideological notions . . . is a process accomplished by the so-called thinker consciously indeed, but with a false consciousness. The real motive forces impelling him remain unknown to him, otherwise it simply would not be an ideological process. (Marx and Engels 1968, p. 690)

So writes Marx's collaborator Friedrich Engels, and underlying his account of ideology is an unquestionably materialist conception of history. *The Communist Manifesto* (authored by both Marx and Engels), commenting on the idea that the intellectual activities of the *philosophes* were an important contributory factor in the French revolution of 1789, says:

> German philosophers, would-be philosophers, and *beaux esprit*, eagerly seized on this literature, only forgetting that when these writings immigrated from France into Germany, French social conditions had not immigrated along with them. In contact with German social conditions, this French literature lost all its immediate practical significance, and assumed a purely literary aspect. (Marx and Engels 1968, p. 56)

An alternative to this materialist explanation is to be found in the idealist one, which explains social and political conditions, their rise and fall, success and failure, in terms of the ideas that they embody. One exponent of such a contention is Michael Oakeshott, a philosopher who shares many of Collingwood's sympathies and is generally regarded as perhaps the last of the British Idealists. Oakeshott, in sharp contrast to Marx and Engels' materialism, explains our contemporary moral and political culture as the outcome of an erroneous, and hence destructive, philosophy, a philosophy he calls rationalism.

> Moral ideals are a sediment; they have the significance they do only so long as they are suspended in a religious or social tradition, so long as they belong to a religious or social life. The predicament of our time is that the Rationalists have been at work so long on their project of drawing off the liquid in which our moral ideals were suspended (and pouring it away as worthless) that we are left only with the dry and gritty residue which chokes us as we try to take it down. (Oakeshott 1962, p. 36)

The first of these sentences expresses a view strikingly like MacIntyre's, but the explanation of our "predicament" that follows clearly lays the blame at the feet of a philosophy, the philosophy of rationalism. So too we might think MacIntyre's thesis idealist. In support of this interpretation it can be noted, first, that several remarks in *After Virtue* seem to suggest that it is the widespread *belief in* emotivism which has generated much of the difficulty. This is because the "characters" that populate our modern drama, and which together make up the social possibilities around which our lives are structured, are the moral representatives of our culture. More than that, they are said to be the social embodiment of "moral and metaphysical ideas and theories" (*After Virtue*, p. 28), of which emotivism is chief. Secondly, what follows the "disquieting suggestion" and the analysis of emotivism is not material history so much as the history of ideas, and the history of philosophy in particular.

How can this be? Why is it *not*, as the analogy would suggest, a history of riots and lynchings? In large part the answer is that the materialist/idealist distinction is just the sort of dichotomy that MacIntyre aims to overcome with his fusion of history and philosophy. Chapter 4 of *After Virtue* begins: "What I am going to suggest is that the key episodes in the social history which transformed, fragmented and, if my extreme view is correct, largely displaced morality ... were episodes in the history of philosophy" (*After Virtue*, p. 37).

Immediately a question arises: are we to suppose that *philosophy* has determined the course of social history? MacIntyre is alive to, and addresses, the problem at once. Chapter 4 continues:

> [H]ow can this be so? In our own culture academic philosophy is a highly marginalized and specialized activity.... Professors of philosophy ... would find it surprising, and the larger public even more surprising, if it were suggested, as I am now suggesting, that the roots of some of the problems

> which now engage the specialized attention of academic philosophers and the roots of some of the problems central to our everyday social and practical lives are one and the same. . . . Yet this might become less implausible if the thesis were cast in historical form. For the claim is that both our general culture and our academic philosophy are in central part the offspring of a culture in which philosophy did constitute a central form of social activity. (*After Virtue*, p. 37)

The need to show this is evident, to my mind. Anyone who wishes to establish that the history of philosophy is also a history of social events must give an account of how the two are interconnected, and the most obvious way of doing so is to show that the activity of philosophizing has at some point had the sort of social significance that politics and commerce are thought to have in the contemporary world. Can this be done? This brings us to the second of the three contentions I identified at the start, that philosophical inquiry and the exploration of ideas can affect the way social history goes. In the subsequent chapters of *After Virtue* we are given accounts of a broad sweep of societies from ancient Athens, through medieval Christendom, to Enlightenment Europe. But the most focused example of a society formed and driven by philosophy – namely eighteenth-century Scotland – is to be found in the next book in MacIntyre's trilogy. It is to this "test case" that I now turn.

2. PHILOSOPHICAL INQUIRY AND SOCIAL ORDER

Was philosophy as an activity ever as important within Western European culture as MacIntyre claims and as his interrelation of history and philosophy requires? If it was, how widespread was this phenomenon? Despite their evident importance for his thesis, I shall eschew these more general questions and ask only whether he makes out the case with respect to just one context and example.

This example, of course, is Scotland in the eighteenth century, the period of the Scottish Enlightenment. Robert Wokler has criticized MacIntyre for ignoring almost completely what appears to be a far more obvious example than Scotland, namely the influence on public affairs exercised by the French *philosophes*. "How is it possible," he asks, "that Voltaire – the godfather of the Enlightenment Project on any plausible interpretation of its meaning – is altogether missing from MacIntyre's cast?" (Wokler 1994, p. 116). This rhetorical question can be answered, however. For MacIntyre's story to work, it is essential not merely that philosophical ideas be in the social air, so to speak, but also that, in some way or other, philosophical thought and reflection be institutionalized. On this point too, Wokler is critical:

> MacIntyre appears to subscribe to the view that only holders of public positions, with socially rooted responsibilities, can exercise any real impact on their followers. But this is surely absurd. To the extent that the Enlightenment was a critically subversive movement, as MacIntyre portrays it, its estrangement from the settled institutions of its day, in France and elsewhere, enhanced its power. By deliberately excluding a French focus from his study, MacIntyre offers his readers an account of peripheries without a core. His Enlightenment Project has been shorn of its projectionism. (Wokler 1994, p. 117)

I shall not explore this objection further, partly because I lack the historical expertise necessary to do so. Suffice it to say, whatever the truth of Wokler's contention about philosophy as a socially subversive force, it is evidently important for MacIntyre's thesis that there be at least some contexts in which philosophy and philosophers enjoyed an established social role of a certain sort. And it is arguable that with respect to the role of philosophy within its social institutions, Scotland was striking among the European nations. An impressive case can be made for asserting that in the time of Francis Hutcheson, David Hume, Adam Smith, and Thomas Reid – in short the period of the Enlightenment – philosophical inquiry and education played a distinctive and highly influential part in the cultural life of Scotland. The evidence for this case, evidence by which others besides MacIntyre have been impressed, is worth rehearsing briefly.

In the eighteenth century Scotland had five universities (in contrast to England's two), one each in Glasgow, Edinburgh, and St. Andrews, and two in Aberdeen. All of these followed a common curriculum, thus giving the country a standard 'university system' that was relatively rare elsewhere. Broadly, this common curriculum preserved the old medieval course structure, once common to Europe, in accordance with which the universities were divided into a "lower" Faculty of Arts and "higher" Faculties of Divinity, Law, and Medicine. All students first took a four-year course in the Faculty of Arts comprising the seven traditional subjects, including courses in logic and in moral philosophy. After completing the arts course, some then proceeded to a training in law, medicine, or divinity.

In reality the picture was not homogenous. The arts curriculum seems to have been fairly uniform, but medical education in Aberdeen and

St. Andrews, in contrast to Edinburgh for example, was erratic. While Edinburgh led the world in anatomy, such that students flocked to it from across Europe, elsewhere in Scotland medical degrees could simply be purchased. The French revolutionary Marat, for example, who had never been to Scotland, possessed a degree in medicine from St. Andrews, and the English public was regularly warned to be on its guard against the medical graduates of Aberdeen, where, it is relevant to note, one Regius Professor of Medicine lectured only once in his twenty-two year tenure of the office. Something of the same may be said of law: the "higher" Faculty of Law in Aberdeen did not come into its own until the nineteenth century.

Nevertheless, by and large it was true of the professional classes, especially the clergy of the national church, both that they comprised the heart of the social order and that they had a philosophical education. This was especially important after the Act of Union of 1707. Thereafter Scotland had no Parliament, but it continued to have its own distinctive ecclesiastical, legal, and educational systems, all of them acting for the most part in independence of the Parliament in London, and all of them staffed by university-trained men. In particular, the General Assembly of the Church of Scotland was a forum for discussion and decision on social, intellectual, and political matters pertaining to "the Church and Nation of Scotland," as the constitutional phrase had it. As a result, it is not implausible to claim, as MacIntyre does, that this was a society in which philosophy played a strikingly important role.

What was that role exactly? *Whose Justice? Which Rationality?* devotes three chapters to this question, the central one expressly entitled "Philosophy in the Scottish Social Order." The general picture MacIntyre paints is this. The academies of Scotland inherited elements of both Aristotelianism and Augustinianism (in its Calvinist form). Moreover, the legal and social order had been hugely influenced by Viscount Stair's *Institutions* (a subject to be returned to). This background is instructive when we consider the conflicts that beset not merely the world of ideas, but the ecclesiastical and moral world in which Hutcheson (and others) had to teach and operate. This was a world where the Evangelical party, persuaded of the preeminence of revealed truth and the corrupted nature of human reason, was ranged against the Moderates. The task of the Moderates was to show, not that revealed truth was irrational or irrelevant (as atheism alleged), but that the important business of sifting truth from error amongst competing *claims* to revelation was the proper business of philosophy. And philosophy, here, should be broadly understood, since the expertise of the philosophers frequently incorporated a wide sweep of learning from biblical Hebrew to Newtonian mathematics. MacIntyre quotes with approval the remark of Colin MacLaurin, one of the premier mathematicians of the day:

> [N]atural philosophy may become a sure basis to natural religion, but it is very preposterous to deduce natural philosophy from any hypothesis, 'tho invented to make us imagine ourselves possest of a more compleate system of metaphysics, or contrived perhaps with a view to obviate more easily some difficulties in natural theology. (Quoted in *Whose Justice?*, p. 250)

In other words, the task of philosophy so conceived is not to displace or eradicate revealed truth, but to provide its intellectual grounding. The point is that philosophy, and especially moral philosophy, has to be the arbiter between competing theological interpretations of Scripture, and that, given the importance of these questions in the society of the time, this arbitration assumes an important social role. Thus it was that the Scottish professors of moral philosophy became principal agents in the outcome of social events. This also explains how, at least in this case, "key episodes in the social history . . . were episodes in the history of philosophy."

There are those who would raise doubts about the historical accuracy of this story, a very important question if MacIntyre's fusion of history and philosophy is to succeed. However, there is an anterior question about the conceptual relations that such a history, even if accurate, can be taken to sustain. The point to be stressed is that for this conception to work it is not enough that philosophers should be shown to have a social role. This in itself is compatible with a much more contingent relation than that which MacIntyre's account requires. The most profoundly materialist philosophy of history can concede that there have been periods when those designated philosophers have exercised considerable influence, just as there have been periods when theologians had a marked degree of social pre-eminence, and as, in our own time perhaps, scientists do. What needs to be shown, rather, is that philosophy, (or theology, or science), *in itself* has been socially influential. And this means, with respect to any of the three, that some demonstration is required that intellectual adequacy is directly correlated with the continuing success of the social institutions which it underwrites. Correspondingly, we need to be able to demonstrate that intellectual inadequacy to the condition of the times is the ultimate explanation of social failure.

It seems to me that MacIntyre is stronger on the former relation than on the latter. He aims to demonstrate, for instance, that Hutcheson's accounts of justice and practical reason had strengths that served their time well. They also had internal, inherent weaknesses that explain the eventual failure of certain social institutions and cultural trends. Perhaps. But there is a less elevated idea to consider. However elegant and intellectually sophisticated such accounts may have been, it is quite possible that the temper of the times first endorsed them with relatively little understanding, and then cast them aside in prejudice and ignorance. To do so was irrational of course, if they really did have the intellectual strengths he alleges, but would have been no less effective for this irrationality. It is, in my view, an intellectualist prejudice to suppose that only coherent ideas can work, or endure, in the end. Unreason may be as powerful, sometimes more so, than rationality.

Interestingly, much of MacIntyre's own account of our past both contends for and sustains just this suggestion. In *Three Rival Versions* he tells us that his account of

> Aquinas's work as the culmination and integration of the Augustinian and Aristotelian traditions is not at all how Aquinas was understood by much the greater part of both his contemporaries and his immediate successors ... What defeated Aquinas was the power of the institutionalized curriculum. Neither theology nor the subordinate *artes liberales* could in the middle or late thirteenth century find room for the Aristotelian system. (*Three Rival Versions*, p. 51)

The same sort of "defeat of reason" is instanced in his claim that the failure of the Enlightenment Project ushered in an era of liberal individualism that, by his own telling, is both intellectually impoverished *and* enduring. The central contention of *After Virtue*, in fact, is that we have a fragmented and incoherent conception of morality, which we have nonetheless succeeded in living with for a considerable period of time. MacIntyre's own analysis of the modern malaise, after all, is that the now dominant language of human rights and individual freedom, which together comprise the most evident product of this conception, are omnipresent, and form the staple of contemporary political language.

To acknowledge their dominance and durability, of course, is not to assert their intellectual adequacy. On the contrary, the most compelling (if not in the end convincing) aspect of MacIntyre's analysis is precisely its implication that we live in an intellectually fractured world. But we do *live* in it. If this were not so, his account of post-Enlightenment modernity would lose most of its interest; if the errors of modernity were *idle*, their analysis would not take the powerful form of social criticism.

Now if all this is true, what it implies is that intellectual failure does not, in and of itself, spell social disintegration; and this in its turn implies that the explanation of social forms – their emergence *or* their continuance – is not always to be explained in terms of the philosophical adequacy and inadequacy of the ideas that underwrite them. Pace Hegel (and several commentators have found a strongly, if unexplicitly, Hegelian element permeating MacIntyre's philosophical history) the real is *not* always rational. Why should it not have been the case that the intellectually better side was defeated by social tendencies of an irrational kind, or even by political *force majeure*? We know from the experience of both tyrannies and democracies that reason does not always prevail. Indeed, this seems to be precisely MacIntyre's story. Modern liberalism is intellectually flawed. Yet it persists, and it is precisely its persistence that generates the modern perplexities with which he is concerned.

Applying this general thought to the particular case of the Scottish Enlightenment seems a simple matter. Even if Hutcheson's account of justice had been intellectually still more robust than MacIntyre alleges, it might yet have been swept aside. And so, it seems, he says it was. Hutcheson's articulation and heroic defense of Scottish philosophy, and its role in the explication of law and theology, could not in the end withstand the acids of "Hume's Anglicizing Subversion" (the title of a third important chapter in *Whose Justice? Which Rationality?*). MacIntyre represents the contest between the Evangelical and Moderate parties in a way which suggests (though it does not actually demonstrate) that the former lost because of its intellectual inadequacy. But in the next part of his story he alleges that the victory of the Moderates was itself short-lived.

The explanation of both its temporary success and subsequent failure, however, is an interesting and important topic in its own right. The Evangelicals were deeply suspicious of human reason; therein lay their weakness. Hutcheson by contrast was a proponent of reason; therein lay his strength. But he was not a Rationalist of Platonic stripe. That is to say, Hutcheson's thinking, at least on MacIntyre's interpretation, did not appeal to an abstract conception of universal Reason, but drew upon a theological and philosophical tradition of inquiry whose strength lay in its ability to recognize challenges both from within and from beyond its own conceptions. It could thus seek, not merely to address them, but to answer them by drawing upon its own resources. This gave it a certain resilience. But more significantly, it allowed it to deploy reason in the service of personal and social formation.

It is this notion of a tradition that comes to be of central importance, not only to this particular episode in the history of ideas, but to MacIntyre's whole project. Tradition is a subject that figures ever more prominently in the succeeding volumes of MacIntyre's work, and especially in *Three Rival Versions of Moral Enquiry*.

Once again, there are reasons to doubt the historical accuracy of this portrayal of Hutcheson. Wokler, for one, questions its veracity.

> Hutcheson was to take up his appointment not as a conservative adherent of a Scottish tradition of higher education but as a critically vigorously critical reformer. His widely attested popularity as a lecturer in Glasgow, partly due to his casual style of delivery in English rather than by way of Latin readings, was even more attributable to the zealotry of his preaching a joyously uplifting moral philosophy in accordance with benign nature and providence, that contrasted with the gloomy precepts around original sin of Augustinian Scholasticism. The Scottish theological tradition which MacIntyre claims Hutcheson affirmed was actually rejected by him. (Wokler 1994, p. 119)

Perhaps, though, there is a deeper story to be told than Wokler here allows, and certainly the context MacIntyre supplies for his interpretation of Hutcheson suggests one. We should not single out Augustinian Scholasticism as the sole or even dominant element in the Scottish intellectual tradition. There were other influential strands. It is at this point that there is occasion to return to Stair's *Institutions of the Law of Scotland* (1681). MacIntyre draws a contrast between the *Institutions* and the *Commentaries on the Laws of England* (1765) by William Blackstone. Though the second appeared considerably later than the first, the comparison provides the vital clue to understanding the later conflict between Hutcheson and Hume.

> What Stair's *Institutions* provided was a comprehensive statement of the nature of justice, of law, and of rational and right conduct, which articulated the presuppositions of what were to be distinctively Scottish attitudes. No one in the Scottish eighteenth century could engage with these topics without in one way or another confronting Stair's theoretical and conceptual scheme, a scheme which expressed in terms of the law of Scotland not only the legal but the key theological and philosophical doctrines concerning justice, law, and rational and right conduct. (*Whose Justice?*, pp. 226–227)
>
> It is instructive to contrast Stair's method of argument with that which was to be followed a good deal later in England by Sir William Blackstone. . . . [I]n in the early sections of the *Commentaries* . . . Blackstone begins by writing as if he too is going to deduce the first principles of the law from theological or metaphysical doctrine. But he at once declares such an appeal redundant by declaring of God that "he has been pleased so to contrive the constitution

and frame of humanity, that should we want no other prompter to inquire after and pursue the rule of right, but only our own self-love, that universal principle of action . . . he has not perplexed the law of nature with a multitude of abstracted rules and precepts . . . but has graciously reduced the rule of obedience to this one paternal precept 'that man should pursue his own true and substantial happiness.' " (*Whose Justice?*, pp. 228–229)

The contrast is plain. Whereas Stair seeks a metaphysical basis to law, rooted in the apprehension of fundamental principles, Blackstone finds a basis for law in the need to coordinate the pursuit of individual desires (the same sort of picture we find in Hobbes, of course). As a result, these alternative conceptions of law both reflect and to a degree strengthen the well-known differences between English and Scots law. While the former is in a sense empirical, since everything turns on case law and precedent, the latter is a descendent of Roman or civilian law, in which cases are decided according to principle and precept.

This difference exists beyond the level of legal theory: it reflects a wider philosophical difference about the relation between reason and passion with respect to action and deliberation. Moreover, it is one that receives explicit expression in the philosophical debates of the Scottish Enlightenment. Whereas Hume, of the Blackstone Anglicizing tendency, asserts that "morality is more properly felt than judged of" (*Treatise* III, Pt.1, §ii), Thomas Reid, the true inheritor of Hutcheson and the Scottish tradition of philosophy, argues precisely the opposite, that "the excercise of my moral faculty . . . are acts of judgement, and not feeling" (*Essays on the Active Powers* V, VII).

In short, Hutcheson, in the spirit of Stair, retains a sense that the role of moral philosophy (and hence social theory) is to discover, or perhaps disclose, rational principles that will form and guide desire. Hume, in the spirit of Blackstone, sees the task of moral philosophy as that of recording the operation of the passions, and correspondingly, his political and social thought is of an instrumental (ultimately utilitarian) kind that accommodates rather than influences the passions.

By MacIntyre's account the difference is of huge significance, and ushers in, eventually, the emotivist impoverishment of moral language and thought. If this is indeed an impoverishment, how are we to recover the ground we have lost? The answer cannot lie with the Enlightenment Project of universal reason, a project which had to fail. Rather we must articulate, recapture, and revitalize the idea of an intellectual tradition that Hutcheson deployed. And here we find a third version of the integration of history and philosophy that is a recurrent theme in MacIntyre's work with which this chapter is concerned.

3. THE IDEA OF AN INTELLECTUAL TRADITION

It is in *Three Rival Versions of Moral Enquiry* that the idea of an intellectual tradition comes to greatest prominence. The rival versions of inquiry contrasted are those of the encyclopaedist, the genealogist, and the traditionalist. The first of these is that of the Enlightenment project, still alive and (so to speak) well in the nineteenth century. This conception of rational inquiry understands the pursuit of truth and the acquisition of knowledge according to the model of compiling an encyclopaedia. It is the conception – embodied, in fact, in the *Encyclopaedia Britannica* – that the pursuit of understanding consists in the timeless, yet progressive accumulation of information. By the consistent application of methods of a sort that must commend themselves to any rational inquirer, humankind has gradually amassed more and more of the truth. Science is unified; its aim and purpose is the steady expansion of knowledge. The picture is something like the regular amassing of coins in a treasury. We are better off the more we have.

The dysanalogy, of course, is that we are not told what to spend them on. What is the *point* of knowledge acquisition? In this encyclopaedist conception, science and understanding are on a par with the filling of the train spotter's notebook. What is missing is context, a context of aim and purpose. In short, the encyclopaedist's conception is ahistorical.

By contrast, the genealogical conception (MacIntyre takes Nietzsche as its representative protagonist) is acutely aware of historical context, and sees the timeless accumulation of truth as an impossible ideal. Truth and understanding are relative to historical period and social purpose. But precisely because he sets scientific endeavor so firmly in the sphere of social life, the genealogist comes to see intellectual endeavor as an exercise of power in defense of interests; its self-professed character as the impartial pursuit of knowledge is a mask, nothing better, in fact, than an amalgam of distortion and illusion that moral thinkers, such as Nietzsche, can at best work to dispel. The genealogist, in other words, subordinates philosophy in history. Because he sees, rightly, that total historical detachment, or radical universalism, is impossible, he swings violently in the opposite direction and concludes that every thought and idea is the creature, and hence the instrument, of its time, to be used or abused in the power struggles of social and political history.

Whereas the encyclopaedist is unrealistically ahistorical, the genealogist is an historical relativist. In contrast to both positions there is a third possibility to be described – that of the traditionalist. Traditionalists – those who self-consciously work within an historical tradition of inquiry – see the pursuit of understanding as a matter not merely of acquiring items of knowledge but of pursuing intellectual questions and problems that they have not invented but inherited. This notion of intellectual inheritance raises the individual inquirer above the peculiarities of his or her own time, but without removing the whole enterprise into the impossible realm of the timeless. It thus implies that "science," broadly conceived, requires membership in a tradition – a movement of thought from and through history. Accordingly, acceptance of this inheritance implies that a large part of the pursuit of understanding is exploration of coherent self-understanding, discovering what we know by grasping who we are.

For the genealogist there is no truth as traditional epistemology understands it; for the encyclopaedist truth is external to the method of inquiry. On both conceptions it is possible to specify the end of intellectual endeavor independently of its methods, and possible therefore to ask, irrespective of the content of those ends, whether the methods are effective. Hume's Anglicizing tendency, following the generalized model of Blackstone's approach to the law, understands the end to be set by passion and desire, and accordingly the efficacy of the method to be determined by preference satisfaction. Hence the resultant emotivism, and the subservience of reason to desire; what point could reason have other than to be the slave of the passions?

MacIntyre has, let us agree, made the inadequacy of this position plain. But in addition there is something positive to be said for the traditionalist account that he wishes to endorse in its place: it simply is more accurate with respect to the realities of intellectual endeavour. In doing philosophy or science we do not, as a matter of fact, invent the problems or questions we address. On the contrary, we *learn* what they are, just as we learn proposed solutions to them. Those who fail to do so, who simply open the encyclopaedia, have neither point nor purpose to guide them, and thus no guard against the wild and fanciful use of the facts they come to possess. They are deluded into supposing that they, uniquely and for the first time, might uncover the "key to all mythologies" (the fruitless pursuit of Mr. Casaubon in George Eliot's *Middlemarch*). On the other hand, it seems perverse to insist, as the genealogist does, that there is really no such thing as inquiry at all, and that those who think there is are the perpetual victims of self-deception and/or manipulation by others. A more accurate description seems to be that, though inquiry cannot "leap over Rhodes" (to quote Hegel), nor is it irrevocably at the mercy of contemporaneous powers and passions.

But if for these reasons we do adopt the traditionalist point of view, then ends and means cannot be specified independently in the way the Humean encyclopaedist required because those things we might identify as the means of achieving the ends at which the tradition aims are necessarily embedded in states of character which are themselves constitutive of the ends – states of character that a large part of education exists to create. Whereas the Humean deliberator, believing that reason is the slave of the passions, asks of the educator "tell me what I want to know," the proper request is "improve my understanding," tell me, in other words, what I *ought to* want to know.

Accordingly, intelligent inquirers seek, pace the genealogist, to pass beyond the immediate and the ephemeral, but they do not expect thereby to be offered (as the encyclopaedist offers them) an accumulation of "facts" with which to fill up the vacuity of their minds, or a set of algorithms by which they may generate more mind-filling facts for themselves. Rather, they seek guidance on how to think, and what to think about. What this implies is that the central source of legitimation and justification in a tradition of inquiry is neither the end result – truth – nor principles of inquiry – Cartesian-type rules for the direction of the mind – but the authoritative practitioner, the one who has mastered the tradition.

So far we have been concerned with intellectual inquiry and with rival conceptions of it. The central point to grasp, however, is that intellectual inquiry is a *practice*, and the same possibilities of conception, and the same points for and against them, can be made with respect to all human practices. In *Three Rival Versions* MacIntyre describes the character of the authoritative practitioner in a way that includes, but is not restricted to, the person who is a master of philosophy or science.

> The authority of a master is both more and other than a matter of exemplifying the best standards so far. It is also and most importantly a matter of knowing how to go further and especially how to direct others towards going further, using what can be learned from the tradition afforded by the past to move towards the *telos* of fully perfected work. It is thus in knowing how to link past and future that those with authority are able to draw upon tradition, to interpret and reinterpret it, so that its directedness towards the *telos* of that particular craft becomes apparent in new and characteristically

> unexpected ways. And it is the ability to teach others how to learn this type of knowing how that the power of the master within the community of a craft is legitimated as rational authority. (*Three Rival Versions*, pp. 65–66)

History is concerned with what has been. Philosophy is a normative inquiry, concerned with what, rationally, we ought to think and believe. It is now possible to see how, on this third account of the connection, tradition fuses historical understanding and normative judgment.

> Because at any particular moment the rationality of a craft is justified by its history so far, which has made it what it is in that specific time, place, and set of historical circumstances, such rationality is inseparable from the tradition through which it was achieved. To share in the rationality of a craft requires sharing in the contingencies of its history, understanding its story as one's own, and finding a place for oneself as a character in the enacted dramatic narrative which is that story so far. (*Three Rival Versions*, p. 65)

If we apply this line of thought to moral reasoning, we can readily see how different it looks once we begin to think in terms of tradition. Determining the right course of action will not now be a matter of applying abstract principles of practical rationality (Descartes or Kant), or estimating likely consequences for happiness (Bentham or Mill), or exposing the forces which, while masquerading as deliverances of truth and rationality, are really devices to suppress the exercise of individual will (Nietzsche or Foucault). Rather, practical reason will be a matter of relying upon the judgments of those well versed in the moral traditions of specific times and places, and by emulation coming to be able to make judgments in our turn. We are accustomed to defining the morally good agent as one who performs right actions; on this way of thinking, the morally right act is to be defined as that which would be performed by the good agent.

The Aristotelian character of this line of thought is evident. Yet MacIntyre has expressly denied that his aim is to restore a "morality of the virtues" in preference to a "morality of rules." The difference is to be found in the last sentence of the passage just quoted, for his account goes beyond Aristotelianism precisely in its appeal to history. The master of a tradition, including a tradition of rational moral inquiry, must find a place "as a character in the enacted dramatic narrative which is that story so far." To do so, obviously, requires a knowledge of what that story is, in short a knowledge of history.

If this third account of the fusion of history and philosophy is to succeed two conditions need to be met. First, understanding must be essentially historical. Second, with respect to philosophy (and moral philosophy in particular), this historicity must not jeopardize its normative character. Can these conditions be secured?

Satisfying the first of them would appear problematic. It seems to be the case that participation in a tradition could be wholly lacking in historical *consciousness*. Future craftsmen must be inducted into the craft by a master, and thereby have their judgments informed by previous (which is to say historical) experience reflected upon. But why must the form of this reflection be itself expressly historical? The origins of the craft, or of a specific project, the names and contribution of predecessors, and indeed the historical development of the craft itself could be quite unknown to a contemporary master. He or she is required only to be imbued with the tradition, not to be able to articulate its history. Arguably, this was precisely the case with the engineers, architects, and stonemasons who contributed to the building of the great Gothic cathedrals of Europe. They were masters of a craft engaged in an inherited project with its special *telos*, one which they in their turn sought to bring to fulfillment and perfection. But it seems reasonable to suppose that they did so without any formulable knowledge or understanding of the past. In a few cases their originating predecessors are identifiable (Canterbury), but not necessarily known to them. If not, were their endeavors any the less consequential?

It is open to MacIntyre to reply, I think, that whatever may be true of other practices, such ahistorical understanding of a *moral* tradition or a tradition of *inquiry* is impossible, since these crucially employ concepts, and the use of concepts implies conscious reflection upon a cultural reality and historical legacy, chiefly that of one's language.

> Every tradition is embodied in some particular set of utterances and actions and thereby in all the particularities of some specific language and culture. The invention, elaboration, and modification of the concepts through which both those who found and those who inherit a tradition understand it are inescapably concepts which have been framed in one language rather than another....
>
> The conception of language presupposed in saying this is that of a language as it is used in and by a particular community living at a particular time and place with particular shared beliefs, institutions and practices. (*Whose Justice?*, pp. 371–373)

It is this view of language that lies at the heart of MacIntyre's criticism not only of emotivist theories of ethics but of the ahistorical semantics that has dominated philosophy in general, and philosophy of language in particular, over the last few decades. To understand language is to understand *a* language in a sociohistorical context. Each tradition of inquiry must employ such a language and hence this context is a condition of the tradition's existence. For this reason the understanding of that tradition, by practitioners themselves as much as by inquirers from other traditions, has to be reflectively historical.

I still think there is a difficulty here. It is true that some practices can be inarticulate in a way that others cannot. Nevertheless, while the understanding of language that ordinary language speakers have is indeed an understanding of a specific language, socially embedded and with its own history, this does not mean that that understanding is itself historical. I should say, in fact, that it only very rarely is. In other words, speakers of a language successfully use concepts with a history, but they do not generally, and do not need to, *know* that history. In the absence of such knowledge, their mastery of the concepts seems largely unaffected.

Of course, it is plausible to hold that the position is different with respect to the philosophical use of that language, which must be reflective in ways that other uses are not. However, to respond in this way to the difficulty that I think I detect is simply to raise another. It seems that there can be a philosophical use of language that is *not* historically informed. Indeed that is the very point upon which MacIntyre criticizes emotivism, and contemporary analytical philosophy of language more broadly; these are engagements in philosophy, after all, whatever else is to be said about (or against) them.

Now someone persuaded of the story so far is unlikely to be persuaded to the contrary by this reference to the mere possibility of an ahistorical philosophical use of and reflection upon language. Such a reference does not seem persuasive precisely because the whole point is that it is *inadequate*. This removes the discussion to another level. I remarked that philosophy is essentially normative, and that any fusion with history (of the sort at which MacIntyre aims) must preserve this normativity. To declare emotivism inadequate is to make a normative philosophical judgment. How does the appeal to history sustain or underwrite it?

The answer given by this third strand in MacIntyre's project is plain: normative philosophical judgments must themselves be rooted in, and derived from, a tradition of inquiry that has its own history. The question then becomes: *which* tradition of inquiry are we to draw upon in making these judgments?

Can there be more than one tradition of inquiry? The answer seems evident, of course there can. Moreover, the liberal/emotivist conception, and with it the encyclopaedist, is just one such tradition. To appeal to it, therefore, would seem to endorse the position MacIntyre declares to be inadequate. If its inadequacy is to be revealed, accordingly it must be some other tradition that is appealed to, and evidently MacIntyre means this to be the neo-Thomist one. But the attempt to do so raises an even more important difficulty. Can a different, more subtle form of relativism be avoided, one in which emotivism is inadequate relative only to one tradition of inquiry?

This is a question John Haldane expressly raised in his essay "MacIntyre's Thomist Revival: What Next?" In a section of the essay significantly entitled "Suspicions of Relativism," Haldane quotes the following passage from *Whose Justice? Which Rationality?*.

> [W]e must first return to the situation of the person to whom, after all, this book is primarily addressed, someone who, not as yet having given their allegiance to some coherent tradition of enquiry, is besieged by disputes over what is just and about how it is reasonable to act, both at the level of particular immediate issues . . . and at the level at which rival systematic tradition-informed conceptions contend. (*Whose Justice?*, p. 393)

Haldane then comments:

> [I]t is worth dwelling on the situation envisaged in the quoted passage. Here we are to imagine someone who has not yet subscribed to 'a coherent tradition of enquiry'. That immediately raises the question of how such a person can choose between rival suitors for his or her mind and conscience. It would seem that his or her choice must be rooted in reason or else be non-rational. But the former is excluded if rational norms are only available to a participant within a coherent tradition, for, *ex hypothesi*, the addressee is a complete outsider. . . . We are prohibited from saying that the rootless addressee can choose on the basis of transcendent norms of practical reason, so that excludes a realist resolution. This returns us to the thought that all choosing is from within a tradition, but if so there is nothing that is to be said by or to such a person, and *a fortiori* he cannot make a rational choice. (Haldane 1994, pp. 96–97)

In *Three Rival Versions* MacIntyre expounds and defends the superiority of the Thomist tradition of inquiry, but if Haldane is right this will not help. To those within it, of course, it comes up with the right answers. To those whose allegiance lies with some other tradition, its answers will be deemed to be mistaken. But to anyone who stands outside these, and outside any such tradition, the answers will be rationally unassessable, even unintelligible perhaps. Haldane is unduly modest in entitling this section of his essay "Suspicions of Relativism"; it seems, rather, that he has shown MacIntyre to *be* a relativist.

Now it needs to be observed that MacIntyre anticipates this criticism in *Whose Justice? Which Rationality?*, where he writes as follows:

> It is not . . . that competing traditions do not share some standards. All the traditions with which we have been concerned agree in according a certain authority to logic both in their theory and in their practice. Were it not so their adherents would be unable to disagree in the way that they do. But that upon which they agree is insufficient to resolve those disagreements. It may therefore seem to be the case that we are confronted with the rival and competing claims of a number of traditions to our allegiance in respect of our understanding of practical rationality and justice, among which we can have no good reason to decide in favor of any one rather than of the others. . . .
>
> Argument along these lines has been adduced in support of a conclusion that if the only available standards of rationality are those made available by and within traditions, then no issue between contending traditions is rationally decidable. To assert or to conclude this rather than that can be rational relative to the standards of some particular tradition, but not rational as such. There can be no rationality as such. . . . Let us call this the relativist challenge. (*Whose Justice?*, pp. 351–352)

In the same place MacIntyre outlines a response to this challenge, one which he elaborates at greater length elsewhere (MacIntyre 1994c). Its basic thrust is that inter-traditional conflicts can in a sense be transcended. This transcendence is not Hegelian – one that, instead of seeing traditions of inquiry as having distinct and distinguishing histories regards them as moments in the unfolding of human understanding across time, such that earlier ones are *aufgehoben* or taken up in those that succeed them, only to be *aufgehoben* by others in their turn. Though this picture fits MacIntyre's account of the emergence of Thomism rather well (for by his account Thomism takes up the rival traditions of Augustinianism and Aristotelianism in a way that produces a new synthesis), here, it seems, the process stops. The resultant Thomism not only stands in opposition to the tradition generated by the Enlightenment Project, as it should in accordance with the Hegelian dialectic, but it does so in perpetuity. In any case, MacIntyre has expressly said (in a reply to critics) that he is "irremediably anti-Hegelian in rejecting the notion of an absolute standpoint, independent of the particularity of all traditions" (MacIntyre 1994f, p. 295).

If we cannot transcend differences between traditions by employing an Hegelian-type absolute standpoint, an alternative would be to find some hitherto undiscovered common ground. Arguably this is what Rawls attempts with his concept of an "overlapping consensus" (Rawls 1993, p. 39). It is also the strategy invoked by ethologists and sociobiologists, whose theorizing may reasonably be interpreted as modern versions of Aristotelian naturalism. The conflict between traditions, and the place of the inquirer innocent of traditional loyalties (around whose possibility Haldane raises his objection), is to be explained in terms of an underlying common nature that all human beings share in virtue of their evolved animality and the condition in which they find themselves.

Once again, though, this appears not to be the line MacIntyre wishes to take. In a 1994 essay (MacIntyre 1994c) he argues that all traditions of inquiry are committed to an assertion-transcendent concept of truth, committed to holding that "the account of morality which they give does not itself, at least in its central contentions, suffer from the limitations, partialities and one-sidedness of a merely local point of view" (MacIntyre 1994c, p. 12) and that this shared commitment implies further that

> if the scheme and mode of justification to which ... appeal [is made] to support [an] account of the moral life were to turn out to be ... incapable of providing the resources for exhibiting its argumentative superiority ... then it must be capable of being replaced by some scheme and mode of justification which does possess the resources *both* for providing adequate rational support for [its] account and for exhibiting its rational superiority to any scheme and mode of justification which supports conclusions incompatible with central theses of that account. For otherwise no claim to truth could be sustained. (MacIntyre 1994c, p. 12; emphasis in original)

In other words, rational superiority is to be found in the circumstances in which one tradition explains the persistent difficulties encountered by another better than the other can itself, and in ways that the adherents of the less successful tradition can recognize. Applied to moral thinking, this means that if natural law theory (for example) can explain why social contract theory encounters the problems it does better than social contract theory does, but in terms intelligible to social contract theorists, then it can be declared rationally superior.

The example of natural law versus social contract is mine, since MacIntyre replies to the relativist challenge in exclusively general terms. Yet to make good the abstract claim and produce some result with respect to the real clash of actual traditions, specific cases have to be explored.

Somewhat curiously, it seems to me, when MacIntyre turns (in his most recent book) to address substantial moral issues, he appears to adopt the second – naturalistic – strategy rather than the third I have just been describing. Though, as I observed, MacIntyre earlier expressly denied that his aim was to restore a "morality of the virtues" in preference to a "morality of rules," this appears to be precisely the line he takes in *Dependent Rational Animals*, in which he revives an Aristotelian conception that is entirely silent on any historical dimension and that takes its cue from the vulnerability and dependence that is the mark of human existence *per se*.

What is very striking about this new work is the difference in orientation from the three books with which this chapter has been concerned up to this point. Even earlier than *After Virtue*, in fact, in *A Short History of Ethics*, the book with which I began, MacIntyre stressed not merely the important, but the crucial role of history to any adequate moral philosophy. In this new book, by contrast, there is no discernible historical dimension. The account he gives us of human nature and the human condition aims to undergird moral philosophy. Indeed his main question is precisely this:

> [W]hat difference to moral philosophy would it make, if we were to treat the facts of vulnerability and affliction and the related facts of dependence as central to the human condition? (*Dependent Rational Animals*, p. 4)

The resulting picture, which, we might usefully observe, derives not from historical but from ethological investigation, seems remarkably static, and in fact wholly lacking in the spirit that declared history to be essential to moral understanding. For my own part I concur with the suggestion (in *Dependent Rational Animals*) that human beings should be regarded as having a (broadly speaking) biological nature, and that the human condition is one of vulnerability. So much we share with other animals. But an important point of difference, which is stressed in the trilogy with which I have been chiefly concerned, seems to be this: Human beings have a history; other animals do not. How does the conception of an adequate basis for moral philosophy advanced in this book cohere with the strongly historical conception advanced in *After Virtue*, *Whose Justice? Which Rationality?*, and *Three Rival Versions of Moral Enquiry*?

MacIntyre has replied to this question (in correspondence) by saying:

> We need to distinguish philosophical work within a tradition that takes the context supplied by that tradition more or less for granted from work that appeals explicitly to the narrative history in which it is embedded or work that defends one tradition and argues for its rational superiority to

> some rival. It is just the same in the natural sciences. Someone at work in quantum mechanics now is able to work ahistorically, presupposing but not making explicit the historical background in Bohr's model of the atom and the stages through which that came to be rejected.

In short, the historical dimension is in some sense *metaethical*, just as the history of science is *meta*-scientific. It is not easy to say, though, whether this distinction can really be maintained consistently with at least one of the important assertions with which the historical exploration of philosophical issues began – that "moral concepts change as social life changes." As it seems to me, it is much more plausible to make this claim with respect to the concepts of justice and honor (for instance) than with the concepts of vulnerability and dependence that are invoked in *Dependent Rational Animals*. No doubt these concepts have a history, but their moral relevance derives not from this history but from a biological nature that human beings share. And insofar as disputed ethical questions can be resolved by the careful delineation and deployment of such concepts, to this extent, it seems, we may disregard the interconnection of philosophy and history that has been so central a part of MacIntyre's enterprise.

2 Tradition in the Recent Work of Alasdair MacIntyre

JEAN PORTER

In *After Virtue*, Alasdair MacIntyre develops a narrative of late modernity in which Enlightenment liberalism, attempting to construct a philosophy and a society on the basis of nonteleological reason, falls into intellectual and especially moral incoherence. The unhappy fate of the modern liberal, left with only therapists for comfort and bureaucrats for security, is contrasted with the happier situation of someone who aspires to a life of virtue in the Aristotelian sense.[1] Yet it is not clear that this is an option today, given that classical and medieval versions of Aristotelian virtue ethics rest on a "metaphysical biology" which is no longer tenable (*After Virtue*, p. 162). MacIntyre accordingly offers a reformulation of Aristotelian virtue ethics in which participation in a tradition plays a role analogous to that played by Aristotle's metaphysical biology – that is to say, it gives a wider purpose and meaning to the narrative that unifies the individual life.

The idea of a tradition continues to play a central role in MacIntyre's works. In *Whose Justice? Which Rationality?* he develops a theory of rationality as tradition-guided inquiry, which he offers as an alternative to the untenable options of Enlightenment foundationalism on the one hand, and postmodern versions of perspectivism and relativism on the other hand. The project of *Whose Justice? Which Rationality?* is further developed in MacIntyre's Gifford Lectures, *Three Rival Versions of Moral Enquiry: Encyclopaedia, Genealogy and Tradition*, in which tradition, as exemplified by the work of Augustine and Aquinas, is defended over and against its other two rivals.

Clearly, any study of MacIntyre's thought must take account of the central place that he gives to the concept of tradition. Yet this task is complicated by the fact that, even though MacIntyre discusses tradition extensively, he never defines the term (so far as I have been able to determine), nor does he situate his account of tradition in the context of other recent discussions.[2] Moreover, as we would expect, MacIntyre's understanding of tradition evolves over the near decade that elapses between the first edition of *After Virtue* and the publication of his Gifford lectures. In each of the three major books that have defined MacIntyre's mature philosophical program, we find a somewhat different account of what a tradition is. Especially in his later works, MacIntyre moves between a wider concept of tradition as an overall social and moral orientation, and a more limited concept of a tradition as a focused scientific or moral inquiry. Nonetheless, we can arrive at an understanding of MacIntyre's account of tradition by attending to the ways in which he uses this idea in developing his overall account of rationality and morality, and that is the strategy that I will follow in this chapter.

1. *AFTER VIRTUE:* TRADITION AS THE CONTEXT FOR VIRTUE

After Virtue is essentially a critical book. MacIntyre's aim is first to develop a diagnosis of what he sees as the malaise of contemporary modern thought, and second to provide a sketch of what a suitably reformulated Aristotelian alternative might look like. This point should be emphasized at the outset, because it reminds us that *After Virtue* is meant to set out a program for future works. As such, it provides a key to understanding what comes after it, even though, as we will see, MacIntyre modifies his program in significant ways as he develops it. Even more important, it reminds us of a point on which MacIntyre himself insists, namely, the tentative character and incompleteness of the account of virtue that he develops in the last third of the book (*After Virtue*, p. 271).

MacIntyre's analysis of the failures of modernity is perhaps the best-known aspect of his work, and only a brief summary is necessary here.[3] In his view we are in the midst of a catastrophic situation, and all the more catastrophic because only a few persons are even aware of it. We have lost the unifying frameworks that are necessary for any coherent moral discourse; what we have instead are fragments from earlier discourses, which no longer make sense now that they have been wrenched out of their contexts, and which can serve only as vehicles for the expression of emotions or as obscuring ideologies for the assertion of power. (That is why, in his view, moral philosophers earlier in the century were so prone to emotivist theories of ethics, and why our contemporaries are so given to the assertion of autonomy through the language of rights (*After Virtue*, pp. 6–22, 66–70.)) In this respect, our situation contrasts unfavorably with that of antiquity or the middle ages, when moral discourse was given coherence through ideals of virtue, which were complemented through reflection on the rules necessary to sustain a moral community. At this point, MacIntyre considers

Aristotle to be the moral thinker *par excellence*; yet (as noted above) he also claims that Aristotle's account of virtue cannot be appropriated as it stands, because it depends on a kind of metaphysical biology that is no longer tenable. Nonetheless, Aristotle speaks from within a wider tradition of reflection on the virtues held together by a core conception of what a virtue is, and MacIntyre does believe that this core conception can be cogently reformulated for our own time (*After Virtue*, p. 186). These convictions set the agenda for the last part of *After Virtue*: MacIntyre attempts to set forth the key elements of this concept of virtue, and to sketch out what a contemporary reformulation of that concept might look like.

As MacIntyre understands it, the core conception of the virtues that unifies the tradition of virtue ethics with which he is concerned is built up in three stages:

> For there are no less than three stages in the logical development of the concept which have to be identified in order, if the core conception of a virtue is to be understood, and each of these stages has its own conceptual background. The first stage requires a background of what I shall call a practice, the second an account of what I have already characterized as the narrative order of a single human life and the third an account a good deal fuller than I have given up to now of what constitutes a moral tradition. Each later stage presupposes the earlier, but not *vice versa*. Each earlier stage is both modified by and reinterpreted in the light of, but also provides an essential constituent of each later stage. The progress in the development of the concept is closely related to, although it does not recapitulate in any straightforward way, the history of the tradition of which it forms the core. (*After Virtue*, pp. 186–187)[4]

MacIntyre goes on to define a practice as follows:

> By a 'practice' I am going to mean any coherent and complex form of socially established cooperative human activity through which goods internal to that form of activity are realized in the course of trying to achieve those standards of excellence which are appropriate to, and partially definitive of, that form of activity, with the result that human powers to achieve excellence, and human conceptions of the ends and goods involved, are systematically extended. (*After Virtue*, p. 87)

Hence, what characterizes a practice, in contrast to a skill or technique, is its orientation toward intrinsic goods that can be attained only through the practice itself, and that require both skill and sensitivity to the aims of the practice in order to be realized. Practices may be found across a wide range of human activities, including skilled games such as football or chess, complex skills such as architecture or farming, intellectual and scientific inquiries, and artistic activities such as painting or music (all these examples are MacIntyre's own; see *After Virtue*, pp. 187–188). MacIntyre does not claim that practices necessarily have intrinsic moral value, or that the attainment of proficiency in any of them is tantamount to moral virtue. Nonetheless, practices are significant because they exemplify forms of activity that are good in themselves, without reference to any further aims toward which they might be directed. In order to attain proficiency in a practice, someone must value, and progressively attain, two kinds of qualities, namely, the goods internal to the practice itself (understood with reference to the individual as a kind of proficiency in, or a sympathetic understanding of, the internal goods in question), and qualities that are essential to any sort of cooperative activity.

Nonetheless, the practices are not themselves virtues, nor are the qualities that they generate in their practitioners necessarily virtues. In responding to misunderstandings on this point generated by the first edition of the book, MacIntyre carefully notes that a quality cannot be considered to be a virtue unless it meets the conditions specified in two further stages (*After Virtue*, p. 275). Practices provide a conception of a kind of good which is intrinsic and not merely instrumental, but the qualities intrinsic to one practice may be useless or even harmful in other contexts (although MacIntyre hesitates to admit that a practice might be evil in itself), and as such, they cannot be considered to be virtues.

In order to move toward a conception of virtue, we must move to the next stage of development, namely, a conception of a human life as a unified whole (*After Virtue*, p. 205). MacIntyre develops this conception through a reflection on the intelligibility of human actions, which on his view presuppose that actions are embedded in an ongoing narrative that gives them meaning and point (*After Virtue*, pp. 207–15). This in turn implies that our lives as a whole are held together by a narrative unity, which is central to the identity of the subject and forms the precondition for responsibility for one's past actions (*After Virtue*, pp. 216–218). At the same time, the narrative unity of an individual life is teleological; it presupposes the possibility of evaluating a human life, in terms of its success or failure, as a life well lived or a life perverted, frustrated, or wasted. This, in turn, presupposes that human lives are oriented toward a good that transcends the individual, and at this point we move to the last stage in the development of the concept of a virtue.

For Aristotle, the ideal of human flourishing provides the orienting good toward which we strive, and provides unity to our individual lives.

At this stage in the development of his thought, however, MacIntyre does not consider this to be a defensible solution today. Nonetheless, he believes that in order for a human life to find the purpose necessary for its successful unification, the individual must be oriented toward a good transcending the individual. For us, this will take the form of a "narrative quest" for the good rather than a predetermined aim to be achieved (*After Virtue*, p. 219). This will necessarily be a communal quest, and as such it will require both devotion to a certain kind of good, and the attainment of qualities necessary to sustain life in community (*After Virtue*, pp. 219–221). The communal nature of the quest for the good, in turn, implies that it has a history extending beyond the life of the individual. It is the historical character of the quest for the good that situates it within a tradition: "I find myself part of a history and that is generally to say, whether I like it or not, whether I recognize it or not, one of the bearers of a tradition" (*After Virtue*, p. 221). It would be misleading to assume that this tradition will necessarily be fixed, or even clearly definable. On the contrary, MacIntyre insists on the open-ended character of traditions and on the fact that they derive their unity from an orientation toward goods which are contested within the tradition itself. He insists that debate is necessary to the life of an ongoing tradition: "A living tradition then is an historically extended, socially embodied argument, and an argument precisely in part about the goods which constitute that tradition" (*After Virtue*, p. 222).[5] Correlatively, "when a tradition becomes Burkean [that is to say, fixed and static], it is always dying or dead" (*After Virtue*, p. 222).

Hence, traditions provide the necessary final stage for developing the concept of a virtue because they comprise communities of inquiry that require virtues for their continued existence:

> The virtues find their point and purpose not only in sustaining those relationships necessary if the variety of goods internal to practices are to be achieved and not only in sustaining the form of an individual life in which that individual may seek out his or her good as the good of his or her whole life, but also in sustaining those traditions which provide both practices and individual lives with their necessary historical context. (*After Virtue*, p. 223)

These virtues will include (but will not be limited to) qualities of judgment and practical reason that enable the individual to discern how the insights and commitments of a tradition might best be extended into the future: "It is rather the case that an adequate sense of tradition manifests itself in a grasp of those future possibilities which the past has made available to the present" (*After Virtue*, p. 223).

It is not necessary for our purposes to review the criticisms of MacIntyre's account of virtue and tradition in *After Virtue* in greater detail because, as he himself notes, this account is only a preliminary to a more developed defense of a particular conception of moral rationality, which he subsequently goes on to develop in his later works.[6] Any assessment of his overall account of tradition must take his latter two books into account, especially since these latter works modify the account of tradition developed in *After Virtue* in significant ways. At the same time, elements of this account continue to inform MacIntyre's later discussions of tradition. Although he drops the claim that a tradition should be seen as a quest, he does retain the sense that a tradition is centrally a kind of open-ended inquiry, rather than offering something fixed and static. And even though he focuses in *Whose Justice? Which Rationality?* on the epistemic functions of traditions, his development of the idea is still clearly governed by moral concerns, which come to the fore once again in *Three Rival Versions of Moral Enquiry*. Finally, and most importantly, he continues to draw on the idea of tradition as a way of reformulating insights drawn from premodern authors into a contemporary idiom.

Before moving on, we should also note that in one of his most recent works MacIntyre repudiates one of the claims on which his development of the idea of tradition in *After Virtue* rests. In *Dependent Rational Animals*, he claims that he was mistaken to reject Aristotle's "metaphysical biology" as a basis for virtue (*Dependent Rational Animals*, p. x). Although he does not want to endorse all the elements of Aristotle's own view, he now asserts that an adequate account of virtue must include some account of human flourishing: "What it is for human beings to flourish does of course vary from context to context, but in every context it is as someone exercises in a relevant way the capacities of an independent practical reasoner that her or his potentialities for flourishing in a specifically human way are developed" (*Dependent Rational Animals*, p. 77). It is perhaps significant that in this book, the concept of tradition plays almost no role, in contrast to each of his other major works following *After Virtue*.

2. *WHOSE JUSTICE? WHICH RATIONALITY?* RATIONALITY AS TRADITION-GUIDED INQUIRY

Whose Justice? Which Rationality? develops the critique of Enlightenment liberalism first set forth in *After Virtue*, but unlike the earlier work, this book is intended to set forth a constructive theory as well as a critique. As its title suggests, the critique in this book takes its starting point from the claim that it is possible to establish universally valid standards of justice, which can be recognized as such by any rational person (*Whose Justice?*, pp. 1–4; cf. the discussion of different conceptions of justice near the end of *After Virtue*, pp. 244–55). MacIntyre attempts to show that this claim is false through a close examination of conflicting ideals of justice that emerged in three societies: ancient and classical Greece, medieval Europe, and eighteenth-century Scotland and England. His argument in each case is that the ideals dividing these societies were not such as could have been resolved through rational argument within a neutral framework of shared beliefs or principles, since in each case the conflicts were at least partly grounded in incommensurable claims that shaped the ways in which the interlocutors evaluated the relevant arguments and evidence (*Whose Justice?*, p. 351; cf. pp. 4–7).

These conflicts among ideals of justice might seem to lead to an impasse, and so long as we stay within the parameters of an Enlightenment ideal of rationality, we will indeed find that they cannot be resolved. It should be noted that MacIntyre does not deny that there are some standards of rationality that can be applied in any social or cultural context – for example, the fundamental laws of logic – but on his view these are not sufficient by themselves to resolve the kinds of substantive conflicts that have emerged in debates over competing ideals of justice. (On the universal validity of the laws of logic and other similar rational principles, and their inadequacy, see *Whose Justice?*, pp. 4, 351.) As MacIntyre argues in more detail later in the book, this situation has led to the emergence of contemporary forms of skepticism about the possibility of establishing genuine truth claims or developing rational arguments at all. But there is another alternative:

> What the Enlightenment made us for the most part blind to and what we now need to recover is, so I shall argue, a conception of rational enquiry as embodied in a tradition, a conception according to which the standards of rational justification themselves emerge from and are part of a history in which they are vindicated by the way in which they transcend the limitations of and provide remedies for the defects of their predecessors within the history of that same tradition. (*Whose Justice?*, p. 7)

The bulk of *Whose Justice? Which Rationality?* is devoted to a remarkably rich and detailed history of three of the four traditions that MacIntyre mentions (liberalism receives a less extended consideration). With respect to the Aristotelian tradition of justice, he shows how it emerged out of the limitations and inadequacies of the Homeric and Platonic views to emerge as one of the strongest traditions available in the medieval period. The

Augustinian tradition is similarly traced up to the point at which it comes into conflict with the Aristotelian tradition in the Middle Ages. This conflict is successfully resolved through Aquinas's synthesis of Augustinian and Aristotelian commitments through a reinterpretation of each in the light of the other. Finally, MacIntyre traces the development of another kind of synthesis, namely, the distinctively Scottish synthesis of Calvinist and Enlightenment perspectives that provided a genuine alternative to European versions of the Enlightenment until it was undermined through David Hume's "Anglicizing subversion." (This narrative comprises the bulk of *Whose Justice?*, pp. 12–348; the phrase "Anglicizing subversion" occurs on p. 281.)

In the closing chapters of his book, MacIntyre turns to the development of his constructive theory of rationality as tradition-guided inquiry. (The basic theory is developed in chapter 18, "The Rationality of Traditions," *Whose Justice?*, pp. 349–369.) Drawing on the narratives of traditions in conflict developed in the first part of the book, he begins by rejecting what he sees as the central claims of Enlightenment philosophy – the claim that it is possible to arrive at a set of rational standards both universal in scope and substantive enough to provide a basis for judging the beliefs and commitments of particular intellectual traditions. On the contrary, he argues, we are in the same situation as the ancient Greeks, medieval Europeans, or eighteenth-century Scots and Englishmen in that we must deal with social and intellectual traditions that are to some significant degree incommensurable with one another. He does not claim that there can be no meaningful communication at all between those who stand in incommensurable traditions. Rather, he claims that for those in such a situation there will be at least some disagreements that cannot be resolved by appeals to mutually agreeable standards of reasonableness and excellence because the disagreements have to do, at least in part, with those very standards themselves (*Whose Justice?*, pp. 4, 351). Hence, MacIntyre contends, since we cannot escape the necessity of arguing from within some tradition or other, we must necessarily turn to the notion of a tradition to provide an alternative framework for speculative as well as practical reasoning.

At the same time, however, MacIntyre also rejects two positions that are so often presented as the inevitable consequences of Enlightenment foundationalism:

> [It might be said that] if the only available standards of rationality are those made available by and within traditions, then no issue between contending traditions is rationally decidable.... There can be no rationality as such.

> Every set of standards, every tradition incorporating a set of standards, has as much and as little claim to our allegiance as any other. Let us call this the relativist challenge, as contrasted with a second type of challenge, that which we may call the perspectivist. . . . [T]he perspectivist challenge puts in question the possibility of making truth claims from within any one tradition. (*Whose Justice?*, p.352)

In contrast, MacIntyre proposes a third alternative, which will allow for strong realist claims for the rationality and truth of specific claims without falling into some version of Enlightenment foundationalism. The plausibility of both relativism and perspectivism derives from the fact that both reflect the inversion of the Enlightenment ideal of a universally valid standard of rationality and truth. Since this cannot be attained (and MacIntyre agrees that it cannot), the only alternative, it is said, is some form of relativism or perspectivism. On the contrary, MacIntyre responds, there is a third alternative, the possibility that the development of traditions, both internally and in relation to one another, can itself be considered to be a genuinely rational process that, if it goes well, moves in the direction of an ever-fuller grasp of reality (*Whose Justice?*, pp. 353–354). He goes on to develop this third alternative through an account of the rationality embedded in the development of traditions.

> The rationality of a tradition-constituted and tradition-constitutive enquiry is in key and essential part a matter of the kind of progress which it makes through a number of well-defined types of stage. Every such form of enquiry begins in and from some condition of pure historical contingency, from the beliefs, institutions and practices of some particular community which constitute a given. (*Whose Justice?*, p. 354)[7]

Initially, these starting points are taken to be authoritative in such a way as to be placed beyond question, or at least beyond systematic questioning. But matters cannot rest there. As the bearers of this tradition continue to reflect on these canonical starting points, internal contradictions will become apparent, divergences of interpretation will emerge, and new circumstances will call into question the significance or the practicality of earlier normative commitments. If the tradition is to survive at all, these tensions must be resolved and the tradition must be reformulated, to some degree at least, in order to retain its relevance and application in changing circumstances.

At this point, a tradition has the resources to generate a concept of truth as the adequation of mind to reality. If the bearers of a tradition succeed in resolving its internal tensions and carrying it forward successfully, they will at some point be in a position to compare the earlier stages of that tradition with its later, more successful stages. But by what criterion will they judge that these later stages are in fact more successful? Whatever the specifics of the answer for a particular tradition, it will imply that the later stage of an ongoing tradition is more adequate because it is in better accord with the realities toward which it is directed. To be more exact, the tradition in its later stages will provide a more adequate framework within which to attain that adequation of the mind with its objects that MacIntyre takes to be the authentic meaning of a correspondence theory of truth – not that the inhabitants of a tradition will necessarily express its greater adequacy in such terms.[8] Once this possibility emerges, however, it implies that the present stage of any tradition (including the inquirer's own) may similarly be inadequate in some yet to be discovered way. And the emergence of this further possibility marks an important intellectual advance because, at this point, one can no longer equate the truth of a given judgment with its adequacy by the best standards of one's tradition. In other words, at this point truth can no longer be equated with warranted assertability.

MacIntyre notes that the development of a tradition is neither Cartesian nor Hegelian: just as a tradition begins from contingent rather than necessary starting points, so its best conclusions are always provisional:

> Implicit in the rationality of such enquiry there is indeed a conception of a final truth, that is to say, a relationship of the mind to its objects which would be wholly adequate in respect of the capacities of that mind. But any conception of that state as one in which the mind could by its own powers know itself as thus adequately informed is ruled out; the Absolute Knowledge of the Hegelian system is from this tradition-constituted standpoint a chimaera. (*Whose Justice?*, pp. 360–361)

MacIntyre goes on to observe that this fact, that tradition-constituted inquiry does not provide for certainty in either its starting points or its conclusions, gives credence to the perspectivist and relativist challenges. In order fully to address these challenges, it is necessary to turn to a further stage in the development of a tradition, which is occasioned by what MacIntyre describes as an "epistemological crisis" (*Whose Justice?*, p. 361).

At every stage in its development, a tradition in good order is constituted by a dynamic process of development and adaptation. An epistemological crisis occurs when this process is in some way stymied: "At any point, it may happen to any tradition-constituted enquiry that by its own standards of progress it ceases to make progress" (*Whose Justice?*, p. 361). At this point, the certitudes of the tradition are called into question and, in order to move forward, its exponents must engage in genuine conceptual innovation. That is to say, they must somehow arrive at new concepts or theories that are not derived from the earlier stages of their tradition, which has so far been inadequate to address the problems at hand; correlatively, these innovations can only be justified in terms of their ability to resolve what had previously been insurmountable difficulties. At this point, any retrospective history of the tradition would incorporate some account of the crisis and its resolution. Because it is (by hypothesis) an account of a successful resolution, this account will include (or imply) a claim to offer a more adequate way of understanding the issues at hand. Correlatively, it will include (or imply) a better understanding of the structures of justification than was previously available, in terms of which the earlier inadequacies of the tradition and their subsequent resolution can be understood. Not only do these claims imply the possibility of making truth claims that go beyond warranted assertability, they actually amount to such truth claims, since they are themselves implicit or explicit claims for truth (both about the subject matter at hand, and about the tradition itself) that go beyond a defense of assertability in terms of the tradition as it exists at any one point.[9] In this way, MacIntyre answers the relativist challenge that truth is equivalent to warranted assertability within the terms of a particular tradition. However, the perspectivist challenge remains to be fully addressed.

In order to do so, MacIntyre considers a further (possible) stage in the development of a tradition in epistemological crisis. That is, a crisis of this kind creates a situation in which a fruitful encounter with a rival tradition can take place and, as a result of such an encounter, proponents of the first tradition may be forced to acknowledge that the rival offers a better account of difficulties which they themselves could not have resolved – better, that is, by *their own* best standards of judgment. As a result, the proponents of these two traditions are able to make a comparative judgment about the relative rational superiority of one tradition over another – precisely the kind of judgment that the perspectivist claims to be impossible. That, at least, is MacIntyre's argument; in order to sustain it, he must offer a convincing analysis of what is involved in the encounter between two traditions and the relative vindication of one over and against the other.

In order for an encounter between two rival traditions to take place, it is first of all necessary that two rival traditions be brought into genuine contact. This requires more than an awareness of each tradition on the part of the bearers of the alternative tradition; it requires that some representatives of each tradition be in sustained contact with the other, and that they remain sufficiently open to consider the claims of the rival tradition seriously.

Furthermore, it presupposes that bearers of each tradition are able to recognize that the alternative represents a genuine rival, that the alternative offers a distinct account of the same realities with which they themselves are concerned. Thus, the conceptual incommensurability between them cannot be so great that proponents of each are unable to agree on at least a partially shared description of the world; otherwise, communication and translation of rival claims between them would be impossible. Before a physician and a shaman can recognize that they have incommensurable views of medical practice, they must at least agree roughly on what counts as sickness. (Otherwise, they would not be able to recognize that they represent two *rival* traditions, which offer two incommensurable approaches to the *same* reality or practical task.) At the same time MacIntyre insists, contrary to Donald Davidson and others, that this level of agreement does not rule out genuine logical incommensurability between the two traditions. (MacIntyre argues for this claim in detail in the chapter of *Whose Justice?* called "Tradition and Translation," pp. 370–388; for Davidson's argument, see Davidson 1974). The shared agreements are not sufficient by themselves to resolve the differences between the two traditions because, in addition, their proponents bring radically different beliefs and standards of judgment to their evaluation of whatever it is that they recognize in common.

At any rate, some degree of communication comprises only a necessary condition for an encounter between rival traditions. In order for such an encounter to take place, there must in addition be some members of each tradition who are able to enter imaginatively into the central beliefs and commitments of the other, at least provisionally. This process involves assimilating the worldview of the rival tradition so that one can consider its claims, at least provisionally, as one's own. Someone who is able in this way to move between two ways of viewing the world is thereby enabled to recognize that the rival tradition offers conceptual possibilities that his or her native tradition does not offer. From this vantage point, it becomes possible to see that problems which arise and appear to be insoluble within one tradition may be resolvable from within the second tradition. And if this is indeed the case, then it makes sense for the proponents of the first tradition to acknowledge that, by their own criteria of judgment, the second tradition offers the possibility of a more adequate grasp of reality in at least some respects. In that case, if the proponents of the first tradition are to be rational *by their own best standards of judgment*, they will acknowledge the superiority of the second tradition, at least in some respects, and will move toward adopting its criteria for judgment, at least partially. Of course, the encounter may go in the other direction. But if an advocate of one tradition is to justify a claim to rational superiority over another tradition, he or she must argue the case on the terms set by that rival tradition, initially at least, showing that by the standards set by the latter, his or her own tradition can better resolve what its proponents themselves feel to be serious difficulties.

This is clearly a more developed and sophisticated account of traditions than that offered in *After Virtue*. It cashes in the promise of the earlier book to offer an account of rationality that does not reject, but on the contrary presupposes, the socially and historically situated character of all practical and speculative reason. Yet MacIntyre's account of rationality as tradition-constituted inquiry also raises questions, both with respect to the relation between the concepts of tradition in *After Virtue* and in *Whose Justice? Which Rationality?*, and more generally with respect to the meaning of "tradition" as MacIntyre understands it.

In comparing the earlier and later treatments, one difference immediately becomes apparent: what had initially been suggested as a moral concept, a part of the necessary framework for developing the idea of virtue, has now been transformed into an epistemic and linguistic concept, which plays a central role in explicating the meaning of truth and rationality. On this latter view, a tradition in good order provides a framework within which the mind approaches, perhaps even attains, that adequacy to its objects that for MacIntyre is the authentic meaning of a correspondence theory of truth. This view, in turn, implies that a tradition is itself referential, at least in a broad sense; it has a subject matter, it is "about" something that it mediates to the intellects of those participating in it. This implication is not necessarily at odds with the view that a tradition is constituted by debates over the good, but at the very least we see a significant change of emphasis here.

In fact, these two different uses of tradition suggest two different understandings of what a tradition is. It is difficult it see how the account of tradition developed in *Whose Justice? Which Rationality*? could apply to all of the examples of traditions that were suggested by *After Virtue*: what is monasticism "about," and what kind of encounter with a rival could lead proponents of such a tradition to conclude that they have an inadequate account of the subject matter of their tradition?[10] This brings us to a more fundamental question: What does it mean to say that any tradition is "about" something in the necessary sense? To put it another way, in what way can a tradition be considered to be referential, to be incommensurable with another tradition, to be revised in light of a more adequate understanding of reality, and the like?

MacIntyre does have an answer to this question, although to my knowledge he does not develop it in these terms. The main lines of that answer are suggested by one of his lesser-known recent works, a monograph based on his 1990 Marquette University Aquinas lecture, *First Principles, Final Ends and Contemporary Philosophical Issues*.[11] On first glance, this monograph would seem to have little relevance to the topic of tradition. MacIntyre's aim is to explain and defend Aquinas' account of *per se nota* principles, arguing that while they are in some sense the starting points for all reflection, they nonetheless do not function as foundational first principles in a Cartesian sense.[12] The key to understanding Aquinas' account, he argues, is found in the Aristotelian conception of a perfect science, which Aquinas takes over and extends (*First Principles*, pp. 25, 28–29). On the Aristotelian/Thomistic understanding of it, a perfected science would consist of a series of propositions perspicuously derived from a set of first principles, which are primary in the sense of being unjustified in terms of the science themselves, although they may be justified in terms of some higher science. This in turn presupposes a hierarchy of sciences in which the highest sciences do rest on principles that are *per se nota*, which correlatively display the implications of these first principles (*First Principles*, pp. 36–37).

So far, this seems to suggest an account of truth and rationality that is not only irrelevant to MacIntyre's account of rationality as tradition-guided inquiry, but actually antithetical to it. However, at this point we need to recall a critical qualification that MacIntyre has already made, namely that the role played by the first principles in a completed science is logical or conceptual, but not epistemic. The claims of the science do in fact follow from its first principles, but this may not be apparent until the science actually is completed, and the relation of its various claims is rendered perspicuous.[13] Matters are very different when we are dealing with a science that is still in the process of development – a condition that would apply to nearly every actual form of inquiry with which we have to deal.[14]

When we examine what MacIntyre has to say about the forms of inquiry appropriate to a science under development, the relevance to his discussion of tradition in *Whose Justice? Which Rationality?* becomes apparent. Even though MacIntyre does not describe a developing science as a tradition in *First Principles*, his description of a science in the process of formation in this book is strikingly similar in several key respects to a tradition as described in the earlier book. It begins from contingent starting points, it develops through a process of self-correction and expansion until it reaches a level of complexity at which encounters with alternative explanations of the same set of phenomena can be fruitful, and it vindicates itself through an ongoing series of encounters with its rivals, showing how its explanations are more successful in terms that proponents of the rival tradition can themselves acknowledge (see, respectively, *First Principles*, pp. 31; 34–35; 37–38; and 32). Finally, to turn to a point not yet remarked, a science in the process of development must be understood teleologically. That is to say, if an incipient science is fundamentally sound, it will develop in a more or less orderly way toward greater comprehensiveness and clarity, although of course MacIntyre does not claim that this will necessarily be a smooth, unbroken progression. Correlatively, a retrospective history of the development of the science will evaluate its various stages in terms of their contributions to, or inadequacies in the light of, the best possible grasp of the aims of the science attained so far (*First Principles*, pp. 47–51). This is at least congruent with MacIntyre's claim, first asserted in *After Virtue* and repeated in *Whose Justice? Which Rationality?*, that the history of intellectual inquiry needs to be written teleologically, in terms of some assessment of its successes and failures.

These points of contact suggest strongly that when MacIntyre speaks of a tradition as a form of intellectual inquiry in the last chapters of *Whose Justice? Which Rationality?*, what he has in mind, at least as the paradigm case of such an inquiry, is a developing science understood in the Aristotelian/Thomistic sense of the term. The chief advantage of this interpretation is that it allows us to speak in a coherent way about the subject matter of a tradition, that which the tradition is "about," and to characterize it in terms of its adequacy to that subject matter. The referent of the tradition will be the object of the science, of which the tradition represents an incipient stage, and towards which its development is oriented so long as it is in good order. Correlatively, this suggests that traditions derive their identity and unity from this object in such a way that, for example, both the Ptolemaic and Copernican traditions take their identity from the movements of heavenly bodies. At the same time, the success of the Copernican tradition relative to the Ptolemaic tradition has the further implication that the latter tradition, but not the former, can be superseded by being incorporated into a wider tradition of inquiry into astronomical phenomena. The Ptolemaic tradition has simply been dropped; the Copernican tradition has been transformed into a partial but (within limits) accurate account of an object that can be more comprehensively understood in another way. (The same might be said of Aristotelian vs. Newtonian physics, seen in relation to contemporary relativistic physics.)[15] Finally, this account has the interesting implication that we may not know what a tradition is about until it approaches its final stages. That is, we may not be able to characterize the identity of a given tradition, or to put it in its proper relation to other traditions, until a fairly late stage in its development; indeed, we may come to realize that our own apparent traditions are not only flawed but are not even traditions at all because they lack any real unified object (perhaps astrology would be an example of a pseudo-tradition of this kind).

What are we to make of the account of tradition developed in *Whose Justice? Which Rationality?* This is clearly a more developed account than we find in *After Virtue*, and it offers an advance in many respects. It provides a way of thinking about the epistemic functioning and rational status of traditions that is interesting and (at least for this reader) persuasive. On this account, genuine conversation and even intellectual conversion between proponents of rival traditions are possible, even though there is no point at which the interlocutors stand outside any tradition whatever. We might say that, on MacIntyre's view, the necessity for standing outside of any tradition whatever is obviated by the possibility of standing within two traditions at once in order to move between them in a comparative assessment of their claims. At the same time, this account of traditions offers a plausible resolution of key questions in contemporary philosophical discussions of truth and rationality, one that preserves a strong meaning for both terms without resorting to a widely discredited foundationalism.

However, it is not so clear that MacIntyre's defense of the rationality of tradition-guided inquiry can be translated straightforwardly into a defense of *moral* rationality, or that it can address the problems of moral pluralism that he raises in *After Virtue*. MacIntyre's own agenda is set by moral philosophy, and he explicitly says that the rationality exhibited in scientific disputes is no different from the rationality exhibited by moral disputes (*After Virtue*, p. 268). Yet this is not evident. In my view, MacIntyre's account of the rational development and encounter of traditions is most plausible when applied to rival scientific traditions, understanding "scientific" broadly to include any kind of inquiry which would fall under the ambit of what Aquinas called the speculative intellect. When these sorts of traditions break down or come into conflict, the resultant dialogue is conducted in a context of observations about, and active engagement with, the natural world. It is true, of course, that disagreements between incommensurable traditions cannot be resolved simply by appeals to observation, since the terms in which proponents of rival traditions describe their observations are themselves in dispute. Nonetheless, as noted above, there must be some level, however rudimentary, at which shared description is possible, or there could be no encounter between rival traditions at all. Correlatively, as conflicts between rival traditions are resolved, the parties to the conflict will find themselves increasingly converging on a shared description of the observed world.

Yet as a number of moral philosophers have argued, moral claims cannot be placed on a par with scientific or observational claims because they are grounded (in some sense) in our own collective commitments and decisions.[16] We, collectively, are the originators (usually not the conscious and deliberate originators) of the basic moral concepts that structure our lives. Of course, it might be said that this view of moral claims is itself a product of a modern division between facts and values that MacIntyre wants to repudiate. But MacIntyre himself agrees that moral claims are at least partially grounded in our collective commitments. In commenting on the influence of Vico on his own work, MacIntyre remarks that Vico was the first to emphasize

> the importance of the undeniable fact, which it is becoming tedious to reiterate, that the subject matters of moral philosophy at least – the evaluative and normative concepts, maxims, arguments and judgments about which the moral philosopher enquires – *are nowhere to be found except as embodied in the historical lives of particular social groups and so possessing the distinctive characteristics of historical existence*: both identity and change through time, expression in institutionalized practice as well as in discourse, interaction and interrelationship with a variety of forms of activity. Morality which is no particular society's morality is to be found nowhere. (*After Virtue*, pp. 265–266; emphasis added)

Given this conception of morality, it is not clear how the rival claims of disparate moral traditions could be adjudicated. Indeed, it is not clear that there could be sufficient genuine conflict between moral traditions for them to count as genuinely rival traditions. (A similar line of criticism is developed in response to *After Virtue* in Bernstein 1984.) You, collectively, arrange your lives in one way, we arrange our lives in a different way. Is it clear that we even *disagree*? What is the shared subject matter of our disagreements? And what would count as resolving these disagreements, since there is no question here of coming to agree on a description of anything? Certainly, we might come to agree on the best way to arrange our lives, but that would represent a change in mores, and not a convergence of thinking about a shared object of inquiry. This need not imply that moral traditions are arational in their internal development or their contact with other traditions, but it does suggest that an account of practical reason cannot simply be read off from the account of rationality as tradition-based inquiry that MacIntyre develops.

In response to this, MacIntyre would probably reply that he does offer extended accounts of moral traditions in conflict in both *After Virtue* and

Whose Justice? Which Rationality?, to say nothing of the subsequent *Three Rival Versions of Moral Enquiry*. (See MacIntyre's response to Bernstein 1984, MacIntyre 1984b.) Certainly, the narratives developed in these books do offer impressive support for his overall thesis. Yet they do not fully address the questions raised above. While the scope of this essay does not allow for a detailed assessment of MacIntyre's narratives, let me suggest three issues that remain to be addressed.

First, the moral traditions MacIntyre discusses are almost always traditions that are contiguous in some way; they represent successor traditions within European society (classical and Hellenistic traditions, Augustinian and Thomistic Christianity), or else they are contemporaneous and have developed in close proximity with one another (Scottish and English traditions in early modernity). At the very least, this suggests that the proponents of these traditions would have had a great deal in common, including (in many cases) a shared past and many common customs and institutions. Of course, this does not rule out the possibility of incommensurability among them; indeed, it may be that some very considerable commonalities of these kinds are necessary if moral traditions are to come into conflict in the sense required for MacIntyre's theory at all. However, this does raise the question of how MacIntyre's theory of rationality as tradition-guided inquiry would deal with the case of moral traditions that did not develop in contact with, or dependence upon, one another, and that therefore do not emerge within a context of shared history, institutions, and customs. Would any rational encounter between such traditions be possible at all, and if so, how might it be resolved?[17]

Second, it is not always obvious that the traditions MacIntyre sees as coming into conflict do in fact conflict as *moral* traditions. This is especially true with respect to the conflict he identifies between Aristotelianism and Augustinian Christianity. Certainly, these do come into conflict on questions of theology, metaphysics, and epistemology, but it is not so clear that they are also incommensurably at odds with respect to moral commitments.[18] MacIntyre claims that every philosophical inquiry has practical implications, and so he might respond that incommensurability at the theoretical level implies incommensurability at the practical level (*Three Rival Versions*, p. 128). But even if we grant that every theoretical inquiry has practical implications (and this is not obvious), the conclusion does not follow. MacIntyre would have to show that the specific points of incommensurability he identifies did in fact lead to specific, incommensurable judgments, and this (in my view) he does not do, at least in the case of the Aristotelian and Augustinian traditions.

Finally, and more specifically, MacIntyre underestimates the extent to which Aristotelian concepts had already shaped Christian moral thought before the reintroduction of Aristotle's philosophical and moral works into Western Europe in the twelfth and thirteenth centuries. As the historian Cary Nederman points out, key elements of Aristotle's moral thought were mediated to Christian theology through a number of classical and patristic sources, and can be identified in medieval writings at least 150 years before the reintroduction of Aristotle's *Nicomachaean Ethics* into the West (Nederman 1991). This may seem like a minor point, and yet MacIntyre himself insists that his historical narrative is foundational to his philosophical argument: "I am committed to maintaining that although arguments of the kind favored by analytic philosophy do possess an indispensable power, it is only within the context of a particular genre of historical inquiry that such arguments can support the type of claim about truth and rationality which philosophers characteristically aspire to justify" (*After Virtue*, p. 265). Furthermore, MacIntyre's analysis of the encounter between Aristotelian and Augustinian thought plays a pivotal role both in *Whose Justice? Which Rationality?* and the subsequent *Three Rival Versions of Moral Enquiry*. Given this, the relevance of Nederman's observation to MacIntyre's project cannot be denied.

I do not mean to suggest that MacIntyre could not address these issues, but only to indicate points at which his theory seems to call for further development. Moreover, it would not necessarily represent a defect in that theory if we were forced to conclude that, in some cases, moral traditions are so profoundly divergent that no genuine encounter, or much less rational engagement and vindication of one over the other, can take place.

3. TRADITION AS A FORM OF MORAL INQUIRY: *THREE RIVAL VERSIONS OF MORAL ENQUIRY*

In *Three Rival Versions of Moral Enquiry*, MacIntyre offers a more extended illustration and defense of the central thesis of *Whose Justice? Which Rationality?* that

> an admission of significant incommensurability and untranslatability in the relations between two opposed systems of thought and practice can be a prologue not only to rational debate, but to that kind of debate from which one party can emerge as undoubtedly superior, if only because exposure to such debate may reveal that one of the contending standpoints fails in its own terms and by its own standards. (*Three Rival Versions*, p. 5)

This book thus continues the trajectory of its predecessor, and in addition, it returns to themes from *After Virtue* that were not so prominent in *Whose Justice? Which Rationality?* At the same time, this latest book also modifies the earlier account of tradition in subtle but significant ways.

In order to trace the outlines of the concept of tradition developed in this third book, we must first place MacIntyre's discussion of tradition within the context of his overall argument. The eponymous three rival versions which he considers are encyclopaedia, exemplified by the authors of the late-nineteenth-century ninth edition of the *Encyclopaedia Britannica*, genealogy, exemplified by Nietzsche and his current postmodern heirs, and Thomism, which properly understood entails an explicit commitment to tradition-based inquiry.

The encyclopaedists were characterized by the belief that it is possible to arrive at a set of universal standards, compelling to all rational persons, within which the rival claims of different cultures and modes of inquiry can be assessed and resolved (*Three Rival Versions*, p. 14). Clearly, this represents a version of the Enlightenment project, and MacIntyre finds it no more persuasive than he did when he wrote *After Virtue*; in his view, the claims of the encyclopaedists have been decisively defeated (*Three Rival Versions*, pp. 55–56). The genealogists, in contrast, appear to him to offer an alternative form of moral inquiry that is still, so to speak, in play, insofar as it has yet to be decisively answered by its strongest antagonists. On the genealogists' view, the development of inquiry reflects social forces beyond it, and more particularly relations of power, which intellectual inquiry serves to both support and conceal. The genealogist attempts to develop an alternative mode of discourse, characterized by the adoption and expressions of a multiplicity of perspectives, none of which is given foundational or definitive status (*Three Rival Versions*, pp. 35–36, 42–43). The genealogist also takes on the task of unmasking, revealing the social arrangements and special interests that seemingly pure theoretical constructs serve to conceal.

Before turning to a closer examination of his construal of Thomism as tradition-based inquiry, we need to consider one other aspect of these two rivals. That is, in what sense are these traditions of *moral* inquiry? When we compare the two, it is striking that, while both have moral implications, these implications are central for the genealogical project in a way that they are not for the encyclopaedists. (And although he does not explicitly say so, this may be another reason why, on MacIntyre's view, the genealogists represent the stronger alternative.) For the encyclopaedists, the paradigmatic moral narrative is exemplified by Agnes Mary Clerke, an astronomer and historian of science who contributed articles on the lives of the astronomers to the ninth edition of the *Encyclopaedia Britannica*. Clerke moved from a sheltered girlhood in Ireland to private study in Italy, eventually to become, in MacIntyre's words, one of "the foremost minds of her age." What is paradigmatic about her story, as he goes on to explain, is its steady progress from cultural isolation to enlightenment, understood in terms of participation in the highest rational discourse of the age (*Three Rival Versions*, p. 21). The genealogists, for their part, clearly bring a moral agenda to their work, driven by the desire to expose the inequities and especially the relations of power and dominion hidden by all forms of intellectual discourse. As this would suggest, they are committed to ideals of equality and individual freedom, seen over against the oppressive structures of control concealed by intellectual discourse – an agenda with which, as we have noted, MacIntyre has a great deal of sympathy.

Having sketched these two alternatives, MacIntyre goes on in *Three Rival Versions* to set forth his own preferred alternative, namely tradition as a form of intellectual and moral inquiry. He takes Pope Leo XIII's encyclical *Aeterni Patris* to be the seminal nineteenth-century statement of this alternative, and he argues that a Thomism that is true to the spirit and intention of Aquinas' own work offers the best option for carrying forward a tradition-based inquiry today (*Three Rival Versions*, p. 2).

Correlatively, the extended example of tradition-based inquiry that MacIntyre offers is taken from Christian thought in late antiquity and the Middle Ages, beginning with Augustine and culminating with Aquinas. On MacIntyre's view, Augustine develops what becomes the canonical formulation of Christianity as an intellectual tradition, at least for Western Europe, through his synthesis of Scripture and neo-Platonism (*Three Rival Versions*, pp. 82–103). This synthesis dominated both intellectual and institutional structures up until the twelfth and thirteenth centuries, including, significantly, the University of Paris, which was structured on the basis of the Augustinian conviction that "rationality [is] internal to a system of beliefs and practices in such a way that, without acceptance at some fundamental level of those beliefs and initiation into the form of life defined by those practices, rational encounter with Augustinianism is ruled out, except in the most limited way" (*Three Rival Versions*, p. 98). At the same time, however, the universities, and above all the University of Paris, provide the institutional setting for a radical challenge to Augustinianism in the form of a revitalized Aristotelianism.

According to MacIntyre, Aristotle's thought challenged Augustinian theology in three fundamental ways: (1) Aristotle defended the natural capacity of the intellect to know its proper objects, whereas for Augustine, a realization of the intellect's incapacity is the necessary starting point for all intellectual and moral progress; (2) Aristotle identifies truth as the correspondence of the mind to its object, whereas Augustine locates it in the source of the relationship between finite objects and the primal truth, that is to say, God; (3) finally, Aristotle has no concept of the will, whereas for Augustine the will exists and is the primary source of moral error. In short, these authors reflect two incommensurable approaches to intellectual inquiry:

> For each contending party had no standard by which to judge the questions about which it differed from the other which was not itself as much in dispute as anything else. And there was no possible neutral standard, since all three key areas of disagreements are part of a systematically different and incompatible conceptualization of the human intellect in its relationship to its objects, to the passions, to the will, and to the virtues. (*Three Rival Versions*, p. 111; the three areas of disagreement are spelled out on pp. 109–111)

At the same time, these rival and incommensurable claims found an institutional setting in the University of Paris, where the philosophers in the faculty of liberal arts tended to defend Aristotelian thought, whereas the theologians defended the Augustinian alternative (*Three Rival Versions*, pp. 112–113).

Aquinas resolved these competing claims through a systematic reformulation of Aristotelian thought in Christian terms (just as Augustine had resolved similar tensions through a synthesis of Neoplatonism and Scripture). Not only did he show that Aristotle's thought need not be inimical to Christian doctrine, he also demonstrated that Christian theology offers a more adequate resolution to problems Aristotle himself recognized but could not resolve. In so doing, he transformed the Neoplatonic Christianity of Augustine, but he transformed Aristotle as well, showing how a properly reformulated Christianity is in fact the best continuation of Aristotelianism as an intellectual tradition. By the same token, he offered a radical challenge to the university structures of his time, since he placed the study of Aristotle within the ambit of the theologians rather than the philosophers (in general, see *Three Rival Versions*, pp. 127–148; in particular, see pp. 122–124; and with reference to Aquinas' challenge to university structures, pp. 132–133).

As this brief summary suggests, and as MacIntyre himself argues, the view of tradition offered here is similar in key respects to that developed in *Whose Justice? Which Rationality?* (MacIntyre summarizes his key claims about incommensurability and the possibility of rational encounter between rival traditions in *Three Rival Versions* at pp. 116–120.) Tradition is seen as fundamentally a form of intellectual inquiry, characterized by its own distinctive form of rationality. As in the earlier book, the development of tradition is seen as a necessarily historical process, driven both by the internal tensions of a given tradition and by the dynamics of encounter with other traditions. The test of adequacy lies in the possibility of carrying a tradition forward; the test of rational superiority is found in the ability of one tradition to offer a more adequate account and resolution of the difficulties and inconsistencies of another than that other tradition can do on its own terms.

At the same time, MacIntyre qualifies his earlier account of tradition in a significant way. That is, in this book he emphasizes the parallels between intellectual inquiry and the practice of a craft, parallels that become evident once we realize that "to be adequately initiated into a craft is to be adequately initiated into a tradition" (*Three Rival Versions*, p. 128). Of course the idea of a practice, presumably including crafts, also played a central role in *After Virtue*. But, at the very least, the parallels MacIntyre draws between intellectual inquiry and the practice of a craft represent a new emphasis in his thought, and they point to two significant modifications of his concept of a tradition.

Why does MacIntyre emphasize initiation into a craft as a paradigmatic example of initiation into a tradition? Most fundamentally, he wants to make the point that initiation into a tradition requires certain kinds of relationships and, correspondingly, certain personal qualities and attitudes, which are particularly apparent when we consider what is involved in becoming proficient in a craft, but which are just as necessary for initiation into a tradition of inquiry. Indeed, rightly understood, moral inquiry is itself a craft requiring certain kinds of relationships and personal qualities (*Three Rival Versions*, p. 63). It is first of all necessary that the initiate stand in a relation of trust to a master or teacher, someone who is able to judge the quality of the initiate's work and to direct him or her on how to go further (*Three Rival Versions*, pp. 65–66). At least initially, the initiate must be prepared to act on the master's directions without him- or herself being able to grasp the point of those directions; that is to say, initiation into intellectual inquiry is impossible except on the condition that the novice be prepared to accept some form of intellectual authority (*Three Rival Versions*, pp. 89–93;

at this point, MacIntyre is discussing the Augustinian tradition in particular, but he clearly believes that the same may be said of tradition-based inquiry in general). This places tradition-based inquiry squarely at odds with both the encyclopaedists and the genealogists since, for the former, rationality demands that from the outset one think for oneself, and for the latter, such forms of authority can only be expressions of power (*Three Rival Versions*, p. 66). Correlatively, the initiate must be open to developing certain personal qualities, namely, an adherence to the goods constitutive of the tradition and a willingness to develop virtues in accordance with those goods. Only in this way can he or she develop the capacities of insight and judgment necessary to grasp the central texts and commitments of the tradition (*Three Rival Versions*, pp. 62–63).

Tradition-based inquiry thus offers direct and fundamental challenges to the conceptions of intellectual inquiry offered by both alternatives. How are these to be adjudicated? As a self-professed partisan of tradition, MacIntyre attempts to defend the claims of tradition in a way suggested by that mode of inquiry: he considers how each of these forms of inquiry has fared in resolving its inner tensions and in defending itself against its challengers. He makes short work of the encyclopaedists, as we noted above. The conflict with the genealogists, on the other hand, is for him still very much an open issue. In his view, tradition-based inquiry will ultimately be vindicated, and he suggests that one point at which its relative superiority will be vindicated lies in its capacity to give a more adequate account of the self. However, he acknowledges that this forecast needs to be defended at more length through ongoing argument and encounter (*Three Rival Versions*, pp. 196–215).

The scope of this chapter does not permit a more extended assessment of MacIntyre's arguments in this brief but ambitious work.[19] To a considerable degree, it represents a defense and extension of the account of rationality as tradition-guided inquiry developed in *Whose Justice? Which Rationality?*, and anyone who finds that account fundamentally persuasive (as I do) will likewise find much of this book to be persuasive. At the same time, this book modifies MacIntyre's earlier accounts of tradition in subtle but significant ways, and these modifications raise questions about the overall direction of MacIntyre's project. Let me focus on one such question, that of the role played by authority in the processes of initiation into and participation in a tradition.

As we have seen, in his earlier accounts of tradition MacIntyre has emphasized the open-ended and even conflictual character of traditions, so much so that he sometimes has been characterized as a crypto-liberal himself.[20] In this book, however, he underscores another aspect of traditions, the essential role played by authority in tradition-based inquiry. This new emphasis is signaled early in the book:

> [The dichotomy between encyclopaedia and genealogy conceals] a third possibility, the possibility that reason can only move towards being genuinely universal and impersonal insofar as it is neither neutral nor disinterested, that membership in a particular type of moral community, *one from which fundamental dissent has to be excluded*, is a condition for genuinely rational enquiry and more especially for moral and theological enquiry. (*Three Rival Versions*, pp. 59–60; emphasis added)

In *Whose Justice? Which Rationality?* MacIntyre mentioned one respect in which authority plays a necessary role in tradition-based inquiry. He argues that every tradition starts from contingent commitments, usually embodied in oral or written texts that are initially given authoritative status. But this form of authority is only provisional since, as a tradition begins to develop, these authoritative texts will be inevitably subject to questioning and reinterpretation; indeed, MacIntyre suggests that this process is a necessary first stage in the emergence of tradition-situated rationality. In *Three Rival Versions* he reaffirms the necessity for this kind of authority (p. 91).

At the same time, in the latter book he adds two further respects in which authority is necessary to the functioning of tradition. One of these is implicit in the relationship between an initiate and master of any tradition-embedded practice. Every apprentice in a craft, including the craft of intellectual inquiry, must learn how to make two key distinctions, first between a course of action that appears to be good and a course of action that is genuinely good, and second between that which is good and best for the individual and that which is good and best without qualification (*Three Rival Versions*, pp. 61–62). In each case, the initiate can only learn through relying on the judgment of a master who is capable of making the distinctions that the initiate cannot yet make, and whose directives must therefore be accepted as authoritative. The authority of the master, correlatively, is not just an authority of expertise or accomplishment:

> The authority of a master within a craft is both more and other than a matter of exemplifying the best standards so far. It is also and most importantly a matter of knowing how to go further and especially how to direct others towards going further, using what can be learned from the tradition afforded by the past to move towards the *telos* of fully perfected work. It is in thus knowing how to link past and future that those with authority

> are able to draw upon tradition, to interpret and reinterpret it, so that its directedness towards the *telos* of that particular craft becomes apparent in new and characteristically unexpected ways. And it is by the ability to teach others how to learn this type of knowing how that the power of the master within the community of a craft is legitimated as rational authority. (*Three Rival Versions*, pp. 65–66)

As this paragraph illustrates, MacIntyre's claim for the necessity of authority in this second sense draws upon the discussion of practices and their relation to tradition in *After Virtue*. MacIntyre has modified the earlier account in some respects; most significantly, he now appears to equate tradition-based inquiry with a kind of practice, whereas in the earlier book the idea of a practice plays a more preliminary and limited role in his overall account of virtue and tradition. Nonetheless, this represents a plausible extension of insights from *After Virtue*, even though the relation between MacIntyre's earlier and later accounts of practices and traditions could be further clarified.

However, this form of authority, like the first we have considered, does not appear to exclude "fundamental dissent." At least on first glance, it would seem to be provisional – apprentices eventually become masters themselves – and moreover it is limited in scope, since it is located within a particular relationship. This suggests a third form of authority, and reading on we find that MacIntyre does assert the need for some authoritative presence that can oversee the development of a tradition as a whole. The functioning of this kind of authority was exemplified by Peter Abelard's willing acceptance of the authority of the church after his condemnation as a heretic: "it is also true that Abelard *did* challenge established authority, but yet by his own obedient acceptance of established authority's response he did as much as anyone to clarify the relationship of dialectic to authority" (*Three Rival Versions*, p. 89, emphasis in the original; MacIntyre goes on to develop this interpretation of Abelard's conflicts with Bernard and others on pp. 90–91). Furthermore, acceptance of this kind of authority is implicit in the other two forms discussed above, since as we progress in inquiry we come to realize that authoritative testimony will always be necessary to intellectual progress:

> So continuous authority receives its justification as indispensable to a continuing progress, the narrative of which we first learned how to recount from that authority and the truth of which is confirmed by our own further progress, including that progress made by means of dialectical enquiry.

> The practice of specifically Augustinian dialectic and the belief of the Augustinian dialectician that this practice is a movement towards a truth never as yet wholly grasped thus presupposes the guidance of authority. Hence when *the very same authority* places restrictions upon dialectic enquiry, it would be unreasonable not to submit. Abelard's submission, therefore, unlike Galileo's was of a piece with his enquiries. The acknowledgment of authority was already an essential element in those enquiries. (*Three Rival Versions*, pp. 92–93; italics added)

So far as I can determine, MacIntyre does not consider this aspect of the Augustinian conception of moral inquiry to have been superseded by Aquinas' synthesizing reformulation, and if this is indeed the case, we may assume that he endorses this conception of authority. Yet it raises questions that go to the core of his account of rationality as tradition-guided inquiry.

The first of these is implicit in the phrase emphasized above: what justification do we have for considering the authority granted to the canonical texts of a tradition, the authority of a master in relation to an apprentice, and a centralized authority that oversees an extended program of research and discussion, to be different forms of one and the same authority? On the face of it, not only is this claim not obvious, it is not even plausible. To take the case of Abelard, it seems clear that Scripture, Roscelin, and the Pope stood in three different relations to Abelard, and exercised three distinct kinds of authority over him. How could it be otherwise? After all, authoritative texts or lore must be mediated through the pedagogy of individual masters or teachers; very few of those who participate in a tradition can have a personal relation with its central authority figures, as they do with their own teachers. Furthermore, within a complex tradition there are likely to be many loci for authority, appealing to different rationales and functioning in different ways. Certainly, medieval theologians distinguished the teaching authority of a master, which depends on his personal competence, from the teaching authority of a bishop, which attaches to his office. (On this point, see Congar 1982 and Rist 1994, pp. 56–63.)

This observation brings us to a further point. It may be that MacIntyre does not argue for his concept of authority because he considers that the history of the period evidently vindicates it. Yet vindication is not evident. MacIntyre's sources for medieval history are fairly dated, and he does not take account of a more recent considerable body of work on the interactions between social and intellectual developments in this period. As a result, he does not take account of the ways in which the location of authority, its scope, and its proper limits were themselves contested in the medieval period.[21] Even when particular authorities were generally recognized, that did not mean that specific exercises of those forms of authority were generally recognized as legitimate. Given this, it is difficult to see how any one institution or individual, even the Pope, could have exercised the kind of final and unquestioned authority that MacIntyre seems to consider to be necessary.

The example of Abelard illustrates this point. On MacIntyre's interpretation of his story, Abelard willingly submits to the accusations of heresy brought against him by Bernard of Clairvaux and accepts the judgment on him implicit in that accusation: "It was clearly pride of will which Bernard discerned in Abelard and which Abelard acknowledged by his submission that he had discerned in himself" (*Three Rival Versions*, p. 91). But this is a very quick – and it must be said, a dubious – summary of a complex story. (In what follows, I rely on Clanchy 1997, pp. 288–325, and Marenbon 1997, pp. 7–35.)

Abelard's works were subject to ecclesiastical scrutiny twice, the first time at the Council of Soissons in 1121, and then a second time at the Council of Sens in 1140. The first of these investigations resulted from accusations from Abelard's fellow scholastics, while the second was due largely (but not exclusively) to the initiative of Bernard of Clairvaux. Abelard did indeed submit to the condemnation of Soissons, but it is not clear why he did so. One of his contemporaries suggested that he did so out of fear of a violent popular uprising, and given the fate of other accused heretics at the time, that would not have been an unreasonable fear. His biographer M. T. Clanchy suggests that he was also broken psychologically by the experience, an interpretation which takes support from Abelard's own later claim that he was in despair and insane at the time (Clanchy 1997, p. 305).

At any rate, Abelard's experiences at Soissons did not keep him from continuing to take what were considered to be heretical views; in the words of Bernard, writing in 1140, "one head, a single heresy of his was cut off at Soissons; but now seven greater ones have grown up in its place" (Clanchy 1997, p. 289). The condemnation of Sens was inconclusive, in part because Abelard appealed to the judgment of the Pope and then left before the council had concluded. Subsequently, Abelard appealed to Peter, the Abbot of Cluny, for protection, thus illustrating on a practical level how different loci of authority could be played off one another at this time. As it happened, Pope Innocent II did condemn Abelard, but thanks to Peter's intervention, the full force of his condemnation appears to have been blunted, and Abelard was allowed to end his days in peace in a Cluniac priory near Chalon-sur Saône. It is not clear that Abelard ever did submit to the condemnation of Sens, as confirmed by Innocent II. In his letter to the Pope, Peter claimed that Abelard had made peace with Bernard, but we are not clear exactly what this means. At any rate, there is little evidence that Abelard ever acknowledged the sin of prideful heresy in himself, as MacIntyre suggests. Clanchy suggests an opposite conclusion: "It cannot be emphasized too strongly that Abelard approved of the prosecution of heretics as much as the pope or St. Bernard did. The difference between them was that Abelard always thought his own opinions were the height of orthodoxy and his opponents were therefore deluded or malicious" (Clanchy 1997, p. 319).

I have dwelt at some length on the question of authority in the latest of MacIntyre's extended discussions of tradition because his insistence on the necessity for an authoritative control on tradition-based inquiry raises fundamental questions for his understanding of rationality as tradition-based inquiry. Why should authoritative interventions be necessary in order to prevent "the development of dialectical argument from fracturing the unity of enquiry into a multitude of disagreements" (*Three Rival Versions*, p. 91)? Why are the processes of self-correction and ongoing reflection outlined in *Whose Justice? Which Rationality?* not sufficient for this purpose? Even more fundamentally, how does MacIntyre see the relation between authority and the emergence and resolution of an epistemological crisis? What is to prevent authoritative prohibitions of dissent from allowing an epistemological crisis to emerge, or from disallowing the kinds of innovations that MacIntyre claims are necessary to the resolution of that crisis? MacIntyre's comparison of Abelard with Galileo highlights the difficulties. On MacIntyre's view, Abelard takes the proper attitude towards authority, whereas Galileo does not; and yet, as MacIntyre himself goes on to acknowledge, it is Galileo who is rationally vindicated by subsequent developments. How can we escape the conclusion that, in this case, authority functioned to undermine, rather than to promote, rationality? It may well be that MacIntyre can answer these questions through a more extended analysis of the warrants and scope of authority within a tradition, but he has yet to do so.

MacIntyre's works have enjoyed a deservedly wide influence, not only among his fellow philosophers, but among theologians, social scientists, and educated men and women generally. It is a mark of the significance and richness of his work that it should suggest so many avenues for further reflection. It is to be hoped that he will return to some of the issues raised here in his future works, developing and extending the account of rationality as tradition-guided inquiry set forth in his recent works.[22]

Notes

1. The moral significance of the role of the bureaucratic manager is discussed in *After Virtue*, pp. 26–27, and the role of the therapist is discussed on pp. 30–31.
2. Julia Annas makes a similar point in Annas 1989, pp. 388–404. As we will see below, MacIntyre does remark, in both *After Virtue* and *Whose Justice? Which Rationality?*, that a tradition is an extended argument over the goods that constitute it; but this observation, while suggestive and important, does not seem to be a definition of "tradition," particularly since MacIntyre later adds the qualification that participants in a tradition must be aware of themselves as such, which would presumably not apply to every historically extended dispute over the nature of the good; see *Whose Justice?*, p. 326.
3. For MacIntyre's own overview of his argument, see *After Virtue*, p. 1–5.
4. These three stages also seem to be recapitulated in the process of individual acquisition of the virtues, although this is not emphasized in *After Virtue*; see MacIntyre 1992b.
5. Similarly, in his next book he asserts that "a tradition is an argument extended through time in which certain fundamental agreements are defined and redefined in terms of two kinds of conflict," namely between proponents of the tradition and its opponents, and internally among those who would interpret its central tenets in different ways; see *Whose Justice?*, p. 12.
6. MacIntyre himself offers a good summary and response to the main lines of criticism in the Postscript to the second edition of *After Virtue*, pp. 264–278. For a particularly valuable set of reflections and criticisms, together with MacIntyre's response, see the papers collected for a symposium sponsored by the British journal *Inquiry*: Clark 1983, Gaita 1983, MacIntyre 1983d and O'Neill 1983; see also MacIntyre 1984a and Wartofsky 1984.
7. In what follows, I rely on MacIntyre's exposition of his theory in *Whose Justice?*, pp. 349–369.
8. MacIntyre emphasizes that the correspondence in question is between the mind and its object, not between a concept or statement and its referent (as the correspondence theory is usually formulated); see *Whose Justice?*, pp. 356–357.
9. My remarks in this paragraph go beyond what MacIntyre explicitly says, but I believe that they are implied by his arguments; see *Whose Justice?*, pp. 363–364.
10. Admittedly, this account would fit at least some of the examples which MacIntyre offers in *After Virtue*, for example farming or medicine; see *After Virtue*, p. 222. But in light of the argument to be developed below, it is significant that these

are traditions in which practical success is closely linked to success in speculative theories about the world.

11. Compare the much briefer, but essentially similar, analysis of deduction, dialectic, and the idea of a science according to Aristotle and Aquinas in *Whose Justice?*, pp. 172–173.
12. A principle is *per se nota* ("known through itself") if the predicate is in some way implied by the meaning of the subject; however, such principles are not necessarily self-evident to us because the meaning of the relevant terms may only be apparent after extensive reflection.
13. On the logical, as opposed to epistemic, priority of first principles, see *First Principles*, p. 10; cf. pp. 34–35. MacIntyre also emphasizes this point in *Whose Justice?*, pp. 172–173. MacIntyre goes on to say that the relation between the first principles and the claims of the science is a result, not a starting point, for investigation at *First Principles*, p. 30.
14. In my view, a plausible case can be made that physics is on the way to becoming a perfected science, and it is conceivable that some other physical sciences (astronomy, geology) and some branches of mathematics might similarly attain this status. However, given MacIntyre's very strong remarks on the impossibility of any intellect to know that it has attained final and definitive knowledge on some subject, he might well claim that no science can be considered to be perfected, even if we may reach a point at which we cannot imagine what a successful challenge to the science would look like.
15. This goes beyond what MacIntyre explicitly says, but I believe it is a straightforward extension of his views.
16. For an early and underrated defense of this view, see Kovesi 1967; for more recent examples, see Searle 1995 and Williams 1985. There are of course significant differences among the views of these three philosophers.
17. MacIntyre does attempt one such investigation in MacIntyre 1990b, but this is little more than a sketch of issues. For an example of an extended study that does attempt to identify and (partially) to resolve conflicts between two widely separated moral traditions, see Yearly 1990.
18. This is particularly evident from his summary of the points of conflict in *Three Rival Versions*, pp. 109–113.
19. In view of the emphasis on medieval history in what follows, I would like to acknowledge my general indebtedness to Kent 1995, pp. 1–38, which is particularly helpful in placing MacIntyre's interpretation within the context of the historiography of the period as it developed in the early twentieth century. I generally agree with her specific criticisms, but pursue a somewhat different line in what follows.
20. By myself, at any rate; see Porter 1993.
21. For MacIntyre's sources, see *Three Rival Versions*, pp. 103–104; the most recent work cited was published in 1985. The following offer useful perspectives on the relation between social and intellectual developments in the twelfth and thirteenth centuries: Constable 1996; Lawrence 1994; Little 1978; Southern

1995; Spruyt 1994, pp. 59–150; and van Caenegem 1988. All of these bring out some aspects of the ways in which conflicts of authority shaped intellectual life in this period. Of course, MacIntyre could not have consulted the most recent works on this list.

22. I would like to thank the Reverend Kevin Lowery for invaluable assistance with the bibliographic research for this chapter.

3 MacIntyre in the Province of the Philosophy of the Social Sciences

STEPHEN P. TURNER

MacIntyre's early writings include a series of books and papers, primarily published from the late fifties to the early seventies (*Unconscious*, *Short History*, *Marxism and Christianity*, *Self-Images*; and MacIntyre 1957a, 1960, 1962, 1965c, 1966a, 1967a, 1967b, 1967c, 1968, 1969, 1970, 1974), but continuing throughout his career (1977a, 1978a, 1978b), in the ill-defined domain of the philosophy of social science. A number of other writings (1986a, 1986b, 1991d, 1994f), including *After Virtue*, rely in various ways on social science concepts, and a final category of writing includes a long series of book reviews of social science and social theory texts and concepts (1978d, 1979a, 1979b, 1979c, 1995c, 1998b). One view of the cluster of early papers is that they are juvenilia that have little to do with the phase of his work that begins with the publication of *After Virtue*. Yet this argument does not square very well with the fact that MacIntyre never stopped writing papers of this kind, or the fact that he continues to refer to the inspiration of such figures as the anthropologist Franz B. Steiner, or the fact that MacIntyre continues to describe his project in social science terms such as "social structure." Nor does it square with the actual content of the notion of tradition as practice, which, as he develops it, is a social theory in which the traditional concerns of identity, selfhood, and intelligibility are understood in terms of social interaction (especially 1986a and 1986b).

Many of the key issues that the later papers address are contained in his 1962 paper "A Mistake about Causality in Social Science," which, I will show, was an important seed bed for his later thought.[1] For the concept of practices MacIntyre developed was itself a social theory: the "philosophical" conclusions are dependent on its validity as an account of practices as a social phenomenon. This chapter focuses on a question of philosophical or social theoretical method that bears on the merits of this theory, one of which is critical: the validity of a form of argument that figures throughout MacIntyre's work, in which characterizations of a topic, "identifications," are used to exclude alternative explanations. In the end, I will argue, arguments of this form are intrinsically misleading or incomplete.

1. THE FIFTIES

The technical philosophical problem at the core of MacIntyre's early writings was the problem of reasons and causes. Anthony Kenny later summarized the conventional account during this period as follows:

> When we explain action in terms of desires and beliefs we are not putting forward any explanatory *theory* to account for action. It is true that desires and beliefs explain action; but the explanation is not of any causal hypothetical form. It is not as if the actions of human beings constitute a set of raw data – actions identifiable on their faces as the kinds of actions they are – for which we may seek an explanatory hypothesis. On the contrary, many human actions are not identifiable as actions of a particular kind unless they are already seen and interpreted as proceeding from a particular set of desires and beliefs. (Kenny 1978, p. 12)

This account was the alternative to, and led to the discrediting of, the idea that "reasons explanations" were a variety of causal explanation. Reasons explanations were descriptions in intentional language of a set of events that the description connected. To be "identifiable as action," in Kenny's language, implied proceeding from particular sets of beliefs and desires. The reason the sets were "particular" was that the connection between them and the actions that "proceeded" from them was not caused but logical: the beliefs and desires were *reasons* for particular actions that also explained the actions. When MacIntyre later wrote of the stock of action descriptions in a society, he meant descriptions of what is "identifiable as action."

What is the status of these descriptions or identifications? An earlier tradition, exemplified by Weber, had put them on the side of the interpretation of meaning, which was taken to be consistent with, and not exclude, causal explanations. The key to the new account of action explanation was that they did. MacIntyre's first major philosophy publication, "Determinism" in *Mind* (1957a), vigorously upheld the claim that

> to show that behavior is rational is enough to show that it is not causally determined in the sense of being the effect of a set of sufficient conditions operating independently of the agent's deliberation or possibility of deliberation. So the discoveries of the physiologist and psychologist may

> indefinitely increase our knowledge of why men behave irrationally but they could never show that rational behavior in this sense was causally determined. (MacIntyre 1957a, p. 35)

Even in the case of the hypnotized person, MacIntyre argued, only if that person acted in accordance with hypnotic suggestion "no matter how good the reasons we offered him" for doing otherwise could we claim that the behavior was produced by the hypnosis (MacIntyre 1957a, p. 38). Reasons explanations, in short, are probative with respect to the truth of causal claims, and, in the absence of unusual circumstances, exclude them: if action is rational, it is not caused.[2]

MacIntyre's first conventional philosophical book, *The Unconscious* (1958), was an attempt to extend the notion of intentional language and the idea of description to account for another class of action explanations thought to be causal, those involving the mechanisms of Freudian theory. He argued that Freud had misconstrued his own achievement by making them into a scientific theory and construing his explanations as dependent on the discovery of a new causal realm. Freud's real achievement was largely a matter of extending intentional language to encompass unconscious motivations. MacIntyre argued that Freud's own causal construal of these explanations was a misinterpretation (*Unconscious*, pp. 71–74). MacIntyre did not argue that the attempt to provide a causal, theoretical account of behavior was in principle mistaken: theorizing about unobservables is legitimate, and theorizing about the unconscious in the normal fashion of hypothetico-deductivism would be legitimate as well (*Unconscious*, p. 46). His question is rather one that can be answered by an analysis of whether Freud's explanations are in fact of this type, and the answer is that they are not. Freud thinks of his unconscious motives as causes, but "in practice, when Freud assigns an unconscious motive to an action he ascribes a purpose" rather than a cause, though a purpose which is inaccessible to the patient (*Unconscious*, p. 61). Thus in practice what Freud has extended into the realm of the unconscious is not causality but intentionality, and in his treatments "the adducing of logically relevant considerations plays an essential part" (*Unconscious*, p. 36). Because the notion of unconscious intention is not causal it does not require the unconscious as a causal entity, and thus does not require causal theory (*Unconscious*, p. 96–97). Freud's usages conceal this. "Repression," for example, appears to be a causal concept, but it is not: it is a metaphor used for descriptive purposes (*Unconscious*, p. 79). The theory of the unconscious, understood as a scientific theory, was, MacIntyre argued, gratuitous, for the discovery of unconsciously motivated actions, which MacIntyre accepted as an important achievement of psychoanalysis, did not require such a theory, nor did it require Freud's complex causal machinery of the mind. The case against the theory is thus an application of the standard account of theoretical entities in philosophy of science.

Showing that Freud's explanations can be construed in intentional terms serves to show why the elaborate and highly questionable structure of mental entities in the theory are not required by the explanations he actually gives. This is a form of the argument that identifying an action as intentional excludes the possibility of causal explanation, or theory, but it is different from certain famous versions of this argument, a difference that is important throughout MacIntyre's discussions of social theory. The difference figures in the contrast between *The Unconscious* and Peter Winch's *The Idea of a Social Science and Its Relation to Philosophy.* Each appeared in the same year, 1958, and in the same series of little red books (Routledge and Kegan Paul's "Studies in Philosophical Psychology"). Winch's book was destined to become a classic. In it, he boldly had extended the "reasons" side of the reasons and causes arguments by arguing that only those reasons that were part of an activity, part (to use MacIntyre's language) of the stock of descriptions available to its participants, could figure in an explanation of the activity. This argument depended on the constitutive role of agents' concepts in the formation of the intention to perform a particular act. The character of these concepts precluded causal explanation, which required concepts of a different type, suitable for generalization.

Causal accounts of actions typically appeal to the notion that the action can be described and categorized independently of the reasons of the agent. In an example that Winch took from Pareto, Christian baptism is described as a lustral rite. Winch argued that this description was an error: the action thus described was falsely described because it was not the action intended by the agents; the intended action was intended in the form of the Christian concept of baptism. An explanation of lustral rites does not explain the actions of the believers because it is not a description of what they did in the strict sense of matching the conceptual content of the actions as they were conceived by the participants. Winch's book extended this line of argument to other figures in the social sciences, showing that they fell afoul of the problem of the constitutive conceptual relationship between the identification of actions and the content of the intentions of the agent. Winch drew the full implications of this argument, and they were radical. To explain the acts of Homeric heroes, or of believers in witchcraft, is to identify the actions in their conceptual terms and then to explicate their concepts. In explaining by explicating concepts one comes to an end, and this was, for Winch, also the end of social science, and its sole end. The goal of causal knowledge of the world of action, the goal of the social sciences, was incoherent, and social science properly understood was a branch of philosophy because it was a form of conceptual analysis.

The tensions produced by this extension of the idea that reasons explain, and explain in some exclusive sense, are multiple and complex, and they appear between MacIntyre and Winch even at this early point. The argument that the concepts contained in intentions were constitutive of action fit problematically with the notion of rational action more narrowly construed, as MacIntyre had construed it in "Determinism." It was plausible to define rational action in the strict sense of rational decision as uncaused, as MacIntyre did in his paper. But MacIntyre's argument there was very limited in one respect: he did not identify any large, actual class of actions as rational according to his definition, and indeed, it would be consistent with his argument in that text to claim that the content of the category of rational action was vanishingly small. The idea that "rational action" involved the adducing of reasons, which figures in *The Unconscious* and "Determinism," was different and had different implications. Argument, like analysis, is potentially interminable, and in any case raises questions about the ultimate grounds of argument. These questions had relativistic implications, since ultimate grounds for us might not be ultimate grounds for someone else. So did the idea suggested in Anscombe's *Intention* (1957 [2000]) that the relevant "reasons" were practical syllogisms, an idea which in any case fit poorly with the idea of rational decisionmaking. The "constitutivity" argument went even further (Weber 1968 [1978], pp. 5–8, 17; see also Turner and Factor 1994, p. 31). To define *all* action as uncaused by virtue of the fact that it is conceptualized by agents led to radical conclusions, conclusions that conflicted with the ordinary usage it purported to analyze.

The link between intention and action, in ordinary usage, is sometimes weak, even if it is backed by practical syllogisms. Weakness of will, multiple relevant motives, and sheer inconsistency are features of human action. Here it does seem reasonable to ask what the real reason was for an act, something that reference to practical syllogisms does not answer, but "cause" might. The idea of ordinary usage, in any case, raises the question of *whose* ordinary usage. Some reasons explanations, especially those in other cultures, seem to be, by our lights at least, systematically false, defective, or unintelligible: the beliefs behind the reasons are false, the categories in which they are expressed (such as Aristotle's categories of food types) are defective, and the cosmologies which underwrite the categories are little better than superstitious gibberish. Even the basic inferences made by agents in these societies (inferences we can apprehend them as making, and even supply the "rules" by which they are made) are not "reasons" for us. Do these reasons explanations – which undeniably are constitutive of the intentions of the agents – count as adequate explanations, or as genuine reasons? Is "of course, he is warding off evil spirits" an explanation? This is not as simple a problem as it appears.

In the first place, this argument creates a problem with the implications that MacIntyre drew from his discussion of rational action. There, very strong truth-claims are being made for the significance of reasons descriptions – claims to the effect that giving a reasons explanation warrants claims about causation – negative claims, claims to the effect that some action was not caused because it was done for a reason. If we accept that a pure, rational decision is by virtue of its character uncaused, does this extend more broadly to *any* action constituted by an intention? Is it really the case that psychologists could discover nothing that had any bearing on, for example, the reasoning involved in the practice of ancient Mayan kings of bleeding their genitals in public, or the actions of criminals, or reasoning about sexual desire, or crowd behavior? This is implausible in the extreme – in effect, it amounts to the claim that social science is unexplanatory gibberish but the practical syllogisms of believers in witchcraft are genuinely explanatory; that ordinary historical explanations of such things as the causes of the Great War were impossible in principle, and that history as practiced by historians was therefore bunk; and that comparisons between institutions were inadmissible, for they violated the constitutivity principle. MacIntyre believed none of this. Indeed, he served as a kind of go-between, continuing to attempt to make the claims of philosophers square with the claims of social scientists. For example, his 1960 paper "Purpose and Intelligent Action" attempts to make sense of the notion of intelligent action in a way that fits both the concept of action and the results of intelligence testing research. The large problem of the relation of social science explanations to intentional action was still there to be solved.

2. MACINTYRE CONTRA WEBER ON RATIONALITY

MacIntyre's first major paper on social science itself was "A Mistake about Causality in Social Science," published in 1962. It represented an extension of the strategy of "Determinism" and *The Unconscious* to this larger problem, and to a figure with whom MacIntyre continued to wrestle throughout his career – Max Weber. The "mistake" to which the title refers is Weber's.

Weber had constructed historical explanations of beliefs, such as the particular "economic ethic" that he described under the rubric of "the spirit of capitalism," by constructing a causal account of the nature of the influence of certain other kinds of ideas, namely the ideas of vocation, predestination, and worldliness that were a part of Calvinistic Protestantism. The explanation as formulated by Weber himself is causal, and this is part of the mistake. It depends on the claim that there is a distinctive psychological connecting link, namely a state of anxiety in the minds of believers, that supplies what Weber thought was the distinctive motive force for capitalist activity of a new kind, in conformity with the novel "ethic" he identified.

Here was an explanation, or apparent explanation, rich in the kind of difficulty that a serious application of the reasons and causes distinction needed to address. It carried with it other intriguing baggage of special relevance to MacIntyre: Weber's account of capitalism had been routinely treated, in the 1950s, as the counterpoint to, and refutation of, the "materialist" view of capitalism and of history generally. The conclusion of Weber's account of the historical course of rationalization had an even more interesting set of implications. His argument that Calvinistic Protestantism represented a rationalization of the Christian tradition was a natural counterpart to the conclusions reached by such Protestant theologians as Karl Barth, whom MacIntyre had other reasons for attacking. For Weber, in the course of the process of rationalization, of which the "disenchantment of the world" was a consequence, the "superstitious" elements of the Christian tradition were gradually stripped away.

MacIntyre does with Weber something similar to what he did with Freud: he reconstructs Weber's explanation by turning it into a pure issue of rationality and contradiction, thus dispensing with the need for cause. Where Weber interpreted the early Protestants as being caught in the grip of a consistent theodicy that had anxiety as a consequence and that had the further causal consequence of strongly reinforcing a particular pattern of reasoning, the "ethic," MacIntyre saw them as in the grip of a theological contradiction, which they resolved rationally. The two lines of argument can be compared very simply. For Calvin and for a rational Calvinist, the recognition of God's omniscient and omnipotence not only posed the usual problem of the existence of evil, the traditional problem of theodicy, but posed it in a very particular form. The revelatory writings taught that there was heaven and hell, and it followed from this that some people were damned, or going to hell, and other people were saved, or going to heaven. We as humans do not have knowledge of whether we are going to heaven or hell, whereas God, being omniscient, knows in advance. This is the basis of the doctrine of predestination. It could be that God grants us free will, and it could also be that we in some sense are allowed by God to earn salvation through the doing of good works. But this "allowing" and "earning" is in the end essentially a sham, simply because God in his omniscience already knows who will be saved by their "good works."[3] In the end, our salvation is entirely a matter of God's grace; we cannot earn it on our own, and certainly not by good works. For Weber this was the transparent consequence of making the Christian theodicy consistent, and it had a predictable causal effect: believers had a deep anxiety about whether they were predestined to election or damnation.

MacIntyre ran this argument the other way around. Good works, he argued, were enjoined in the revelatory writings. Protestant theology thus was placed in the untenable position of arguing that what the revelatory writings commanded was in some sense irrelevant to God and God's nature (which they supposed themselves to have theological access to through their own theorizing). This contradiction between theology and revelation could only mean that the Calvinists were mistaken about God's nature and that Protestantism was a false doctrine. They found a way out of this contradiction by embracing the notion of good works in practice while denying it in theory.[4] Thus, contra Weber, it is Protestantism rather than Catholicism that arises out of irrationality and contradiction. The consequences of this contradiction, and people's response to it, is thus explained not through the kind of psychological mechanism that Weber invokes but rather through the logical fact of contradiction – something that occurs at the level of belief, and also needs no further explanation, because it is "rational" to resolve the contradiction.

MacIntyre's argument is relentless in placing his historical account on the *reasons* rather than the *causes* side of the line. "The relationship which [Weber] in fact manages to pinpoint is indeed a rational one. Weber in fact presents us with capitalist actions as the conclusion of a practical syllogism which has Protestant premises" (MacIntyre 1962, p. 55). Weber's concern with causal alternatives – the cases of India and China – "is entirely out of place" (MacIntyre 1962, p. 55). The statistical material Weber presents is relevant, but only in that it shows that there were people whose behavior corresponded to the practical syllogism – that is to say, people who conformed to the description. The fact of conformity to the description is sovereign, and causally probative: because it is rational to resolve the contradiction as MacIntyre constructs the practical syllogism there are no causal facts of the matter. The "mistake" supposedly made by Weber, and by social scientists more generally, is to think otherwise.

This is an application of the claim MacIntyre made in "Determinism," but one for which we can see how much might fall into the category of rational action. The sharp line MacIntyre draws in that text between behaving irrationally and behaving rationally, in which rational behavior is the case in which the agent would change the course of action if and only if "logically relevant considerations" were adduced, now is extended to an example that is more realistic – the case in which the agent has various reasons, and the determinants that select what the operative reasons are from these available reasons may be (and were hypothesized by Weber to be) conditions, such as anxiety, that are unlike "reasons" or "information," the terms MacIntyre uses in "Determinism" (MacIntyre 1957a, p. 35). MacIntyre's response was to acknowledge the problem of inconsistency between beliefs and actions itself. Real human action rarely works as neatly as the simple relation between a belief, a good, and an action modeled in the practical syllogism "Dry food suits any man," "here's some dry food" → the action of eating it (MacIntyre 1962, p. 53). But the model does solve a problem. It accounts for the constitutive or "internal and conceptual" character of the intention-action relationship. The idea that practical syllogisms provided logical backing for the intention-action link allowed MacIntyre to assimilate action explanations to the decision-oriented model of rational action in "Determinism." This avoided the claim that action was shown to be uncaused simply by virtue of the fact that it was conceptually constituted. It also allowed him to make sense of the problem of false practical syllogisms. He argued that we can imagine a dialogue with the practical syllogizer in which the beliefs of the agent can be revealed, and the false ones corrected. When the subject in this dialogue "insists on simply affirming the premises and denying the conclusion, he becomes unintelligible: we literally do not know in the one case what he is saying or in the other case what he is doing" (MacIntyre 1962, p. 53). The use of "intelligible" is telling, for it persists – twenty-four years later MacIntyre was still wrestling with the notion of intelligibility (MacIntyre 1986a). Here, the later conclusions are foreshadowed. This style of explanations comes to an end not in concepts but in the intelligible agent.

Weber's explanation had singled out one strand of the plethora of desires, beliefs, and decisions that early capitalists made, and tried to explain why this strand proved to be so causally significant. This was a question that MacIntyre's approach could not address, except through the insistence that the strand of reasoning he described was the *only* possible account, given the evidence, rather than *a* possible account among others, that evidence would decide between.

One may observe again here a characteristic of MacIntyre's style – his reliance on a particular kind of winner-take-all reasoning – which we may characterize as "exclusive identification." He himself characterizes this form of argument, in a different context in the same paper, by saying that "what I have been concerned to do is to *identify* rather than to *explain*. But if one accepts this identification then we will have to take out a widely accepted class of explanations" (MacIntyre 1962, p. 69). The new context is the problem of alternative conceptual schemes, and here we see MacIntyre attempt for the first time to provide a systematic alternative to Winch. MacIntyre's approach concedes one of Winch's points about the conceptual constitution of action, that "if the limits of action are the limits of description, then to analyze the ideas current in society is also to discern the limits within which action necessarily moves in that society" (MacIntyre 1962, p. 60), from which he draws the conclusion that "the theory of ideology appears not as one more compartmentalized concept of the sociologist, but as part of his central concern with society as such" (MacIntyre 1962, p. 60). However, consistent with his earlier accounts of rational action as action open to the adduction of reasons, he argues that the descriptions in the stock of descriptions available in a given social group at a given time "occur as constituents of beliefs, speculations, and projects and as these are continually criticized, modified, rejected, or improved, the stock of descriptions changes. The changes in human action are thus intimately linked to the thread of rational criticism in history" (MacIntyre 1962, p. 60). This approach in turn becomes the distinction between two types of ideology.

One is represented by the Azande, who had been discussed by Michael Polanyi in his magnum opus *Personal Knowledge*, also published in 1958. The Azande were striking for having had a conceptual system in which witchcraft beliefs were central, and which had ad hoc answers to any evidence that might be given against it, and was thus closed to criticism. MacIntyre claims that in primitive societies closure is characteristic: "they have their concepts and beliefs; they move in a closed conceptual circle" (MacIntyre 1962, p. 63). But while "[a]ll primitive societies, especially isolated ones, tend to be closed ... [m]ost later societies are open; there are established modes of criticism" (MacIntyre 1962, p. 63). MacIntyre draws the line between "open" and "closed" in such a way that Marxism is not a closed scheme, but Stalinism was. The difference is that Stalinism represented "a concerted attempt to delimit the available stock of concepts and beliefs and at a certain point to return to a closed circle" (MacIntyre 1962, p. 63). We can distinguish the two kinds of case because for Stalinism closure can be accomplished only by recourse to irrational devices that exclude rational alternatives. Closure, in short, can occur "rationally" only for primitive societies that have never known openness, but elsewhere closure must be forced, or irrationally induced. This is an intriguing move, in light of what follows, not least because it suggests that "ideology" always has an act of "irrationality" in its historical pedigree. MacIntyre argued that Stalin's terror, which could "remove physically all traces of alternative" arguments, was necessitated by the fact that ideological closure is not possible in a modern industrial society. Even in Stalin's Soviet Union there were the Old Bolshevists, "who in their own theories and practices, were the bearers of an alternative wider conceptual scheme (it is in the light of our canons of rationality that we can see it as wider), which prevented consciousness being closed to non-Stalinist alternatives" (MacIntyre 1962, p. 68). Terror, he thought, is bound to fail, even though in Stalinist terms "the whole thing is rational; it can only be challenged by leaving this closed circle" of ideas (MacIntyre 1962, pp. 68–69). This "identification" of Stalinism as rational on its own terms meant that classes of explanation that appealed to such notions as "cult of personality" are wrong (MacIntyre 1962, p. 69). But it did not mean that it was immune to explanation, since the devices that sustained it are irrational by our standards.

3. ENTER KUHN

The cultural tsunami that was Thomas Kuhn's *Structure of Scientific Revolutions* (1962) was published in the same year as "A Mistake about Causality in Social Science." Kuhn's argument maps on to the problem of the Azande as follows: science is like a primitive society in that its concepts also move, for long periods of time, in a closed circle. Anomalies are dismissed, just as they are by the Azande, with ad hoc explanations – of the failures of the oracles, for the Azande, and of unexplained but possibly relevant results, for scientists within their paradigm. The rational alternatives to the existing paradigms that emerge are treated by scientists not with openness but with endless attempts to exclude them from serious discussion. These attempts seem irrational only in retrospect, once a scientific revolution has occurred and replaced the previous closed system with a new one. The revolution itself is not and cannot be a matter of rationally considering alternatives, at least if they are fundamental alternatives, because the only relevant "rational" criteria are internal to the closed system of concepts. In this respect scientists are in the same position as the Azande. There is no such thing in the history of science as an explanation to the effect that some belief is true or rational simply because it is true or rational. It is only true or rational according to our standards or theirs, and there is no way of explaining our standards as rational – to say they are rational simply because they are is itself an instance of reasoning within a closed circle of concepts. The open/closed distinction is a sham, or perhaps it would be better to say a relative distinction, that operates internally to a system of concepts, not between them. The only way out of a paradigm was a "revolution" that could not be construed as rational in the past paradigm, and conversely the past paradigm could not be properly understood in the language of the new.

MacIntyre's discussions of Stalinism and the Azande, his insistence on the conceptually relative character of action-explanations as always rational and always restricted to the "stock of descriptions" in the explainee's society, his apparent equation of our standards of rationality with rationality as such, his invocation of Popper's distinction between open and closed, and his depiction of Stalinism as an attempt to secure closure, all read in retrospect like a man walking into a trap.

MacIntyre argued that "the beginning of an explanation of why certain criteria are taken to be rational in some societies is that they *are* rational." Presumably he meant that "our" society was among these societies, for in the next sentence he adds: "And since this has to enter into our explanation we cannot explain social behavior independently of our own norms of rationality" (MacIntyre 1962, p. 61). MacIntyre characterized the process of changing someone's views by argument as follows: "I appeal to impersonal canons of rationality and the relationship between us can only be elucidated by an account of the established features of rule-following" (MacIntyre 1962, p. 68). This suggests that he thought at this time that impersonal standards of rationality were universal, their application governed by locally established procedures of rule-following. He might have avoided making such an assumption simply by leaving out the notion of "criteria" of rationality or the idea that we have "our own norms of rationality." Instead, by making an unargued identification of "our own norms of rationality" with rationality as such MacIntyre opened the door to the full form of the puzzle of rationality and relativism: appealing to "our norms" makes the explanations explanations *for us*; appealing to rationality *as such* raises the question of how we are to affirm our criteria of rationality without circularity.

The term "paradigm" included the notion of a rational standard among its multiple meanings, and Kuhn's discussion made it clear that when scientists made substantive judgments of rational adequacy of evidence, and of whether an anomaly was significant in science, they relied on paradigms. Within paradigms justification was circular – evidence supported the paradigm, but the paradigm defined what counted as evidence; paradigms were validated by explanatory and predictive successes, but they defined what counted as explanation and what success amounted to. But Kuhn's case was historiographic and historical: for him incommensurability was simply a fact, shown by the reactions of incomprehension of scientists adhering the old paradigm in the face of the new paradigm. Moreover, according to Kuhn, what MacIntyre in this paper characterized as unusual and "slightly self-contradictory" (MacIntyre 1962, p. 63) about ideological thinking, namely the attempt to close the circle of concepts, to "prevent any criticism which does not fall inside the established conceptual framework" is what scientists normally do in the course of solidifying the triumph of a paradigm and dealing with anomalies.

The naive idea that divergence in conceptual schemes was error, that there was unproblematic progress with respect to rationality, or truth, in the course of the replacement of conceptual schemes or in the comparison of divergence schemes, validated by personal canons, was over with Kuhn. For better or worse, this was a cultural transformation to which MacIntyre, and every other thinker of the era, was compelled to respond. To fail to do so would lead to a relativism in which Stalinism was merely another paradigm with its own rationality, and in which our judgments about the nonrationality of its methods of self-justification or closure would be merely expressions of "our" paradigm. The distinction between ideology and rational adequacy would collapse. Reasons explanations of action would be explanations only for us. But vindicating "our" standards faced its own problems. A claim that the explanation of the fact that certain criteria are taken to be rational by us is that they are rational would simply be circular – a justification of our standards by reference to our standards. The Azande and Stalin could say the same.

4. WINCH'S NEW CHALLENGE

MacIntyre had no wish to escape from this problem, which, in various guises, was to be the central subject of his later career. Winch posed a new problem, a problem of the logical conditions of understanding. Winch now argued that there could never be grounds for judgments of rationality of the beliefs of other cultures, no matter how outré the beliefs, because such judgments about beliefs seem necessarily to involve pressing the concepts in question where they would not naturally be taken and thus misconstruing them. The case was the now familiar Azande. The facts of the matter, reported by E. E. Evans-Pritchard, were these. The Azande employed a particular method for answering a wide variety of questions. They asked a question that could be given a yes or no answer while they poisoned a small domestic fowl. If the bird lived, the answer was "yes"; if the bird died, the answer was "no." The method was used for making decisions but also for answering causal questions such as: "Is Prince Ndoruma responsible for placing bad medicines in the roof of my hut?" (Winch 1970, p. 86). Oracles, however, can conflict: the implications of the oracular pronouncements are often inconsistent with one another, and future experiences do not always square with predictions. Witch powers were supposed by the Azande to be hereditary, so discovering through the oracle that someone is a witch implied that the person's whole family line are witches. But other oracles might, and do, contradict this by answering "no" to the question of whether a given person is a witch. The Azande supplied various explanations for the failure of oracles; for example, that a bad poison was used or the ritual was faulty. These ad hoc explanations were, as the Europeans who studied them understood, not sufficient to overcome the endless contradictions that belief in oracles produced.

The way in which Evans-Pritchard had described the Azande involves a basic principle of logic, the principle of noncontradiction, that had figured among MacIntyre's "impersonal canons of rationality." But it is not clear, as Winch points out, that Evans-Pritchard is entitled to do so in this case. Evans-Pritchard's challenge is first to *understand* the concepts of the Azande and that judgments about contradiction seem to depend on correct understanding. Our understanding of concepts is first a matter of understanding how they are used. In the case of the Azande, as Evans-Pritchard himself tells us, the people who engage in the practice of oracles do not have any interest in the problem of contradiction, or indeed any theoretical interest in the subject. For Winch, this suggests that there is no mystery about the contradictory character of Azande thinking, only an error that creates a false problem. It is the interpreter, Evans-Pritchard, who is in error, and his error is conceptual: he wishes to use the concepts in ways that the Azande do not use them. Evans-Pritchard is guilty of attributing to the Azande a concept other than the one they use. Pushing the concept into uses that are unnatural to the Azande, to the point of contradiction, is the same as misconstruing the concept, and the appearance of contradictions in a reconstruction of their thought shows no more than that the reconstruction is faulty.

So Evans-Pritchard failed to understand the Azande, and consequently failed to describe their mode of thought. This seems to mean that understanding these concepts precludes judgments about their beliefs and assertions about the rationality of these beliefs, and that, in the case of concepts that figure in developed forms of life, to make a claim that the concepts are "irrational" amounts to misunderstanding them as they are used by the participants in that form of life, where in fact their use in practice does not lead to collapse in the way that a contradiction leads to the collapse of a theory. In short, claims about the "rationality" of other cultures or their contents are inevitably misdirected – directed at a false reconstruction of the concepts of the other culture rather than the concepts as the people of the culture employ them. MacIntyre began promptly and explicitly to extricate himself from the trap created by Winch's arguments by abandoning some of his earlier arguments and acknowledging some previous, unacknowledged conflicts. The strong version of the constitutivity argument, with which MacIntyre flirted in 1962 (cf. esp. MacIntyre 1962, pp. 60–62), it was now evident, had relativistic implications: if identification of action was explanation, and identification could only be on the terms of the society in question, we would be limited to these explanations; rational criticism, which MacIntyre had then thought allowed freedom from these limitations, did not escape the circle of local concepts; the exclusion of all other explanations of action meant that we are deprived of any means to account for their beliefs. To say that Stalin's methods were irrational was not merely to apply our standards of rationality, but to misunderstand his. Appealing to impersonal canons assumes understanding; showing his beliefs are contradictory shows we have not understood.

MacIntyre's new approach appears in his papers "The Idea of a Social Science" and "Rationality and the Explanation of Action," both of which he included in *Against the Self-Images of the Age* (1971). Each of these was in large part a commentary on Winch. MacIntyre now argued that the reasons and causes distinction was overdrawn, and that his previous view of the significance of some of the key arguments in the reasons and causes literature was mistaken: "we shall be in conceptual error if we look in the direction of the causes of the physical movements involved in the performance of the actions. It does not follow that there is no direction in which it might be fruitful to search for antecedent events that might function as causes" (MacIntyre 1967a, p. 200; see also p. 215).[5]

The hypnosis example reappears, now to make a novel point, *against* Winch's use of the identification argument. MacIntyre now argues that possessing a reason, which is what the identification establishes, is not enough for explanation – possessing a reason may be a state of affairs identifiable independently of the performance of the action. Recall that in "Determinism" MacIntyre had used the example in support of the claim that the agent's action in this case was not "rational behavior" and that "to show that behavior is rational is enough to show that it is not causally determined in the sense of being the effect of a set of sufficient conditions operating independently of the agent's deliberation or possibility of deliberation" (MacIntyre 1957a, p. 35). In the case of the hypnotized person, it is causally determined, and consequently considerations of rationality do not apply. In the later paper, the issue is whether a given reason is "causally effective," and this is a question that presupposes that the hypnotized subject possesses a reason, but one that is not the cause of the action. In this case the question of whether the reason caused the action "depends on what causal generalizations we have been able to establish" (MacIntyre 1967a, p. 117). So Weber, it now appears, was correct in his methodological self-conception, at least in this respect: the question of whether a particular belief is the cause of a particular action is not a category mistake.

In the passage in which MacIntyre connects the problem of reasons to the problem of the status of nonrelative social science concepts he is still concerned to vindicate the notion that there can be cross-cultural generalizations, a commitment he soon curtailed. But he also has his eye on two other issues that had figured in "A Mistake about Causality in Social Science" (1962): the problem of explaining the change from one set of beliefs to another, and the problem of false consciousness, which MacIntyre understands in this context to be a form of the problem of error about the actual causes of one's actions as distinct from the rationalizations one provides for them, as well as the problem of erroneous belief, such as the witchcraft beliefs in the time of King James and among the Azande. The problem here was whether rationality, the criteria of rationality of a society, falsity in the sense of false consciousness, and coherence, to list a few of MacIntyre's favorite usages, could be extricated from the closed circle of concepts or were simply part of the circle. The problem was not Kuhn's or Winch's alone, nor was it merely a matter of the philosophy of social science. MacIntyre now addressed it in the form of religion and the familiar Christian puzzle, known as Tertullian's paradox, that understanding was a precondition of belief but belief was a precondition of understanding, which he turned on its head in a surprising way.

The argument of "Is Understanding Religion Compatible with Believing?" (1970) starts with the *religious* form of the problem of incommensurability: are the skeptic and the believers talking about the same thing? Or, as some Protestants would say, is it that the skeptic has not rejected Christianity, but instead failed to understand it, and thus rejected something else? This latter argument depends on a strong notion of understanding that implies acceptance, or at least "sharing." But, as MacIntyre notes, "anthropologists and sociologists routinely claim to understand concepts they do not share. They identify such concepts as *mana*, or *taboo*, without themselves using them – or so it seems" (MacIntyre 1970, p. 64). The problems are parallel, and also, MacIntyre shows, so are the solutions: anthropologists wind up with various approaches that parallel positions in the philosophy of religion. The key case is again Evans-Pritchard, whose *Nuer Religion* (1956) describes the concept of *kwoth*, and, as MacIntyre puts it, by identifying the rules governing its use in a "social context of practice" is "able to show that the utterances . . . are rule-governed" (MacIntyre 1970, p. 65). MacIntyre's point is that while this enables him to "show us what the Nuer idea of intelligibility is" and "why the Nuer think their religion makes sense . . . this is not to have shown the Nuer are right" (MacIntyre 1970, p. 65).

Can we judge intelligibility, incoherence, and so forth independently of the Nuer – or alternatively the Christian believer – and arrive at the conclusion that their beliefs do not make sense? Or is this necessarily to have failed to understand them, as Winch supposed? If the idea of one overall norm of intelligibility is a metaphysical fiction, is the only alternative total relativism? The point was of course at the core of philosophical discussion generally in the last quarter of the twentieth century, so it is all the more striking that, on the page following MacIntyre's elaboration of this problem, he appeals to Franz Steiner's discussion of taboo.[6]

The point MacIntyre makes against Winch in elaborating the problem is that "criteria have a history," which bears directly on "the suggestion that agreement in following a rule is sufficient to make sense" (MacIntyre 1970, p. 68). Taboo, it appears, is a concept that we can provide rules for using, but cannot, at least on the basis of current usage, make meaningful, intelligible, rational, and so forth (MacIntyre 1970, p. 68). On the basis of present usage alone, we might say that taboos are prohibitions where no further reason exists, and as he jokes, "the temptation to tell anthropologists that taboo is the name of a non-natural quality would be very strong for any Polynesian who had read G. E. Moore" (MacIntyre 1970, p. 68). Steiner's solution, as MacIntyre construes it, is to say that taboo formerly *did* make sense, but that the usages recorded by anthropologists no longer do. As MacIntyre puts it, Steiner has "constructed from the uses of taboo a sense which it might have had and a possible history of how this sense was lost" (MacIntyre 1970, p. 68). With this phrase, one sees the key insight of *A Short History of Ethics* and ahead to *After Virtue* and the rest of the later project. Where does it leave us with religion? As with ethics, we must accept the realization that our troubles with our concepts in the present are a matter of their separation from embodied social practice and from the history in which they made sense. In the case of religion it leads to MacIntyre's novel conclusion that Christians don't understand the religion they profess. Barthian theologians, G. E. Moore, and taboo thinkers are in the end no different.

Steiner's account of taboo is one in which something intelligible, namely the sense of the dangers of things and places, turns into something unintelligible – apparently pointless prohibitions – which can be understood only by constructing its historical origins in the context of which it is intelligible. The trope recurs in MacIntyre's thought in many forms, notably in the problem of morality in *A Short History of Ethics*, which accounts for moral theory as a means of making sense of substantive moral notions whose original moral context of social practice has disappeared. Thus, with Stoicism, for which virtues that made a particular kind of sense in a social order in which practicing these virtues had visibly good results, in the disordered public world of the Roman Empire, had to be practiced, if they were practiced at all, without regard to consequences, as purely private virtues – a notion that would have been oxymoronic for Aristotle (*Short History*, pp. 100–109). Here we see Steiner's basic strategy brilliantly applied: to make sense of the Stoics, it is not enough to find intelligible analogues between their beliefs and beliefs in our own culture that are already intelligible to us. As a matter of interpretation this may be sufficient; as a matter of history it is not – history, in this case the history of moral ideas and moral philosophy, would become a parade of bizarre inventions. What is needed is a rational reconstruction of the irrational that makes the inventions intelligible as attempted solutions to real problems at the level of ideas – problems such as what the authoritative basis of morality might be in the face of diversity in practice – and existential problems, such as how one can use power in a violent and disordered society in which acting on old ideas of decency produces defeat and suffering.

The same kind of arguments cannot of course apply to science, or to any ongoing tradition of inquiry in which coherence is not lost. But these too "have a history" and, in these cases, a certain kind of history has a crucial role. This is the argument against Kuhn that MacIntyre deployed in "Epistemological Crises, Dramatic Narrative and the Philosophy of Science" (1977a). The article deals with the issue of commensurability, which had been critical to the philosophical impact of Kuhn. Paul Feyerabend, in 1962, published a lengthy paper in *Minnesota Studies in the Philosophy of Science* III that made the issues very explicit: the traditional account of theoretical advance involved subsuming old theories under new ones, and this required meaning invariance – that is, that the terms had the same meaning in both theories. Feyerabend argued that they did not. Without a logical account of the connection between theories, the "logical" analysis of theory change was doomed, and soon unraveled. The "revolutions" account presented by Kuhn implied that successive paradigms were not *strictu sensu* about the same things. But scientists thought their theories were, and also that they were advances.

MacIntyre argued that the scientists' historical accounts, narratives of scientific change, were themselves part of science properly understood, and that the value of a theory *in science* depends on, and is shown by, its role in narratives of progress.

> The criterion of a successful theory is that it enables us to understand its predecessors in a newly intelligible way. It, at one and the same time, enables us to understand precisely why its predecessors have to be rejected or modified and also why, without and before its illumination, past theory could have remained credible. It introduces new standards for evaluating the past. It recasts the narrative which constitutes the continuous reconstruction of the scientific tradition. (MacIntyre 1977a, p. 460)

5. TRADITION

Tradition, continuously reconstructed by narrative, was MacIntyre's solution to the puzzle of rational continuity in Kuhn. The question of whether "only standards to which anyone can appeal in judging what is a good and what is not are the standards embodied in the ordinary language of each particular group" (1992a, p. 18) was left to be solved. Whether MacIntyre solves them or exacerbates them is a matter of dispute: Winch believed he did not solve them (Winch 1992). There is, however, another question that arises, on MacIntyre's own terms, about the status of this account of tradition in its aspect of social theory, and this is a question that may be more fruitful. The concept of the scientific tradition was associated with Michael Polanyi, and MacIntyre was at pains to distinguish his views from Polanyi's. For MacIntyre, "what constitutes a tradition is a conflict of interpretations of that tradition, a conflict which itself has a history susceptible of rival interpretations. If I am a Jew, I have to recognize that the tradition of Judaism is partly constituted by continuous argument over what it means to be a Jew" (MacIntyre 1977a, p. 460). Similarly for science. Degenerate traditions, in contrast, erect "epistemological defenses which enable [them] to avoid being put into question by rival traditions." Liberal Protestantism, some forms of psychoanalysis, and modern astrology are examples (MacIntyre 1977a, p. 461). Psychoanalysis, Marxism, astrology, all are Polanyi's examples as well, as is the argument that "any feature of any tradition, any theory, any practice, any belief can always under certain conditions be put in question, the practice of putting in question, whether within a tradition or between traditions, itself always requires the context of a tradition" (MacIntyre 1977a, pp. 461–462; Polanyi 1958, pp. 269–297). If we are to accept MacIntyre's account as the best or only account, we need grounds to do so – grounds that rule out rivals, or show their inferiority. In the smaller intellectual space of theories of tradition, there *are* alternatives, and MacIntyre has a case against them. To understand the case we must understand the rivals. Polanyi, according to MacIntyre, erred because

> he does not see the omnipresence of conflict – sometimes latent – within living traditions. It is because of this that anyone who took Polanyi's view would find it very difficult to explain how a transition might be made from one tradition to another or how a tradition which had lapsed into incoherence might be reconstructed. Since reason operates only *within* traditions and communities according to Polanyi, such a transition or reconstruction could not be a work of reason. It would have to be a leap in the dark of some kind. (MacIntyre 1977a, p. 465, emphasis in the original)

> Natural science can be a rational form of enquiry if and only if the writing of a true dramatic narrative – that is, of history understood in a particular way – can be a rational activity. Scientific reason turns out to be subordinate to, and intelligible only in terms of, historical reason. (MacIntyre 1977a, pp. 464)

Michael Oakeshott's "Rationalism in Politics" was published in 1948. It is striking that the example of Stoicism was discussed, in largely the same terms and in the same way as MacIntyre, by Oakeshott in the late twenties (Cowling 1980, p. 253). Michael Polanyi published *Science, Faith and Society* in 1946, *Personal Knowledge* in 1956, and in between published a stream of articles and commentary. T. S. Eliot's *Christianity and Culture* (1949) defended a notion of the European tradition as essentially Christian. One of the major themes of several of these works was the rehabilitation of the contribution of medieval Catholicism to the forming of this tradition. Christopher Dawson, editor of the *Dublin Review*, wrote *The Making of Christian Europe* (1932) and engaged closely with the London scene. Even such figures as Popper were briefly caught in this current. His paper "Towards a Rational Theory of Tradition" appeared in 1949.

MacIntyre's comments on this tradition are infrequent but interesting, and they cluster in the late seventies though Popper's article was mentioned in 1962 (MacIntyre 1977a, pp. 465–466, 468; 1978b, pp. 26–27). He had been caustic about Polanyi, whom he considered to be a Burkean, a term MacIntyre used to designate a kind of conservatism that was the intellectual analogue of Stalinism – a concept of tradition that was closed and "unitary." One may observe that this comment is misplaced as applied to Polanyi, who made the point that the relevant cultural ideal was "a highly differentiated intellectual life pursued collectively" (Polanyi 1962, p. 219), "a continuous network – of critics" (Polanyi 1962, p. 217). Similarly for the tradition of tradition as a whole: T. S. Eliot argued that too much unity was a bad thing (Eliot 1949, p. 131). Oakeshott would have argued that the notion of closure as applied to tradition is a capitulation to the French Revolution's notion of tradition that the tradition tradition rejects. Indeed, it may be the case that the notion of unity in this tradition is weaker than MacIntyre's own.

Others have pursued the question of the similarity between MacIntyre's concept of tradition and its rivals (for example, Flett 1999–2000). The more pressing question is one of method. Given that there are rivals, and that at least one of these rivals, MacIntyre's, presents itself as not only different but superior, how are we to assess this claim? Here we come to a small puzzle. MacIntyre himself employs a variety of standards, depending on what sort of claim is being assessed, and in his relatively rare remarks on alternative concepts of tradition there are two kinds of argument. One, to which I will return, is an identification that excludes alternatives. The other is to assess the theory, as any other theory in science or social science is assessed, to see whether it accounts adequately for the appearances it is designed to account for without adding too much problematic baggage.

The concept of practices (for example, in *After Virtue*, pp. 187–203) is a straightforward example of a theoretical deployment: it is a theoretical entity posited to account for various features of human activity. It is supported by its consilience with other things that are known about human activity, with what is known about human psychology, and so forth. We can ask the usual questions about these theoretical entities in the usual way. These are not, for MacIntyre, questions from outside. His own writings, from *The Unconscious* to his writings on social science in the eighties, provide ample grounds for holding him to this test. He argues that it could not have been known *a priori* that the project of Durkheim and of positivist sociology would fail (MacIntyre 1986b, p. 92). And this means that nothing *a priori* guarantees the validity of alternatives, either. Philosophy is not autonomous in this respect: philosophical doctrine can be evaluated only as contributing to specific inquiries (MacIntyre 1986b, p. 87).

It will seem like an evasion to say that an assessment of MacIntyre's approach to tradition, or that of any of his rivals, in these terms is not a simple matter. The problem is tangled up with some of the central mysteries of present thought, notably the problem of normativity – of whether there is such a thing to be explained, and what would count as an explanation. The problem of theoretical baggage is largely a problem relative to this. The features of MacIntyre's account, its teleology and its doctrine of internal goods, which are shared with some other accounts of tradition and constitute its heaviest pieces of baggage, are there because of it. I do not propose to solve it here. But I will observe that a crucial kind of argument in MacIntyre, "identification," which leads to the exclusion of alternatives might be taken as an alternative to the weighing of theoretical baggage, both as an approach to vindicating MacIntyre or to interpreting his own arguments for his concept of practice and tradition. I question whether this is a form of argument at all, or at least a complete one: identification, one may say, is never theoretically innocent. There are no appearances that we may simply "identify," no prerogative interpretations which exclude all others.

Nevertheless, the way in which MacIntyre makes his case, for example in "The Intelligibility of Action"(1986a), his most complete discussion of the traditional concerns of social theory (which has a similarity to G. H. Mead and Charles Horton Cooley on the self [cf. MacIntyre 1986a, p. 77]), rests almost entirely on an identification of the concept of intelligible action that is shown to require practices, thus good reasons, and thus the concept of the good (MacIntyre 1986a, p. 75), and to exclude such things as intelligible action by machines, which "lack the relevant kind of history and the relevant kind of social relationships" (MacIntyre 1986a, p. 79). He says, correctly, that this is not a "demonstration of a conceptual truth to the effect that intelligible action cannot be predicated of machines" (MacIntyre 1986a, p. 79). But this claim, like the case for tradition as a whole, seems to fall into the long series of arguments in which MacIntyre's identifications of what is to be explained do the work of excluding rivals. If these arguments are problematic, so is the structure as a whole.

Notes

1. One of the features of his style that is illustrated by his work on the issues of social science as a whole is the use of the outlying province of philosophy of the

social sciences as a base for attacking the fashionable issues of the metropole (cf. MacIntyre 1978b, p. 21).

2. Of course there are qualifications – the probative force of the identifications is not absolute. It may be, MacIntyre suggests, that there are unnoticed, glandular conditions that would validate the claim that an action was really caused rather than rational (MacIntyre 1957a, pp. 35–36).
3. This line of reasoning has a fascinating history. The Catholic side of the problem has recently been reconstructed by Leszek Kolakowski in his book on Pascal and his context, entitled *God Owes Us Nothing* (Kolakowski 1995), which deals with Jansenism. The phrase "God owes us nothing" cuts to the heart of the problem. There is no such thing as cashing in on God's promises of salvation simply because the notion of owing does not apply to God as omniscient and omnipotent, and the idea that we can bind God to promises in this way is absurdly presumptuous.
4. MacIntyre's argument is this:

   > Weber describes this as if the psychological pressure of the need to know if one were saved had distorted the logical consequences of Calvinism. But in fact Calvinism and Calvin himself had always had to accommodate the commandments to good works in the Bible. Calvin was committed to the following propositions: 1. God commands good works; 2. It is of the highest importance possible to do what God commands; 3. Good works are irrelevant to what is of most importance to you, your salvation or damnation. It is a requirement of logic, not of psychological pressures, that one of these propositions be modified; the alternative is contradiction. Moreover, unless it is the third proposition which is modified, preaching and legislation on morals, two central Calvinist activities, which are also rationally backed up by doctrine, lose their point. (MacIntyre 1962, p. 55)

5. MacIntyre returns to the problem of causality in the social realm and history in "Causality in History" (1976). Weber's account of the causes of the Great War, from a letter MacIntyre does not identify, which targeted Slav expansionism as the key contributing cause, is taken as an example of a bad explanation. The Marxist view that the war was inevitable, given certain long-standing conditions, is claimed by MacIntyre to be correct. The methodological grounds on which the claim is made, however, involve a revision (and application to history) of the account of legal causality in Hart and Honoré (1959). The new revision is actually very close to Weber's own views, with this difference: Weber regarded causal claims of this kind as claims that the presence of a given factor, relative to a reference class of preselected factors, increases the probability of the outcome, and thus he saw all causal claims of this type as relative to the selection of the reference class. MacIntyre argues, consistent with this model, that the particular cause Weber selected did not meet this criterion since the outcome would have happened anyway, but he seems to have failed to recognize that the claim that the reference class produced the inevitable (presumably meaning a very high probability) result of war itself is a causal claim that needs to be warranted by comparison to a preselected reference class, and thus misses Weber's point: that this selection, like all such selections, is a result of the historian's interest, and not given in history.

6. The significance of this text, which figures in a central passage in *After Virtue*, is pointed up much later, in MacIntyre's interview with Borradori, in which he discussed the influence on his thinking of Franz Steiner, an anthropologist. He dates this influence, interestingly, to the early fifties. MacIntyre says:

> [Steiner] pointed me toward ways of understanding moralities that avoided both the reductionism of presenting morality as a mere secondary expression of something else, and the abstractionism that detaches principles from socially embodied practice. Rival forms of such practice are in contention, a contention which is neither only a rational debate between rival principles nor a class of rival social structures, but always inseparably both. (MacIntyre 1991d, p. 259)

4 Modern(ist) Moral Philosophy and MacIntyrean Critique

J. L. A. GARCIA

> We have to describe and explain a building, the upper story of which was erected in the nineteenth century; the ground floor dates from the sixteenth century, and a careful examination of the masonry discloses the fact that it was reconstructed from a dwelling-tower of the eleventh century. In the cellar we discover Roman foundation walls, and under the cellar a filled-in cave, in the floor of which stone tools are found and remnants of glacial fauna in the layers below. That would be a sort of picture of our mental structure.[1]

1. INTRODUCTION

My title and topic here call to mind both the title and themes of G. E. M. Anscombe's article, now almost half a century old, "Modern Moral Philosophy" (1958). In one of the twentieth century's most widely reprinted and influential pieces of philosophical writing, which gave us the term (and the topic) consequentialism and helped spawn both the line of inquiry later called philosophy of action and the revival of interest in the moral virtues, Anscombe defended three principal theses. First, she urged philosophers not to explore moral philosophy until possessed of an adequate philosophical moral psychology. Second, both they and the rest of society should abjure conducting moral discussion using the discourse of "morally right/wrong," of "morally ought," of moral obligation, the morally required/forbidden/permitted, and so on, because those terms mean nothing substantive today, retaining only what she memorably called "mesmeric force." Third, the differences among modernist moral philosophers, much discussed by her predecessors and contemporaries in the profession, not least in their elaborations of C. D. Broad's contrast between "teleological" and "deontological" theories, are in fact of little importance, masking agreements that, though deeper and more significant than the overblown disputes, had gone largely neglected, unacknowledged, unnoticed, and undefended.

Much of Alasdair MacIntyre's work on ethics can be read as addressing the matters that Anscombe had thrust into the foreground, whether or not her work figured in his thinking intentionally, thematically, systematically, or even consciously. From his book *The Unconscious*, published the same year as Anscombe's article, through his more recent work on moral virtues, MacIntyre has sought to help provide us a more philosophically adequate psychology, informed, in a way that distinguishes it from most of that by Anscombe and her philosophical colleagues in Britain and the United States, by wide reading in social and individual psychology and in other parts of the social and biological sciences. Similarly, his account, especially in *After Virtue*, of our moral discourse as, in effect, emotive, and his view of our talk of moral rights, duties, and so on as "survivals" that lack coherent and accepted conditions of application, both serve to amplify, flesh out, and defend a position close to Anscombe's second thesis. Here too, as illustrated by his treatment of Polynesian "tabu" in *After Virtue* (pp. 111–113) and *Three Rival Versions of Moral Enquiry* (pp. 182–186), MacIntyre draws on the empirical social sciences. Finally, though today MacIntyre seldom directly addresses topics classed under the rubrics of moral problems or practical/applied ethics, from *Marxism and Christianity* through *Whose Justice? Which Rationality?* he works to undermine both utilitarian and neo-Kantian accounts of justice and practical rationality, the very accounts that underlie the *de facto* consensus on normative issues that Anscombe decries in expounding her third thesis. There she points out that both the utilitarian followers of G. E. Moore and the *soi disant* Kantian followers of W. D. Ross and Henry Prichard agreed that the goal of avoiding possibly unwelcome consequences could justify even the most patently unjust and immoral actions – anything from taking for others' use someone's vital organs to framing innocent parties, blasphemy, betrayal, and sexual perversion.

MacIntyre's critique of modernist moral philosophy, for all these similarities, does not at all simply recapitulate Anscombe's. His criticism is more detailed, deeply informed by his ties to Marxism and his reading in the social sciences and by elements distinctively his own. Introduced and developed over more than four decades of texts, his critical examination covers more ground than I can hope to examine here. Instead, this chapter explores just four themes. Before getting to their specifics, I should interject some remarks about my aims and methods. I mean to offer a reading of some of MacIntyre's arguments and positions, to concentrate on articulating their content and assessing them. I do not try to defend the accuracy of my interpretations of MacIntyre's texts, or examine the accuracy of his own readings of particular moral philosophical texts from the modernist epoch. What is, I think, more interesting is what his texts suggest to us, whether and how those suggestions are helpful, and the extent to which they may be correct and even insightful. Those latter topics provide my focus, and the interpretive matters – both mine of MacIntyre and MacIntyre's of modernity's great thinkers – will be treated in only cursory fashion.

2. MacINTYRE'S CRITIQUE OF MODERNIST MORAL PHILOSOPHY: EXPOSITION

At the end of *After Virtue*, MacIntyre pairs a striking disjunction with an even more startling conjunction. Nietzsche or Aristotle? he asks provocatively (p. 256). As signposts to his answer, he points to Leon Trotsky and St. Benedict. What does he mean by this question and this answer? Consider, first, what MacIntyre calls "the Enlightenment Project" (p. 36), which aims to justify, in a secular way and for a secular age, retaining a moral code much like traditional Christian morality, especially its emphasis on benevolence and mercy. The project rooted morality in human practical rationality, which it understood largely as instrumental or as autonomously legislative, or in human nature, which it understood in a rigorously nonteleological mode (p. 52). (Especially in the past century, this new moral approach became increasingly forthright in repudiating traditional Christian sexual morality.) MacIntyre thinks that this project can now be seen to have failed and, in counterposing Aristotle to Nietzsche (pp. 109–120, 256–259) and linking Leon Trotsky to Benedict (pp. 261–263) I think MacIntyre means that in its wake we face only two choices.

On one hand, we can more frankly reject morality altogether, appealing only to natural passions and drives, some idiosyncratic and capricious, some social, and some universal but wild. This is the alternative to which Nietzsche points us. On the other hand, we can undertake the arduous task of reevaluating and ultimately modifying the modernists' turn against teleology and attempt to reconceive morality along lines similar to Aristotle's. This will be a lonely task, because so many, including many intellectuals, have convinced themselves that, while some reforms remain to be implemented, our moral order and our moral thought are basically in good order and without need of fundamental reconstruction. MacIntyre thinks those in his more radical project, then, will need largely to do their thinking within groups sharing the same fundamental standards and objectives, while reading much more widely beyond these traditions of inquiry.[2] This confronts them with two chief options on how to relate to those outside: the Trotskyan model of active, subversive engagement with the larger world and the Benedictine model of withdrawal from it to ordered privacy. MacIntyre realizes neither has a great chance of success in modern conditions because, despite its self-image of tolerance, liberal society will brook neither certain forms of challenge nor withdrawal.

In the passage I prefixed to this discussion, Jung uses the image of an old house, with sections dating from different centuries and foundations containing still older elements, to help us in thinking about the mind. We could readily apply the same image to MacIntyre's conception of both Western societies in the modernist epoch and also the vocabulary and forms of thought they use to conduct their discourse.[3] As with the house's parts, the disparate provenance of the different components may not be obvious and may have been forgotten. It is also likely that over time the fissures become deeper and the structure less stable, even if the joints are hidden to all but the trained eye. Thus, like Anscombe, MacIntyre has long complained that, in our moral discourse, we freely shift from concepts of natural law to natural rights, from obligation to virtue, from self-interest to sacrificial charity, from consideration only of overall consequences to compassion for immediate victims to interest in one's own higher interest and long-term self-improvement, without noticing the very different histories and, he thinks, incompatible bases and presuppositions from which these concepts and vocabularies emerge. MacIntyre thinks this modern moral 'order' a mess approaching a deeper crisis of its own internal contradictions, as in Marxist eschatology, and he thinks the project that hides its messiness an exercise more in obfuscation than in its self-described enlightenment.

I will explore five claims I think MacIntyre makes against the forms of moral philosophy that have predominated in the West from the time that the medieval epoch started giving way to the modern, and especially since the Enlightenment cemented the triumph of postmedieval forms of thought. I neither claim, nor presuppose, nor even think that these exhaust the intellectual bases for MacIntyre's dissatisfaction with the theories of Smith, Hume, Kant, Mill, and their admiring successors. Mine is only a selection. However, I do think that the claims I attribute to MacIntyre and examine below are among the most significant, both in the way they target theses that lie deep within those philosophies and are characteristic of it, and in the ways they provide grounds for several of MacIntyre's distinctive elements in the more positive vision of moral philosophy he developed during the past century's last two decades.

The first of these claims is that the modernists' moral philosophies ignore the dependence of both justice and moral reasoning on (fairly specific) standards and thus on (group) traditions. I call this one single part of his critique, but it should be clear that it involves several distinct claims. First, MacIntyre seems to reject the project of deducing substantive moral judgments from the meaning of very general evaluative terms such as 'ought' or 'right' or 'good'. This was a major contention of his early book *A Short History of Ethics*, rethinking whose claims, he recently said (see MacIntyre 1991a and 1991d), was the source of his moral philosophical project since the mid-1970s, and it animates several of the essays, especially on the meaning and use of 'ought,' collected in *Against the Self-Images of the Age: Essays on Ideology and Philosophy* (1971). Rather, MacIntyre maintains that someone can figure out what she ought or has to do only by determining her responsibilities within her situation.[4]

This might be uncontroversial when narrowly construed. No utilitarian or Kantian thinker denies that an agent's circumstances affect what she ought to do. For MacIntyre, however, the way in which the agent is pertinently situated includes not just whether she has made any promises now coming due or stands to help or harm many people by her choice. Rather, it extends also to the relationships in which she stands to other people, the roles she occupies, and therefore – this is the second important claim – he thinks that it can include the expectations her society's traditions properly vest in them (and, therein, in her). This pushes MacIntyre's thought toward relativism, and the charge that his position is relativist has frequently been lodged (see, for example, Haldane 1994). Below, I turn more fully to MacIntyre's relation to relativism. Here it is important to note that his recent position requires a complex background against which any judgment that someone ought to do something needs to be legitimated in order for it to be rationally acceptable. This judgment must be tied to pertinent virtues, and the virtues to what he calls "practices." Further, because "no individual lives her or his life wholly within the confines of any one practice," the practices and their goods also need to be brought into such harmony as to yield coherent and potentially fulfilling lives for the people participating in them (see, for example, MacIntyre 1992b, esp. pp. 7–8). Finally, this fulfillment needs to be understood as such by some tradition of moral inquiry into human flourishing, which tradition is itself rationally superior to its rivals.

MacIntyre contrasts the bare, untethered moral 'ought', which has plagued Western thought and confounded its philosophers from Hume onward, with the 'ought'-judgments of Homeric and medieval times (*After Virtue*, pp. 121–130, 165–180; see also MacIntyre 1971d, pp. 143–145). In those days, anyone could normally tell what a person ought to do because what she was to do was so to behave as to fulfill herself as a warrior, or a citizen, or a husband or wife, or a Greek, or a monk, or a Christian, or as occupying some such social position. That is not to say there could not be conflicts. However, even then someone knew that, to borrow a familiar example from the mythological tradition, Agamemnon owed it to Menelaus as a brother, a fellow king, a Greek, to help him to regain his wife, while he also owed it to Iphigenia and Clytemnestra to act protectively toward his family and daughter, even if there was some tension between these two socially recognized debts. Indeed, as MacIntyre sees it, these debts were not merely recognized by society, but largely created by its structure and practices, which themselves provide the moral vocabulary necessary to give the responsibilities content and specificity. In this Homeric morality, there is nothing that Agamemnon ought to do, nothing virtuous for him to be, no projects incumbent upon him except as occupying one or another of these roles, which his society creates, shapes, and defines, and whose *telos* it furnishes. This is the chief reason MacIntyre thinks much of our normative discourse, especially in morality, operates emotively. As in the past, to be legitimate our 'ought'-judgments need backing by reasons and thus by practical rationality. However, unlike some historical epochs, MacIntyre believes that, in this society and time, our rationality (that is, we, reasoning) cannot get sufficient purchase to supply fully defensible grounds. Our reasoning lacks the social context needed to give moral judgments clear and determinate content and to provide adequate standards for their rational assessment. This point naturally leads into his view of the deductive gap between factual judgments and moral judgments that Hume is thought to have noticed and that drew great attention from MacIntyre's colleagues within analytical philosophy, especially in the last century's middle third (*After Virtue*, pp. 56–57).[5]

A second element in MacIntyre's critical analysis of the modernists' moral philosophies is that they so divorce what they regard as 'facts' from 'values' that our moral practice becomes operationally emotivist, with different factions within society arguing against others in ways that tend to turn both desperate and self-righteous (see, for example, *After Virtue*, pp. 6–8, 23–25). Desperate, because each senses that (though not *why*) it cannot conclusively establish its position's correctness; self-righteous, because each knows that (though, again, not *why*) its position cannot be conclusively exposed as incorrect. Facts and values, as we understand them today, MacIntyre holds to be Enlightenment inventions, designed precisely to contrast with each other in such ways as to create between them a gap that cannot be bridged. Like the noncognitivists, MacIntyre insists on this gap and on our inability to eliminate it. Unlike them, he thinks this is not a general logical phenomenon, but a historical peculiarity of our epoch (*After Virtue*, pp. 18–19). For MacIntyre, there are no resources simply internal to reason as such that can justify our normative judgments. Rather, he thinks both moral reasoning and moral concepts are inherently historical artifacts requiring a certain social context for people to recognize and employ the relevant concepts in a clear, determinate way, and for their applications to be rationally defensible according to accepted standards.[6]

A third line of criticism that MacIntyre directs against the thinking of the major moral philosophers of modernity is that it promotes and acquiesces in the *fragmentation* of the modern subject into disparate (and, it appears, sometimes conflicting) roles without providing any basis or method for her *reunification*, *coherence*, and *integr(al)ity*. Here, MacIntyre's position seems to be that we moderns recognize elements of our plight, tacitly and implicitly if not as such, and that we allow for it in our practical thinking, again even if not in our theories of practical rationality. We accommodate this breakdown in our moral discourse chiefly by taking refuge in other kinds of evaluation where things seem not so bad. Specifically, we see our less controversial responsibilities within the roles we occupy, and focus on them, sometimes unifying them when we need to under some general and seemingly clear, determinate, and uncontroversial managerial concepts, such as those of efficiency, profit maximization, health, and 'pragmatism'. MacIntyre dismisses such concepts' claims to be either uncontroversial or useful in settling ambiguities or conflicts (MacIntyre 1977b). They make sense only within certain assumptions, which themselves are controverted and need support we cannot provide them. As for the roles themselves, they are disparate, can pull in different directions, and stand in need of some larger justifying purpose. So, if I understand him, MacIntyre sees us moderns fulfilling our various roles, when we do, with no adequate grounds for thinking we are therein living fulfilled and worthwhile lives.[7]

A fourth of MacIntyre's grounds for rejecting modernist moral theories is that these philosophies permit, and even encourage, the subject to see her private (and her faction's) self-interest as pitted against both the good of other individuals and, more important, the good of the larger political community. MacIntyre hopes to call into question and reduce the scope of, if not wholly to overcome, the familiar opposition between the good of the individual and that of her group (see, for example, *Dependent Rational Animals*, pp. 108–109). These can be reconciled, even partially, only when the private, the small group's, and the larger community's goods are objectively and properly understood as interdependent both in principle and in fact. When each decides its good for itself, there is manifest potential for wide and deep conflict. MacIntyre's concern here may be both theoretical and existential. Theoretically, we cannot accurately understand someone's welfare except as constituted by her flourishing as a member of some definite community. Indeed, there may be no such thing as her flourishing except her flourishing *as* such a member. Existentially, we cannot live fulfilled lives in the context of the radical alienation and anomie that characterize modernity. However, none of the totalitarianisms that have attempted to provide a larger sense of meaning, a sense of being part of something important beyond ourselves, has yet succeeded in justifying itself, even if some have temporarily avoided sociopolitical oppression.

The fifth and last of the issues that we will raise from MacIntyre's critique resides in his view, retained and adapted from his Marxist days, that much of the vaunted rationality and freedom on which liberal thinkers have prided their culture since the Enlightenment masks sinister interests of some groups over others. Some of what are frequently presented as features of universal reason or as uncontroversial values (e.g., efficiency) function to serve (and to conceal) these groups' interests by delegitimizing any opposition as parochial, romantic, narrow, mystical, dogmatic, unscientific, or otherwise irrational, illiberal, and unjustified. Here, MacIntyre sides with the genealogists and other postmodernist "masters of suspicion" in challenging this intellectual hegemon. Unlike them, however, MacIntyre never deprecates rationality, objectivity, justification, or ordered liberty as such. Rather, he questions the identification of these with their recent modernist social manifestations and theoretical conceptualizations. For him, challenge and pluralism are stages on the way to a reconceived reason and truth, which are never fully attained, but may better be approximated.

3. MacINTYRE'S RESPONSE TO MODERNIST MORAL PHILOSOPHY: SUMMARY

From his earliest writings, MacIntyre set himself in opposition to the liberal order of modernism. Like others before him, and in keeping with his deep belief in the communal and the historical, he consistently maintains that a nonliberal order would have to draw heavily not only for its critique of liberalism, but also for its positive alternative to liberalism, on sources of which some were plainly premodern and others we might today classify as postmodern. The two chief sources were Christianity and Marxism. Thus, he later wrote of his book:

> Then [in 1953, when *Marxism: an Interpretation* was first published] I aspired to be both a Christian and a Marxist . . . now [1968, when its revision was issued under the title *Marxism and Christianity*] I am skeptical of both, although also believing that one cannot entirely discard either without discarding truths not otherwise available. Then [1953] I envisioned the beliefs of both Christians and Marxists as essentially the beliefs of organizations . . . Now it is clear that for both Party and [Roman Catholic] church the relationship of belief to organization has become much more ambiguous. But one still cannot evade the question of relationship. (*Marxism and Christianity*, pp. vii–viii)

However, he recognized, as a Hegelian would, that one could not expect to reinstate either Christianity or Marxism as they had earlier existed. While both articulated insightful criticisms of the extant order, neither, he thought at the time, either attempted or could withstand subjecting itself to the same sort of critique it effectively advanced against modernism. "Christians and Marxists both wish to exempt their own doctrines from the historical relativity which they are all too willing to ascribe to the doctrines of others" (*Marxism and Christianity*, p. ix).

Eventually, he came to think that a form of Christianity could survive such critique, and he formulated a new moral-theoretical vision from within it. In this chapter, my interest lies chiefly in MacIntyre's criticism of the major modernist philosophers' moral thought, not in what he offers to put in its place. Nonetheless, a brief consideration of several of his positive proposals can help clarify just what it is to which he objects. As a physician's diagnosis can sometimes be better understood by looking to the treatment prescribed, so may we better grasp pertinent elements of MacIntyre's critique if we consider alternatives MacIntyre envisions to each of the ills that, as interpreted here, he claims to have detected.

In response to the first of the concerns I cited above, the fact (as he sees it) that justice and moral reasoning depend upon fairly specific standards of application and, because of that, also depend on social groups' practices and traditions, MacIntyre proposes that we consciously work within the most defensible tradition available, which he identifies as Thomas Aquinas' synthesis of Aristotle's virtues-oriented, self-perfectionist naturalist teleology with Augustine's conception of moral life as centered in conformity and obedience of will to natural and divine laws (*Whose Justice?*, pp. 164–208; *Three Rival Versions*, pp. 127–148). I put the project this way to highlight the magnitude of the work Aquinas set himself.

As an alternative to the second concern above noted, that our moral philosophies and our moral thinking so disengage 'values' from 'facts' that we retain no capacity for objectively grounding our normative judgments, MacIntyre proposes that we evaluate options teleologically, and thus see value-judgments as factual. He urges a more sociological, practice-based teleology in *After Virtue* (see esp. p. 196), and a more biological teleology in *Dependent Rational Animals* (see esp. p. x), in such a way that we evaluate a moral subject and her actions always in relation to some *telos* – the kind of fact that incorporates the basis of certain value judgments.

To counter the disintegration of the moral subject, briefly described in the third of MacIntyre's criticisms of modernist moral philosophizing, he now proposes that we subordinate any "role teleology" to more comprehensive conceptions of human nature and flourishing, and of the good human life as a coherent narrative now understood, especially in *Dependent Rational Animals*, to be rooted and revealed in the *dependence* and *vulnerability* we share as humans (pp. x–xi, 1–9).

In response to the fourth problem, the alienation of the individual and her welfare from that of her group and its communal life, MacIntyre proposes that we conceive of the individual's fulfillment and flourishing as a consummation she achieves only *as* a member of a particular political community, so that her good cannot be separated either factually or conceptually from that of her political community, which community itself needs to be shaped so as adequately to respond to humans' natural needs as social animals.

The fifth and last part that we identified in MacIntyre's critique of modernist moral philosophy and the cultural patterns it attempts to rationalize and justify was the problem of the supposed ways in which liberalism's familiar rhetoric of rationality, justice, freedom, and rights may function to conceal group interest in maintaining domination. Predictably, this kind of response has exposed MacIntyre to the charge that his criticism collapses into a form of relativism about morality, at least, and perhaps about reason itself.[8]

MacIntyre's rebuttal is as radical as it is ingenious.[9] It is, in effect, to outrelativize the relativist. Rather than recoiling from relativism, as I understand his strategy, MacIntyre plunges so deeply into it as, we might say, to fall out the other side. Let me explain what I mean. A crucial step is to define the issue in such a way as to turn the tables on the relativist. Thus,

MacIntyre holds first that the proper issue is not the attainment of moral knowledge or certainty, but only the rational superiority of a certain position or, better, the rational superiority of a certain tradition. To demand more is unrealistic. He holds second that the notion of rational superiority can only be applied against the background of some particular set of standards, which we cannot assume to be everywhere accorded the same status. Third, the comparison explicit in talk of rational superiority already implies a second term, which further limits the objective. The most that can ever be established is that accepting a certain tradition is rationally superior to accepting this or that other one, and all the ones comparatively evaluated *so far*. Thus, MacIntyre never entirely abandons his historicism. Fourth, the verb 'accept' requires us to specify a mental subject, and (fifth, sixth, and seventh) the Hegelian in MacIntyre is loath to allow her to float free of all temporal, personal, and social context. So, the question must always be whether this subject, in the particular situation she occupies within her society and her time, is rationally justified by her standards in making this choice among these options.[10]

On this basis, as I reconstruct it, MacIntyre's rejection of relativism about morality and reason (really about moral reasoning) amounts so far to the following. Contrary to what he sees as the relativist's hasty and facile assumption, MacIntyre insists that it is not necessarily (nor always) the case that everyone is so situated that there is no position whose adoption *by her* at *any* time would be rationally superior to some particular *set* of alternatives. Adapting (in MacIntyre 1977a) the Kuhnian notion of "epistemological crises," MacIntyre suggests that it is possible for (at least) some of us, by wide study and deep reflection, to come to be in such a position, relative to our own and to some other moral tradition(s), that it may be rationally superior/preferable, even by our own criteria of rationality (C1), for us (people in group G1) to accept some tradition (T1) over another tradition (T2) in our social situation (S1) and temporal location (L1). As the indexical terms indicate, that is a highly relativized claim. MacIntyre, as I understand him, uses it to place the strong relativist in the extreme position of having, implausibly, to deny this possibility in principle. Now the tables are turned, and it is the relativist who appears the dogmatist, claiming to know in advance and *a priori* that no one can be so situated. Note that MacIntyre forecloses what might seem the most appealing way of defending a strong relativism. For that defense would insist that standards of rationality are themselves relative to different traditions or conceptions of rational inquiry, and MacIntyre concedes (indeed, insists on) that claim at the outset.

Of course, to rest with this would constitute phony victory over a straw man. Not every form of relativism need be so strong. This victory would allow the purportedly vanquished relativist still to say that no one in the actual world, or no one in our Western traditions of moral inquiry, or no one for the past several hundred years, has been in a situation rationally to discern or choose as superior any from a limited number of seriously contending traditions. The relativist might well find that a defeat to savor. So it is important for MacIntyre's strategy to insist that science (as illuminated by its philosophically understood history) gives us historical examples of epistemological crises and how people have responded to them rationally. That provides him a model for his view that modernity has also plunged this society into a kind of prolonged, epistemological crisis in the moral realm. MacIntyre is not eager to claim that we are all in a position easily to resolve (or even to recognize) our crisis. In fact, it nicely jibes with his dismissive stance toward much recent philosophy to say that many of us, his academic colleagues – narrowly read, ignorant of the natural and social sciences, unschooled in history, whose cramped specialization leaves us unfamiliar with the details and even the languages of many of the West's moral traditions let alone those of distant lands – have no hope of finding a resolution unless we change our ways radically. Relativism is wrong in that it is false – indeed, as MacIntyre has reversed the expected order, it is narrow minded – to assume that there is no hope, in principle, for us to get to a point from which a rational choice among traditions can be made. However, nothing in that means it will be easy, or that most of us are already in a position to make one.

Moreover, MacIntyre distances himself from relativism by rejecting what he seems to see as the most appealing form of relativism for us today – that is, Nietzschean genealogy – because of what he regards as its inconsistent and inadequate account of the self (*Three Rival Versions*, pp. 205–215). There are several aspects to this critique, most of which I will not explore here.[11] One chief point, however, is that genealogists go too far, treating not just the human being *qua* individual (as conceived in the Enlightenment), *qua* rights-bearer, and so on, as social inventions or "constructs," but regarding humans as social constructions "all the way down," to adapt Richard Rorty's phrase. Against this, the MacIntyrean wants to remind us that the process of construction must have both an agent and an input. These, of course, are already human beings, and they must have constitutive and other qualities antecedent to the constructive process. This raises the possibility that these qualities and the nature that grounds them can already serve as the basis of moral virtues. Likewise, the fact that even genealogical deconstructive analysis needs some norms of rational inquiry raises the possibility of more constructive applications of these norms. The genealogist's very notions of manipulation, distraction and fetishization, masking and unmasking, all likewise suggest some more humane forms of interaction and more honest and truthful forms of social organization. Finally, for genealogy and deconstruction to lead to improved understanding and appropriate action, for unmasking to have either a theoretical or a practical point, there need to be norms of reasoning and moral conduct that, even if themselves critically examined, are not thereby undermined.[12]

4. MacINTYRE VERSUS MODERNIST MORAL PHILOSOPHY: CRITIQUE AND ASSESSMENT

Thus far, I have essayed some sketch of several of MacIntyre's principal misgivings about many of the West's chief moral philosophical presuppositions, arguments, and positions from early modernism through the present. While my task in this essay is chiefly expository, it may prove useful for us to undertake a few steps towards assessment. It is often the case, and especially in philosophical writing, that it is in subjecting it to criticism that we come not only to appreciate a position's strengths and weaknesses, but better to understand its content.

On the first issue, MacIntyre is surely correct that evaluation of an option as just or rationally superior requires fairly specific standards. However, it is not obvious *why* or *that* (a set of) standards need (1) have come into existence publicly, (2) have developed over time, or, more important, (3) be an accepted and continuing project of some social group. That I need to use standards to make a value or normative judgment hardly shows that I need to use socially established, lasting, and accepted ones. Nor has MacIntyre shown that no fairly specific standards are internal to the only (or to the most) defensible understanding or specification of reason or justice. He has marshaled arguments against Kantian, Humean, utilitarian, and other conceptions of rationality, some more powerful than others, but the issue is hardly settled. MacIntyre may be impatient and unrealistic in insisting that if philosophy has not yet resolved the matter, then we ought consider it beyond resolution and move on. Indeed, this presupposes his view that to establish a thesis must be to establish it by socially recognized standards. That, however, is just what may be in dispute. Nevertheless, we should recognize that MacIntyre has an important point in reminding us that it is difficult to defend the rationality of trusting any such conception until it has been tested *by many* and *over time*.

As to the second matter, MacIntyre rightly observes both that we invented *the terms* we use in moral reasoning and also that the related *concepts*, such as (and especially) those of fact and value, came to be recognized in time. However, it does not follow, and seems strange to maintain, that we invented either facts or values, let alone that an intellectual tradition is the key to overcoming their bifurcation.[13] Again, though, it seems to me that MacIntyre is basically correct that we need something *like* (along the lines of) an Aristotelian teleology, in which a valid value judgment is a species of factual judgment, in order to yield defensible, productive, objective, rational, convincing, and noncontroversial evaluation.

On the third issue, that of the fragmentation of the modern self, we can certainly allow that MacIntyre's conception of the individual's good as that which she has *qua* member of a political community with a tradition of rational inquiry is, doubtless, *one* way of overcoming ultimate fragmentation. However, there are alternatives we would need carefully to consider before we could be fully justified in rejecting them. Germain Grisez, for example, has recently suggested that an overarching project internal to the good of religion can lend unity to human life, and it may also be that even within pluralistic, role-centered moral theory, a certain comprehensive role-relationship – such as that of God's creature – which encompasses the other roles that constitute moral life, could overcome such fragmentation (see Grisez 2001; also Garcia 1997). Still, it may be that MacIntyre can allow for these possibilities if he allows that the fact that someone's living morally may promote her individual self-interest is neither her *motive* nor her behavior's moral *justification* (Meilaender 1999).

The fourth matter concerned modernism's balkanized, atomistic psychology. This certainly appears to be something socially harmful and otherwise undesirable. However, it is doubtful that we can eliminate *all* conflict between your individual welfare and mine or (what is different) between yours and (y)our group's. It is, moreover, dangerous to look to politics and to *political* community and tradition for this total absorption of the individual into something larger.[14] For all that, we should admit that MacIntyre is correct to think that someone can be good (i.e., *act* well) and (what is different) can flourish (i.e., *fare* well) only *as* this or that, even if he is too restrictive in his view of what can serve these roles.[15]

Finally, the kind of response to the charge of relativism that MacIntyre makes concedes that both morality and its rational evaluation (both internal and external) are relativistic, limiting only the latitudinarian implications of this claim. I suspect MacIntyre concedes too much to the relativist here, relativizing standards of both morality and rationality to social forms. More important, his concessions seem not to be required by the strength of the relativist's arguments, but rather driven by his own prior intellectual sympathy for Hegelian relativization of rational and moral norms to historically embodied forms of social life. That said, the sort of critique I attribute to MacIntyre is unusually helpful in exposing forms of dogmatism internal to the supposedly tolerant (and, nowadays, pragmatic) doctrines of cultural relativism in morality.

Summing up, then, MacIntyre's claims for tradition's necessity may well be overstated.[16] Still, he is surely correct that we need to be more aware of disputable and hidden assumptions and to avoid smug modernism, even those of us who continue to think we can make genuine progress by the now hoary techniques of conceptual analysis. Charles Taylor suggests we need to know those intuitions' sociohistorical origins (Taylor 1989, pp. 3–4). I suspect this is particularly true in questioning temporally and class-limited (or class-concentrated) views about what either is valuable or is entitled to protection from interference, social discouragement, or regulation. There is no pretending any more that even utilitarianism can somehow manage without appeal to our moral intuitions. Certainly, we must be more aware of how those intuitions can be shaped by history, class, and circumstance. This is an important hedge against the low-minded "deontologism" of those who strive merely to articulate and defend received elite opinion and current prejudices – about mercy killing, sexual perversions, medicalized mutilations, monstrous experiments in cloning, and so on down the new agenda – of their own comfortable and educated class.

I suspect MacIntyre is also correct that we should look to humans' personhood, needs, interpersonal relationships (Homeric 'ought's), and virtues rather than to duties and principles as keys to moral life – what we fundamentally want and need in and from others and ourselves as and because we are humans. Robert Adams has recently pressed the old complaint that the traditional conception of natural law draws too much from this minimal truth (Adams 1999, p. 365). Perhaps we can continue, as MacIntyre does, to call these deep features of ourselves "natural," but acknowledge that this is a rather modest use of the term, less grandly teleological and functioning more like one of J. L. Austin's "trouser words," chiefly to exclude the possibility that these preferences are rooted merely in social convention, idiosyncratic subjective preference, and so on (see also Adams 1999, pp. 307–308, 365–366).

5. CONCLUSION

Anyone who has had occasion to teach Aquinas' *Summa Theologiae*, especially if she has taught it to undergraduates, will have had occasion to note, regret, and make public apology for the book's confusing and vexing format. Its so-called "questions" are but the names of topics, its "articles" are in the form of questions, and each major discussion begins with a battery of arguments – usually bolstered by erudite quotations from (and sometimes controversial interpretations of) an array of authorities from Scripture, scriptural commentators, church fathers, more recent theologians, as well as from pagan philosophers – arguments severally and collectively making a case *against* some thesis the author holds. Only after this prologue to each "article" does Aquinas articulate and defend his own position on the issue, proceeding then to laborious rebuttals of each "objection." We are not surprised such a work was never finished; the wonder is that it was ever begun.

It is the maddening thoroughness of this give-and-take, so irritating to today's short-attention-span readers, that seems to draw MacIntyre to Aquinas and his great *Summa*, not only as a principal source of truth and wisdom but also as a model of what he sees as the communal intellectual work of philosophical and theological inquiry. Some aestheticians have exploited the ambiguity in the term 'painting', which can refer both to an activity and its finished product. We might note just the same ambiguity in the word 'work'. Part of what seems to appeal to MacIntyre in Aquinas' great work is the way its author lets us see him working, a mind at work in wrestling with other minds in a common striving for the truth. Despite the oft-heard and glib dismissals of Aquinas and his Christian colleagues for dogmatism, the *Summa Theologiae* is anything but a calm, imperious, context-free, and ahistorical recitation of the truth. The truth for which it strives, and into which it sometimes offers glimpses, may be outside time and space. However, the book itself is unmistakably and unapologetically a work of its time. It is a *summation*, as its name makes explicit, of what has so far been said on the issues it treats and an interpretation of the progress that has been made, sometimes by revealing the dead ends to which some lines of inquiry have proceeded. This is MacIntyre's Aquinas, the paradigm of the intellectual inquirer, guided along the pathway by the lamps of tradition, but continually looking into what flickers in the darkness to help us see why the lamps marking the path's edge stand where they do. Even if truth is eternal, we inquirers are placed in time and place, and can only attain those truths by reflecting with, and often by arguing against, others who have gone before us. This is not always pretty, but it is necessary if we are to learn from our history and from others' wrong turns as well as their progress. It is as if MacIntyre sees in Aquinas' work an intellectual embodiment of a recent poet's injunction:

> whatever you have to say, leave
> the roots on, let them
> dangle
>
> And the dirt
>
> Just to make clear
> where they come from (Olson 1987b)

Jung compared the mind to a house, and I suggested above that we could profitably employ this metaphor in grasping MacIntyre's view of parts of our modern social order and its moral vocabulary. In this conclusion I have shifted to a metaphor of inquiry as night hiking along a lantern-lit path, and the poem I cited regards our speech as if an uprooted plant. Perhaps we should see these three images in play – house, uprooted plant, night-lit path – as corresponding to three moments in MacIntyre's analysis. In examining what MacIntyre regards as our current moral babble, the poet's metaphor of the uprooted plant helps us understand our discourse as composed of pieces torn from the intellectual and social context they need for intelligibility as plants need soil for sustenance. In examining the larger intellectual edifice of our moral thinking, the metaphor of the house helps us discern that what now seems to fit may have been merely plastered together or covered with a common carpeting, concealing deeper differences in materials and underlying foundations, differences which may mean differential capacity to bear loads, etc. In considering how we ought respond to these facts, or what is to be done, the metaphor of the lamp-lit path at night, where skeletons in the dark mark paths that did not work, helps us remember that we may be able to make progress only along paths lit by others' successes and marked by others' failures. What is important to take from MacIntyre's critique is the emphasis on process and our situatedness. Now, as a Christian in search of what he has reconceived as timeless truth about our nature and origin, as earlier when, as a Marxist, he repudiated the class-based and imperial assumptions he discerned within European Enlightenment thought, MacIntyre has wanted to puncture the pretension of our time's little preoccupations and rules, which present themselves as eternal truths and inherent structures of reason itself. Whatever the truth about truth itself, we approach truth through a dialectic process, and it is at our own peril that we delude ourselves into believing that we can do it entirely on our own and cut off from time and space, as Descartes imagined in his warm little chamber. We can see how to proceed, MacIntyre thinks, only by continually reviewing the places from where we have come. Not for our minds is the Crystal Palace, which so excited the pulse of the Victorians in the last glory of Enlightenment innocence that MacIntyre explores at the beginning of *Three Rival Versions*. If these minds of ours are to witness such perfect limpidity, it must be in some future realm MacIntyre now thinks better envisioned by John the Divine than by Karl Marx. For our minds, even in their highest intellectual achievements, there is no leaving behind the roots and the dirt because we need "to make clear where they come from."[17]

Notes

1. Jung 1928, pp. 118–119; quoted in Alston Conly, "House: Charged Space," catalogue of an exhibition at the McMullen Museum, Boston College, June 11–September 16, 2001.
2. MacIntyre realizes the problematic inherent in his contrast of liberal modernism with tradition. As liberals seem to have their own great texts, powerful images, accepted avenues of thought, et cetera, why is not liberalism itself a tradition? His answer is not readily discernable, but seems to boil down to the claim that while liberalism may have some of the trappings of "tradition" and may even be called a tradition, it is not a tradition *of inquiry* in the relevant sense. Especially because of the stark opposition it presupposes between rationality and authority, even the authority of tradition, liberalism cannot comfortably accept itself as a tradition, and more important it cannot adequately *operate* as a tradition of inquiry that makes progress.
3. The house image is an old one. Descartes puts it to very different use from MacIntyre in Part 2 of his *Discourse on Method*, in which he stresses the need for knowledge, like a house, to have good foundations, and complains about houses and towns (and, by implication, mental structures) built in different parts by different architects and in different styles. For MacIntyre, the issue is not just that of the firmness of foundations, but of the history and concealment of ill-fitting elements, seams, and joints, and of different foundations and even their possible absence beneath some sections later added.
4. That philosophical attention to these most general terms may be misplaced was a point Anscombe made and on which she has been joined by Bernard Williams, among others.
5. MacIntyre himself proposed a more limited reading of Hume (1959a), but later revised this in *Whose Justice?*, pp. 311–322. It is not clear to me the extent to which in the latter revision MacIntyre joins the standard interpretation of Hume as denying any inference from what he deemed factual judgments to moral ones.

6. In so talking of facts and values, and even sometimes of the "individual," as social inventions ("constructions," some would say today), MacIntyre makes a move characteristic of the postmodernist heroes of today's cultural studies. Thus, Michel Foucault pointedly and influentially insisted in *The Order of Things* (1974 [1966]) that "man" himself was an invention of recent vintage, adding that he was also one that would not last long. Here, the poststructuralist Foucault outdid his structuralist predecessor Claude Levi-Strauss, who had a decade earlier reminded his readers that there were no human beings at the world's outset and there would be none at its close. See also Lilla 1998.
7. This difficulty also afflicts the system of Homeric 'ought'-judgments and makes it impossible for us to return to anything like it as adequate for our purposes.
8. See, especially, Nussbaum 1989. This assumed opposition persists. In a recent exchange, scholars dispute whether Edmund Burke, in his rejection of the French Revolution, was siding with tradition against reason (see McElroy et al. 2002). While the disputants allow that things are not quite so simple because instrumental reason might indicate some value or short-term efficiency in relying on tradition, they do not address the stronger possibilities MacIntyre envisages – that a tradition can itself be a tradition of rationality nor, more strongly, that practical rationality may require a tradition in order to flesh out its conception of the good life and to turn vague desiderata such as adequate consideration into determinate criteria for use. Consider also Nozick on the parallel difficulty in theoretical assessment:

   > Are there procedures for choosing among alternative and competing scientific theories of the same phenomena; do the norms or methodology of science determine such choices among theories, so that all who follow these norms must agree in which theory they select? There are different virtues in a scientific theory, different dimensions along which it can be evaluated: explanatory power, goodness of fit with the data, breadth and diversity of evidential support, degree of testability, range and diversity of phenomena it covers, simplicity, fit with accepted theories, and so on.... Judgments of how a theory falls along each of these dimensions are largely intuitive. Moreover, there is certainly no adequate systematic proposal about how these different desiderata of a theory are to be combined in an overall evaluation, about how two competing theories are to be comparatively evaluated or ranked when one is better along one of these dimensions, while the other is better along others. (Nozick 1981, p. 483)

   MacIntyre would demur chiefly regarding Nozick's appeal to private (and unconfirmable) intuition, where MacIntyre would invoke a time-tested tradition of inquiry to set standards and make comparisons, and regarding Nozick's apparent assumption that a theory's epistemic adequacy can be determined outside of such tradition-relative standards.
9. My discussion is chiefly an interpretation of *Whose Justice?* See also MacIntyre 1999b.
10. We might stress that, though she faces this decision by herself in an important sense, she will have gotten there only through joint inquiry conducted by continual consultation of other efforts in both her own tradition and others. For

more on inquiry's social dimension and as modeled as a kind of Aristotelian friendship founded on a common good, see Burrell 2000.

11. See Gutting 1999, pp. 107–110.
12. "[B]oth Christianity and Marxism are constantly being refuted; and the point here is . . . that those who lack any positive coherent view of the world themselves still have to invoke Christianity and Marxism, even in the acts of criticism and refutation, as points of ideological and social reference" (*Marxism and Christianity*, p. viii).
13. Judith Thomson has recently suggested that teleology may not be necessary for factual evaluation, though being good *in ways* (or *qua* this or that) is needed (see Thomson 2001, ch. 1). We ought also point out that the fact/value gap does not suffice for emotivism, as MacIntyre appears to presuppose in *After Virtue*, because prescriptivism and versions of intersubjective ethics taking moral terms to express group endorsement are also available and alternative possibilities.
14. The problem also besets some of MacIntyre's more effective critics. It seems to me exacerbated within Gutting's (1999) "pragmatic liberalism."
15. Certainly, this is a more sensible approach than some recent efforts to understand human benefit. Judith Thomson, for example, offers a bifurcated analysis of what is good for someone, referring most forms of benefit, especially those we share with lower animals, to our functioning as humans, but deferring others to subjective desires, insisting only that the latter be filtered in various ways to ensure that they are serious, informed, voluntary (see Thomson 2001, ch. 1). What is startling here is that Thomson never raises the obvious question of how someone's wanting this or that itself fits with desire's function in human life.
16. Moreover, the historicism MacIntyre thinks internal to tradition may clash with the locality he also emphasizes. For more on this, see Gutting 1999, pp. 99–101.
17. I express thanks to Patrick Byrne, Sarah Harper, Mark Murphy, and Jason Taylor for helpful comments on an earlier draft.

5 MacIntyre and Contemporary Moral Philosophy

DAVID SOLOMON

The task of this chapter is to give a general account of Alasdair MacIntyre's views in moral philosophy. This would be a difficult task to carry out in the short space allowed for any major moral philosopher, but there are well-known reasons why it is even more formidable for MacIntyre. MacIntyre has been publishing important work in moral philosophy for over half a century, and in the early years of the new millennium he shows no signs of slowing down. His views in ethics have changed in important respects during this period and they continue to develop, sometimes in surprising ways. These difficulties in interpreting MacIntyre are compounded by the fact that he does not neatly separate his work in ethics from his work in action theory, philosophy of language, and philosophy of the social sciences. And, notoriously, his systematic views in ethics are developed against the background of a rich and controversial account of the history of ethics. Moreover, his work in ethics has engaged in a number of different ways most of the large-scale cultural developments in the last half century, including especially the cold war conflicts between Marxism and liberalism, the cultural turmoil of the sixties, and radical changes within the Roman Catholic Church (of which he has been a member since the 1980s).

These characteristics of MacIntyre's views, however, should not be exaggerated. Although his views have developed in important ways, there are a number of themes that have not changed. Indeed, it will be part of the thesis of this chapter that the continuities in MacIntyre's ethical thought are more important than the changes in it. MacIntyre himself has frequently mentioned that his objections to liberalism have remained constant throughout the development of his thought, although they have been made from slightly different perspectives at different times. He has also consistently rejected emotivist and relativist approaches to ethics, while at the same time rejecting the main foundationalist alternatives to these approaches. Throughout his career he has shown an openness to a robust naturalism in ethics, while always (unlike some others who have championed the cause of virtue) emphasizing the centrality and ineliminability of moral rules in the moral life.

It also seems to me that MacIntyre's reputation as an outsider to mainstream academic moral philosophy is misleading. Although he often writes in a manner that contributes to the myth that he is an outsider hoping to pull down the house of academic moral philosophy, careful attention to his work throughout his career belies this reputation. MacIntyre has indeed been almost a model philosophical citizen. He has carefully and fairly reviewed the books of his most important philosophical opponents and responded patiently to their criticisms of his own work. No contemporary moral philosopher has made a greater effort to open himself to dialogue with his opponents, nor has any moral philosopher been more gracious in acknowledging his debts to others.

In suggesting that MacIntyre is a good philosophical citizen, and not the *enfant terrible* he is sometimes held to be, I do not intend to deny that he is distinctive in a number of respects among contemporary Anglophone moral philosophers. As already noted, he pays much more attention to the history of ethics than do most other contemporary moral philosophers, and he does not simply combine his superb historical learning with a distinct capacity for systematic ethical theory. It is impossible to separate his theses in systematic moral philosophy from his historical claims. In criticizing the Enlightenment Project, he is also criticizing the Enlightenment. His defense of Aquinas is inseparable from his careful historical scholarship on Aquinas. Some of MacIntyre's most astute critics recognize that to criticize his ethics it will be necessary to criticize his history.[1] MacIntyre also, of course, pays much more attention to the social sciences than do most other contemporary moral philosophers. He not only says that "every moral philosophy presupposes a sociology," he also claims to investigate the sociology presupposed by the moral philosophies he discusses. Like many continental philosophers, he engages the thought of Marx and Freud and brings their work into contact with the projects of moral philosophy. He has been also influenced, in ways that are unusual for most Anglophone moral philosophers, by the thought of such continental figures as Gadamer, Maritain, and, more recently, Edith Stein and Husserl.

In spite of the many ways in which MacIntyre's work differs from that of most off-the-shelf Anglophone moral philosophers, his work in ethics can be understood in relation to the standard divisions within twentieth-century analytic moral philosophy's metaethics, normative ethics, and applied ethics. In the first half of the twentieth century, academic moral philosophy came to be dominated by a set of questions about the meaning of key ethical terms and the logical structure of moral arguments. This set of questions, and a variety of semantic and logical techniques for answering them, defined what came to be called metaethics. This problematic lives on in contemporary ethics, although in a slightly chastened and less central form. In the 1960s, and especially in the early 1970s, there was a revival of the kind of large-scale normative theorizing characteristic of such historical figures as Kant, Bentham, Hobbes, and Aristotle. Disputes within normative ethics came to dominate most academic discussions in ethics in the last quarter century, and the classical arguments between Kant and Bentham – or Hobbes and Aquinas – are being refought by their twentieth-century surrogates. At about the time that philosophers started turning their attention to the project of normative ethics, they also began commenting on particular moral quandaries arising in particular social and professional contexts – medicine, the environment, the relation between men and women, the obligations of citizenship, and so forth. Applied ethics then became a third context, characterized by a set of questions and increasingly by a set of competing theoretical approaches, for discussion among contemporary moral philosophers.

MacIntyre's relation to contemporary discussions in metaethics, normative ethics, and applied ethics is complex. On the one hand, he has made important contributions to all three areas. He has defended a robust cognitivism in metaethics, a rich Aristotelianism in normative ethics, and a number of particular views within applied ethics. At the same time, he has been critical of the framework that has shaped much of the discussion in these three areas. It is the somewhat Janus-faced aspect of MacIntyre's contributions to these three areas, I want to argue, that makes his role in contemporary philosophy open to such differing interpretations. MacIntyre the outsider is critical of the pretensions of metaethics and normative ethics and of their ideological and self-deceived roles, as he sees them, in many contemporary discussions. MacIntyre the good philosophical citizen nevertheless models the right way to do metaethics and normative ethics. Discussions in each of these areas of ethics arise out of genuine questions, and these questions demand answers that it is the duty of philosophers to pursue. MacIntyre has pursued these answers as vigorously and with as much integrity as any contemporary philosopher. At the same time, he is fully alive to the possibility that the framework within which these questions arise may itself be distorted by ideological pressure, by bureaucratic forms of organization, or by other forces that the philosopher's cultural and historical naïveté ill suit him or her to recognize. MacIntyre sometimes can give the impression of being engaged in a perverse Neurathian project – trying to rebuild the ship of ethics while simultaneously loudly claiming that it cannot actually be rebuilt – and further charging that, even if it could, it would certainly sink at its mooring.

In what follows, I will structure the discussion by examining MacIntyre's contributions to two of the three areas of ethics I have distinguished here – metaethics and normative ethics. For reasons of space, I will largely ignore his contributions to applied ethics. While examining his particular contributions, however, we will be also examining the ways in which he is critical of the framework of discussion in each area and his suggestions about how the questions and techniques in each area should be transformed.[2] In the final section we will turn briefly to a discussion of two significant criticisms of MacIntyre's work in ethics.

1. METAETHICS

There is a perennial distinction in moral philosophy between abstract questions of conceptual structure and meaning in ethics, and concrete questions about the content of moral principles or rules – or the appropriate lists of virtues and goods. It was left to the twentieth-century metaethical tradition, however, to sharpen this distinction into an orthodoxy so rigid that it almost strangled creative ethical thought. It was presupposed by almost everyone in this tradition that there was something distinctive about moral language and moral argument, and that it was the primary (or possibly exclusive) task of moral philosophy to explore these special semantic and logical features of the moral. Metaethical investigations in this tradition were sharply distinguished from normative ethics (which took up substantive ethical questions), and it was frequently suggested that moral philosophers, as philosophers, should confine their activity strictly to metaethical investigations.[3]

The story of the history of classical metaethics from G. E. Moore to its transformation in the final third of the twentieth century has been frequently told, not least by MacIntyre himself in the penultimate chapter of his *Short History of Ethics*. It is common now to distinguish three main phases in this history:

1. The intuitionism of Moore, Prichard, and Ross, which focused on the autonomy of the ethical and the evaluative and, in Moore's case, on the indefinability of the most basic ethical terms.
2. The noncognitivist reaction to intuitionism made popular by the work of Stevenson and Ayer, and developed in a later, more sophisticated

form by R. M. Hare.[4] The noncognitivists shared the intuitionists' objections to "naturalistic" definitions of evaluative terms, but rejected the intuitionists' view that the main task of ethical discourse is to ascribe properties to actions or persons. The noncognitivist emphasis on the action-guiding role of the ethical led them to attribute a special form of meaning (variously, emotive meaning, evaluative meaning, or prescriptive meaning) to ethical terms and to argue that moral argument should be understood as embodying an irreducible rhetorical component which could not be captured in any purely cognitive metaethical view.

3. The "naturalistic" rejection of the excesses of both intuitionism and noncognitivism by such thinkers as Foot, Geach, Toulmin, Searle, and MacIntyre himself in the 1950s and 1960s.

MacIntyre's first important work in ethics, his master's thesis[5] (1951), was written very much in the spirit of classical metaethics and attempted to move beyond what was already being called an impasse between cognitivists and noncognitivists in this metaethical discussion. In this thesis, *The Significance of Moral Judgments*, he develops a number of themes that figure in his discussion of metaethics in the decades to follow. Almost half of the thesis is taken up with close criticism of Moore's intuitionism and Stevenson's emotivism. While he rejects both intuitionist and emotivist metaethical views using familiar arguments, he also argues that the intuitionists and emotivists shared a number of views about the metaethical project itself that he regards as mistaken. Indeed, he argues that all participants in the metaethical discussion shared a tendency to oversimplify the metaethical project by supposing that it is possible to discover a relatively simple characterization of the meaning of moral discourse. MacIntyre argues, however, even at this early stage in his thought, that the meaning of such discourse will not conform to a single pattern. As he says in summing up this point:

> The most important step in the understanding of the significance of moral judgments is taken at the point when we cease to look for a referential meaning for them, naturalistic or non-naturalistic. The temptation is, of course, to go on from this to deny them anything but an emotive or psychological significance as interjections. But once we have seen that significance does not derive from reference, that every kind of sentence has its own kind of logic, and that these logics are the logics of languages *in use*, we can formulate the sense in which moral judgements have significance by exhibiting the logic of their usage. (*Significance of Moral Judgments*, p. 73)

There are places in the thesis where MacIntyre seems to lean toward a broadly naturalistic view of moral language, as when he says:

> Frequently when all the facts have been related, nothing more remains to be said. At the end of "Madame Bovary" we do not want Flaubert to say, we do not want to say ourselves, "Emma Bovary was a bad woman." We are more likely to do as the French have done and cease to use the word "bad" to describe that kind of woman in the future, using instead a word coined from her name. (*Significance of Moral Judgments*, p. 65)

There is no non-natural property to be added to the facts in this case, nor need there be an emotive overlay. MacIntyre makes it clear, however, that even the naturalistic accounts of moral language that most tempt him oversimplify the "logic of moral discourse."

In the final chapter of the thesis, MacIntyre turns his attention from his criticism of the standard metaethical positions to constructive suggestions about how an exploration of the "logic of moral language in use" might work. He carefully dissects a number of moral arguments drawn from literary texts by, among others, E. M. Forster, Virginia Woolf, D. H. Lawrence, and Aeschylus. By looking carefully at these arguments, MacIntyre attempts to establish the diversity of forms of moral argument and the dangers of any attempt (as he later puts it in "Ought") to "homogenize" our moral vocabulary or forms of moral argument. In the end his claim is that intuitionism, emotivism, and naturalism each pick out some feature of moral judgment and moral argument and elevate it to a kind of paradigmatic status. The central mistake made by the classical metaethicists is one of oversimplification, a mistake that can only be made good by attending to the variety and complexity of moral language and moral discussion. He ends the thesis with this characteristic MacIntyrean flourish:

> It is because they enable us to solve problems of appraisal and of action that moral judgements possess significance. They are part of a pattern of language and action, continually to be adjusted and criticized, and just because they are never exempt from criticism to be accorded the title of reasonable or unreasonable, as the case may be. Above all they arise out of the way in which we see the world and the way in which our language allows us to see the world. We cannot sufficiently emphasize the direction given to our appraisals by the language which happens to be available for our descriptions. It is as we see the facts that we judge the world. But even within the limits of our language, vague and imprecise as it so often is, there is better and worse reasoning, there are correct and mistaken

> decisions. But on this topic one can only be conscious of how little has been said, how much remains to say. (*Significance of Moral Judgments*, p. 92)

MacIntyre attempts to say over the next half century much of what he regards at mid-century as remaining to be said. His later work continues to emphasize themes clearly enunciated in this early work: (1) that moral judgments are important because of their connection with "problems of appraisal and of action"; (2) that moral judgments are never beyond criticism and dispute and that just for this reason the categories of the reasonable and the unreasonable apply to them and the arguments for them; (3) that moral judgments grow out of how we *see* the world, and that vision is more central to moral judgment than attitude; and (4) that the contours of our moral thought and action are constrained by "the language which happens to be available for our descriptions."

MacIntyre pursues both his critical and constructive metaethical suggestions at many places in his later works, particularly in the last chapter of the *Short History*, a number of the essays reprinted in the second half of *Against the Self-Images of the Age*, and, of course, in the opening chapters of *After Virtue*. In all of these discussions he shows respect for the integrity of the work done by the classical metaethicists while sharply criticizing many of their conclusions and, more importantly, their self-understanding. His particular criticisms of the intuitionists and the noncognitivists in this tradition differ little from many of those raised by other critics at the time (Strawson's criticism of intuitionism and Geach and Foot's criticisms of noncognitivism were particularly influential). His reaction to classical metaethics is distinctive, however, in at least two ways. First, unlike most other critics, he is concerned to explore in some depth why the views of intuitionists like Moore and emotivists like Stevenson were so persuasive; second, he is interested not only in assessing particular metaethical views but also in assessing the enterprise of metaethics itself. His most important conclusions about the metaethical enterprise are threefold: (1) the main metaethical views are mistaken as metaethical views; (2) nevertheless, these views illuminate important features of the cultures in which they were put forward; and (3) the enterprise of metaethics as conceived by most of those engaging in it embodies mistaken views about how moral concepts are related to their cultural setting.

MacIntyre's discussion of metaethics in *A Short History* once again provides brief criticisms of all of the main positions in the metaethical tradition.[6] His overall diagnosis of metaethical disagreement in this work, however, is more narrowly specified than it was in his thesis written a decade and a half earlier. In *Short History* he argues that the central metaethical disagreement between cognitivist and noncognitivist metaethical views is best understood as growing out of a conflict between persons speaking from outside any moral view and those speaking from within a particular moral view.

> Conceptual conflict is endemic in our situation, because of the depth of our moral conflicts. Each of us therefore has to choose both with whom we wish to be morally bound and by what ends, rules, and virtues we wish to be guided. These two choices are inextricably linked. . . . Speaking from within my own moral vocabulary, I shall find myself bound by the criteria embodied in it. . . . Yet I must choose for myself with whom I am to be morally bound. I must choose between alternative forms of social and moral practice. Not that I stand morally naked until I have chosen. For our social past determines that each of us has some vocabulary with which to frame and to make his choice. (*Short History*, p. 268)

He puts the point even more pointedly when he says,

> It follows that we are liable to find two kinds of people in our society: those who speak from within one of these surviving moralities, and those who stand outside all of them. Between the adherents of rival moralities and between the adherents of one morality and the adherents of none there exists no court of appeal, no impersonal neutral standard. For those who speak from within a given morality, the connection between fact and valuation is established in virtue of the meanings of the words they use. To those who speak from without, those who speak from within appear merely to be uttering imperatives which express their own liking and their private choices. The controversy between emotivism and prescriptivism on the one hand and their critics on the other thus expresses the fundamental moral situation of our society. (*Short History*, p. 266)

In this discussion, MacIntyre seems primarily interested in combating the view that moral concepts are timeless and unhistorical, a view that he regards as giving support illegitimately to a range of "absolutist" views held by philosophers as different as Jean-Paul Sartre, the British emotivists, and the British naturalists. Emotivists and prescriptivists typically, according to MacIntyre,

> try to absolutize their own individualist morality and that of the age, by means of an appeal to concepts, just as much as their critics try to absolutize their own moralities by means of an appeal to conceptual considerations. But

> these attempts could only succeed if moral concepts were indeed timeless and unhistorical and if there were only one available set of moral concepts. One virtue of the history of moral philosophy is that it shows us that this is not true and that moral concepts themselves have a history. To understand this is to be liberated from any false absolutist claims. (*Short History*, p. 269)

These are the concluding words of the *Short History* and they again represent an important MacIntyrean theme – that moral philosophers of all stripes, absolutist or skeptical, cognitivists or noncognitivists, frequently attempt to defend their views by appealing to some features of the conceptual structure of moral thought and talk. MacIntyre has always contended that such arguments that depend on the primacy of the conceptual in ethics fail. His claim is not that conceptual investigations are not important, but that they cannot be first philosophy in ethics. Concepts are prey to historical development and philosophical transformations just as much as forms of life and particular practices are. Moral language and styles of argument are just one entrée into understanding the moral life – an important way in, to be sure, but not the only way and certainly not a privileged way. The investigations of historians and social scientists, as well as the imaginative works of literature that use these concepts, are as important as the bare examination of the concepts. There is no privileged access to the structure of moral thought. Concepts always have a history and are subject to pressures of various sorts.

This general picture of metaethics that emerges in the *Short History* is explored in much more detail and extended in important respects in a series of essays that MacIntyre writes over the next five years or so and that appear in the second half of *Against the Self-Images of the Age*. In these essays, he is especially concerned to come to grips with the prescriptivist views of R. M. Hare, who had inherited the noncognitivist mantle from Stevenson and the emotivists and who was the dominant figure in metaethics throughout the late 1950s and 1960s. His criticisms of Hare focus – as one would expect – on Hare's view that the two central semantic features of morally evaluative language are universalizability and prescriptivity. Hare argued that one could identify these as the central semantic features of moral language from a position that is neutral with regard to any substantive moral views. Hare also claimed that, while the results of this semantic investigation were morally neutral (i.e., did not entail, even together with additional "factual" premises, any substantive moral views), these semantic facts about moral language nevertheless gave us access to a distinctive method of approaching moral conflict and moral uncertainty that goes some way toward resolving these conflicts in a reasonable fashion.

MacIntyre's particular criticisms of this view (as found especially in "What Morality Is Not" and "Imperatives, Reasons for Action and Morals") are complex and subtle, but grow out of two central points. First, he continues to argue, as we have seen above, that it is mistaken to suppose that "moral language" can be regarded as a timeless object of analysis existing outside historical change and differences in social practice. Hare talks about "our moral concepts," but MacIntyre argues that we must recognize the indexical character of this phrase. In support of this point, he discusses in some detail particular historical episodes (as he had already done in *Short History*) in which we can see moral language developing and changing under the pressure of historical contingency and philosophical argument. There is no simple truth about "the" meaning of our moral concepts, and any attempt like Hare's to defend some simple truth on this matter will substitute ideology or conventional moral opinion for genuine semantic analysis.

Second, MacIntyre argues that even if there were some hope of giving "the" correct account of the meaning and use of moral language, Hare's particular attempt to characterize the meaning of moral language as essentially one of prescribing behavior or attitudes overlooks the rich variety of uses of this language, even if we restrict ourselves to the uses of language in contemporary cultures. As MacIntyre says, "there are a great variety of uses to which moral utterance may be put, none of which can claim the title of 'the' function of moral valuation" (1957c, p. 101). He goes on to list "some of the tasks which even so familiar a form of moral judgment as 'X ought to do Y' may be set." These tasks include:

1. The expression of indignation or other violent or mild emotion.
2. The expression of commands or exhortations.
3. The appraisal of actions.
4. The giving of advice.
5. Persuasion.
6. The expression of one's own principles.

MacIntyre comments after giving this list:

> This incomplete catalogue of uses of "ought" in simple sentences such as "X ought to do Y" has one main point: moral philosophy to date has been insufficiently lexicographical. Even a partial enumeration of the differences already noted between first-, second-, and third-person uses of

> "ought" . . . should make us conscious of the need for a far wider range of patterns of analysis than any contemporary writer has so far offered. (1957c, p. 102)

It is important to note about this line of argument that MacIntyre is not developing the kind of argument that was frequently brought against Hare and the metaethical tradition generally – the argument, that is, that metaethics was mistaken in placing semantic investigations at the heart of ethics, thereby diverting the attention of moral philosophy from its real concerns, such as concerns to develop comprehensive normative theories or to discuss genuine moral dilemmas present in contemporary culture. MacIntyre's grounds for objecting are rather that the semantic investigations have not been done well enough – or as he puts it in the quotation above, "moral philosophy to date has been insufficiently lexicographical." Hare goes wrong not in aiming to clarify the meaning of moral and more broadly evaluative language and, by doing so, to illuminate the structures of moral argument; rather, he goes wrong in doing so badly. He is insufficiently attentive to the historical changes in our moral language and to the variety of uses of moral language. An adequate ("genuinely lexicographical") account of moral language would need to be more historically aware and more nuanced in its approach to the variegated uses of our vocabulary for moral conversation and deliberation.

MacIntyre goes some way in the direction of modeling a genuinely lexicographical investigation of moral language in the work that follows his largely critical work of Hare. This later work, first introduced in two remarkable articles, "Ought" and "Some More About 'Ought'," and then later developed in the opening chapters of *After Virtue*, attempts simultaneously to illustrate what it would be to do genuine metaethics and why the deep failures in metaethics in the twentieth-century are symptoms of important features of our moral situation. MacIntyre's concern in "Ought" is to investigate a particular case of metaethical disagreement – that between Harean prescriptivists and Footean naturalists – and to attempt to draw from this investigation some general lessons for thinking about procedure in metaethics. He is struck, as were many at this time, by the deep impasse between these two views. Both prescriptivism and naturalism had been developed and elaborated by able philosophers using highly sophisticated arguments. Each was familiar with the other's objections to the favored view and armed with responses to these objections. The arguments for and against each view had been honed in countless philosophical articles and been tested in dialectical exchanges at philosophical meetings.

MacIntyre, writing in the early 1970s after this debate had been in full swing for over a decade, is skeptical, however, that we are even in sight of a resolution to this dispute. While he admits that "there has been no lack of peacemakers attempting to patch up things between them," he is confident that "no conclusive argument is found at any point in these exchanges; conclusive, that is, in terms other than those of the party that propounds them" (1971d, p. 140). The reason for his confidence that, given the present terms of the dispute, no resolution of the disagreement will be forthcoming, is that each of the sides in this disagreement are so expert at redescribing the facts that would resolve this disagreement – and redescribing them, of course, in a fashion that tends to support the favored conclusions of their side. Prescriptivists, in developing their arguments, are allowed to describe the "linguistic facts" in a way favorable to their view of the conceptual landscape, while naturalists play the same game from their quite different naturalistic perspective. Given this situation, MacIntyre argues that it follows that

> if the argument between prescriptivism and naturalism is not to be an empty and pointless contest, which has by the very virtuosity of the contestants in the performance of the task of redescription been deprived of that independent subject matter, the characterization of which was the sole point of the whole enterprise, one prerequisite is that as far as possible both theories are matched against the facts, so far as these can be independently delineated, and the tendency to redescribe the facts in accordance with the requirements of the rival theories must be curbed as far as possible. (MacIntyre 1971d, 141)

MacIntyre's suggestion, then, is that the seemingly interminable disputes within metaethics in twentieth-century Anglophone moral philosophy can be settled only if we can hold these theories up to the facts, "independently delineated," where independence is to be understood as independence from the presuppositions and biases of the contending theories. But what could be this perspective, independent of improper philosophical influence, that might serve as the neutral arbiter in these debates? Not surprisingly, MacIntyre opts for a historically and sociologically sophisticated lexicography. What is required, that is, is that we approach

> the linguistic facts at first as much as possible in the mode of the lexicographer rather than of the philosopher; by next setting the linguistic facts in their social contexts; and finally by asking whether this does not enable us to discriminate, in relation to the theories of both prescriptivism

and naturalism, the types of moral situation of which each doctrine is the natural and convincing explanation and analysis from the types of moral situation which one or the other doctrine has to distort. In so doing we shall treat these doctrines as hypotheses, which invoke a stylized model of argument to explain the actual patterns of moral speech and controversy. (MacIntyre 1971d, p. 141)

In both "Ought" and "Some More About 'Ought'," MacIntyre strives to put on the table some of the sociological and historical materials that will open up the kind of genuinely lexicographical investigation that he has argued will be necessary if progress in settling metaethical disputes is to be possible. In "Ought" he introduces and develops in great detail a taxonomy of uses of 'ought' rooted in close attention to social practices and historical contingencies. He suggests that there are three stages in the use of the English word 'ought': "a first in which 'ought' and 'owe' are indistinguishable; a second in which 'ought' has become an auxiliary verb, useable with an infinitive to give advice; and a third in which the use of 'ought' has become unconditional"(MacIntyre 1971d, p. 143). He further suggests that there are particular social contexts in which these different uses of 'ought' most naturally find their home and within which the nuances of their usage can be examined. He looks in some detail at the Icelandic culture of the Norse sagas as a place where linguistic equivalences of our 'ought' never go beyond his first stage of usage, the culture of classical Greece as a place where usage never goes beyond the second stage, and modern culture where "it is only perhaps that we have 'oughts' of all three stages marked by the dictionary" (MacIntyre 1971d, p. 152). MacIntyre's discussions of the different social contexts in which these usages of 'ought' most naturally find their homes is subtle and detailed, and it is impossible to summarize it briefly without oversimplification.

The main conclusion of this discussion of relevance to MacIntyre's general attitude toward metaethical disagreement, however, is that "naturalism and prescriptivism are most plausibly understood not as rival accounts of the whole field of moral or even of evaluative discourse, but as accounts of different types of moral and evaluative discourse" (MacIntyre 1971d, p. 154). Oversimplifying grandly, we can say that MacIntyre's claim is that neither naturalism nor prescriptivism can adequately account for the first stage of 'ought', that naturalistic theories give a plausible account of the second stage of 'ought', and that prescriptivist theories give a plausible account of the decayed form of the third stage of 'ought'. But since both views claim to give an adequate account of 'ought' *simpliciter*, both are wrong. MacIntyre rejects not only the metaethical views of the prescriptivist but also those of their naturalistic rivals – and he rejects them both for the same general reason. They are one-sided in their focus on a narrow range of examples and fail to appreciate the full complexity of the use of moral language in modernity. Of the naturalists who refuse to take seriously the late-developing, unconditional 'ought', he says, "The nursery, like classical Greece or medieval Europe, is one of the natural homes of naturalism. But societies change and people grow up" (MacIntyre 1971d, 154).

His criticisms of the prescriptivists, however, are even harsher. In "Some More About 'Ought'," he focuses on the unconditional 'ought' of modernity, especially as it appears in the secularized moral vocabulary of ninteenth-century moral earnestness and is canonically analyzed in Prichard. Of this 'ought', MacIntyre argues that it is so cut off from the presuppositions that could have made its use intelligible that it can at most express a kind of superstition and be used to bully and deceive. Of the "Prichardian or distinctively moral 'ought', " MacIntyre says, it

> was a ghost and it is a ghost that still walks in certain quarters, although more and more obviously, like other ghosts, a survival. Yet so long as it survives, morality involves a degree of bluff and deception that can only have the effect of engendering cynicism whenever it is once more expressed. This paper is therefore not only an attempt at analysis; it is also hopefully an exorcism. (MacIntyre 1971f, pp. 171–172)

Prescriptivist views – and noncognitivist views, in general – go wrong in that, while they correctly diagnose intuitionist expressions of the moral 'ought' as mere bluff and deception, they replace the mistaken views of the Prichardian intuitionists with the view that all attempts to give 'ought' judgments a cognitive role are equally mistaken. MacIntyre says of Stevenson's emotivist view on this score what he might well have said about Hare's prescriptivism: "His theory is not a true theory of moral utterance, but a true theory of intuitionist moral utterance, if we understand by intuitionism not merely the doctrine of a group of philosophers, but the doctrine of a social milieu" (MacIntyre 1971f, p. 171). So in the end, prescriptivists attempt to elevate to a general account of the meaning of 'ought' a true account of the meaning of 'ought' as it is confusedly used by certain moderns, while naturalists attempt to elevate to a general account of the meaning of 'ought' a true account of a certain usage of 'ought' at home in classical Greek culture and the contemporary nursery. Both theories are right about something, but neither is right about what it claims to be right about. Both views aspire to give a general account of the meaning of moral concepts and to draw from this account general methodological guidelines for moral argument and deliberation. But both fail through their parochial attention to only certain usages of our moral vocabulary, and both defend approaches to moral argument that can only appear as one-sided and out of touch with the real cultural situation of contemporary moral discussion.

MacIntyre's metaethical journey from his first groping approach to these problems in his master's thesis to the sophisticated historical and sociological discussions in "Ought" and "Some More About 'Ought' " is one in which the results of his work are largely negative. He argues that both the particular metaethical views on offer in contemporary philosophy and the whole enterprise of an ahistorical metaethics are mistaken. Although he produces some examples of what a sufficiently rich lexicography might be in these articles in *Self-Images*, it is clear that the investigations he is there undertaking go beyond the bounds of anything that can any longer be called metaethics. These developments in his views of metaethics throughout the 1950s and up to the 1970s are simultaneous with his intellectual engagements with contemporary Marxism, contemporary theology, and contemporary psychoanalysis and the therapeutic professions more generally. He also explores issues in action theory and the philosophy of the social sciences during this period. Although these investigations are explored in other chapters in this volume, we must note here that they all come together in a powerful way in *After Virtue*, which MacIntyre was writing in the 1970s. In this book – clearly the most important and influential statement of MacIntyre's views up until its publication – results from his metaethical investigations come together with views he had developed in other areas of his work in an exposition and defense of a radical attack on most of what constitutes modern moral philosophy and in the beginning of a constructive account of a new kind of moral philosophy. In some sense, the narrowly metaethical investigations of the first quarter century of MacIntyre's work are left behind in his work in *After Virtue* and later, but in another sense that work is taken up into a larger synthesis of thought. This synthesis moves MacIntyre's work quite radically from the metaethical context in which it began into the context of the disputes among comprehensive normative theories that come back to center stage in moral philosophy with the publication of John Rawls's *A Theory of Justice* in 1971.

2. NORMATIVE ETHICS

When *After Virtue* appeared in 1981, the revolution in normative theory had been underway for a decade or so. John Rawls and his students had been the primary proponents of a sophisticated and updated Kantian rationalism that aimed to provide a philosophical foundation for liberal-democratic political systems and to address some of the social dislocations of the 1960s. New forms of consequentialism were also developed by a number of moral philosophers, especially students of Hare's such as Derek Parfit and Peter Singer, who seemed to understand before Hare did that his allegedly morally neutral metaethical theory had mutated into a consequentialist normative theory. The revival of these Kantian and consequentialist theories seemed to many philosophers to exhaust the normative possibilities. Just as the metaethical field had been dominated by the impasse between naturalism and prescriptivism, it appeared that the normative possibilities would be exhausted by broadly deontological and consequentialist possibilities.

It is one of the main themes of *After Virtue* that this picture of the normative landscape as divided between warring deontological and consequentialist alternatives is deeply flawed. In contrast, MacIntyre argues that the contending deontological and consequentialist normative theories are themselves to be understood as the decayed forms of Enlightenment ethical theories that share much in common. In developing these views, he deploys a complex set of considerations – historical, sociological, and conceptual – that permanently expand the repertoire of contemporary ethical theory. The appearance of *After Virtue* clearly marks a critical moment in MacIntyre's philosophical development. In the synthesis of his views presented there, he draws together a number of strands of his thought developed over the previous thirty years and molds them into a powerful and comprehensive attack on central features of modern culture and the style of moral philosophy dominant within it.

In the twenty years since the publication of *After Virtue*, MacIntyre has refined and extended the comprehensive view first deployed there. In *Whose Justice? Which Rationality?*, he refines his historical account of the development of ethics in a number of different ways and develops a comprehensive account of how rational dialogue among competing traditions of normative thought can occur. In *Three Rival Versions*, he applies some of the lessons taught in *Whose Justice?* to examine in detail the arguments among three particular traditions of ethical thought – the genealogist, the encyclopedist, and the traditionalist. In his most recent book, *Dependent Rational Animals*, he turns to a more detailed account of the human good and the virtues associated with it. In all three of these books, he does not hesitate to correct mistakes he acknowledges in his earlier work and to take his view in directions that seem to depart from earlier statements, but he is for the most part still filling in the outlines of the comprehensive view first adumbrated in *After Virtue*. It is the urtext for MacIntyre's later work.

A natural way to begin a discussion of MacIntyre's mature contribution to normative ethics would be to sort out the central questions and concerns of contemporary normative ethics, to examine MacIntyre's answers to these questions, and to compare them with the answers given by his main competitors in the contemporary dialogue. Since the normative revolution in moral philosophy began some thirty years ago, there has developed a certain canonical view of the field and its central questions into which some have tried to fit MacIntyre in this way. The received story (vastly oversimplified) goes something like this. There are four central contending positions in the arena of normative ethics: (1) a deontological view, rooted in Kantian rationalism or some form of contractarianism, which gives priority to the right over the good and places rules in a privileged place at the heart of normative theory; (2) a broadly consequentialist view, which places the notion of maximizing good states of affairs in the privileged place at the heart of normative theory; (3) virtue ethics, rooted in some broadly Aristotelian or Humean conception of the virtues, which places the notion of a virtue and the companion notions of human flourishing or well functioning at the heart of normative theory; and (4) anti-theory with regard to ethics, which is skeptical of the ambitions of any of these views and skeptical especially of the claims of moral philosophy to be able to vindicate rationally some substantive conception of the good life for humans.

The contemporary literature in moral philosophy is replete with developments and slight variations of this taxonomy, and the standard introductions to normative ethics explore the arguments and counterarguments brought by proponents of one or another of these normative conceptions against their rivals. Normative ethics is largely constituted by this set of positions and debates, and to characterize someone's views in normative ethics is to locate them within this framework. Like all taxonomies of areas of inquiry or academic debate, this one gains plausibility from the fact that it no longer merely describes the landscape in normative ethics but also functions normatively to guide discussions. It is not part of the purpose of this chapter to criticize this received view of the field of normative ethics, but it is important to notice that MacIntyre's views do not fit neatly into it. He is frequently identified as a proponent of virtue ethics, but many of those whose views are regarded as instances of virtue ethics are wary of his views – and rightly so. Unlike the idealized virtue theorist of the canonical view, MacIntyre gives rules a central place and returns to the topic of the place of rules in an adequate theory repeatedly. He is also frequently identified as an anti-theorist, but his strong commitment to moral realism and his rejection of postmodernist perspectivist and relativist views put him at odds with many others characterized in this way, although he shares many of the anti-theorists' critical views of the pretensions of much contemporary normative theory.

If one cannot find a way into MacIntyre's views on normative ethics by locating him within the textbook categories in normative ethics, how should one proceed? Without claiming that it is the only way, or even the best way, I will proceed by examining the broad outline of the views that he deploys in *After Virtue* and develops in his later works. With this outline in place, we can turn briefly to some critical remarks on the overall shape of MacIntyre's project.

After Virtue begins and ends on an apocalyptic note. It opens with an evocation of a picture of contemporary culture as one of moral and ethical fragments, the product of some cultural disaster, now forgotten by most, but one which was responsible for the current disordered state of moral discourse in contemporary culture.[7] This disordered state, though invisible to the untrained eye, is most in evidence in the deep moral disagreements that characterize contemporary moral discussions.[8] MacIntyre examines three areas of moral dispute in contemporary culture – debates over the moral character of war, of abortion, and of economic justice – and argues that in each case valid arguments of various sorts can be brought for a variety of conflicting positions on each of these issues. Though these arguments are valid, their premises differ and are in fact incommensurable and drawn from different historical sources. The depth of moral disagreement endemic to contemporary culture, and the failure of the standard techniques for resolving these disagreements, are the primary data for MacIntyre's analysis of contemporary culture and for the approach to normative ethical theory that rests on this analysis. Those theorists who disagree with MacIntyre about this matter will find much of what he claims to follow from it unconvincing.

MacIntyre argues that there are four different responses one might make to his claims about the depth of moral disagreement. One might, of course, simply deny that moral disagreement is as deep and irresolvable as he suggests. This would be, on his view, simply to deny the obvious. Second, one might agree with his description but argue that this is always and inevitably the case, since the expression of moral views is simply a matter of the expression of moral attitudes that are a function of one's upbringing and the social forces impinging on one. Even if there were agreement in these attitudes it would be merely a contingent matter, but, given the complexity and diversity of environments within which human beings are socialized, we should not expect such convergence. Since this second response is that favored by emotivists and other noncognitivists who had been so influential in the metaethical debates earlier in the century, we can call it the emotivist response. Third, one might admit that moral disagreement is deep, but deny that it is impossible to rise above these disagreements, and appeal to certain rational principles, available to everyone, with the capacity to bring agreement on even the most contested moral disputes. The resources of the Enlightenment moral theories, Kantian rationalism, or Benthamite consequentialism would be the prime examples of such theories that attempt, as it were, to put the fragments back together. The contemporary resurgence of normative theory (and its extension into the area of applied ethics) bears witness to the fact that this hope is alive and well in contemporary culture. This response might be called the Enlightenment Response. Finally, one can claim, as MacIntyre does, that the current state of moral disagreement is as he described it, but that it is neither a universal feature of ethical discourse as the emotivist claims, nor a problem remediable by the proper application of normative ethical theory as neoKantians and consequentialists claim. It is rather a particular malady of contemporary culture to be explained by the history of this culture that will vindicate the "fragmentation thesis." Moral disagreement is so deep and so little amenable to the techniques of rational discussion because discussants are beginning with ill-assorted fragments of a traditional, largely coherent approach whose coherence was shattered by certain events in the history of modernity. This approach need not deny that there are more or less rational ways of holding and defending ones moral views. It must, however, deny that these rational techniques are of the sort favored by the Enlightenment response.

The agenda of MacIntyre's ethics is set by this picture of contemporary moral disagreement and the cultural and philosophical responses to it. The major themes in his later views on ethics emerge from his attempt to vindicate this picture of moral disagreement and also to defend an appropriate response to it. MacIntyre says that the two major tasks of *After Virtue* are to defend his particular characterization of modernity as a culture of fragments and incommensurable disagreement and to "identify and describe the lost morality of the past and evaluate its claims to objectivity and authority" (*After Virtue*, p. 22). The sweep of MacIntyre's argument in carrying out these tasks is breathtaking and its details and nuances far exceed the capacity of this survey paper to capture. It is important to look, however briefly, at the manner in which MacIntyre pursues these two tasks.

MacIntyre's Characterization of Modern Culture

As we noted above, MacIntyre takes the fact of fundamental and incommensurable moral disagreement to be the most obvious feature of contemporary moral discourse. We have also seen, however, that he rejects the emotivist view that attempts to explain this moral disagreement by defending the view that the meaning of moral terms is exhausted by their role in expressing speakers' attitudes and evoking similar attitudes in others. While he rejects emotivism as an account of the *meaning* of moral terms (and draws on familiar arguments in the literature to do so), he argues that emotivism is an accurate portrayal of the *use* of moral terms, at least within certain dominant social groups in contemporary culture. While moral terms retain a meaning that allows them to assert moral claims that enjoy a certain independent and objective force, they are typically used in contemporary culture simply to express subjective aims.[9] There is a tension then in the use of moral language in contemporary culture between an objective meaning and an emotivist use. MacIntyre characterizes what such a tension in the contemporary use of moral language would be like in the following way:

> The meaning and use of moral expressions were, or at the very least had become, radically discrepant with each other. Meaning and use would be at odds in such a way that meaning would tend to conceal use. We could not safely infer what someone who uttered a moral judgment was doing merely by listening to what he said. Moreover the agent himself might well be among those for whom use was concealed by meaning. He might well, precisely because he was self-conscious about the meaning of the words that he used, be assured that he was appealing to independent impersonal criteria, when all that he was in fact doing was expressing his feelings to others in a manipulative way. (*After Virtue*, p. 14)

MacIntyre argues for this complex condition of moral language in modernity in two different ways. He argues against the emotivist account of *meaning* using standard philosophical arguments familiar in the metaethical discussions; he argues for the emotivist account of *use* by developing a comprehensive picture of contemporary social life that can only be explained, he thinks, if we live in an emotivist culture in which moral terms are characteristically used simply to express one's attitudes in a manipulative way. Since "every moral philosophy presupposes a sociology," all genuine moral philosophies must be capable of being socially embodied, and every society will embody some moral philosophy. And he claims that a close examination of contemporary culture suggests that it socially embodies emotivism, even if the moral language we use in contemporary culture retains a kind of meaning that suggests impersonality and objectivity in our moral discourse.

MacIntyre argues that the key mark of an emotivist culture is "the fact that emotivism entails the obliteration of any genuine distinction between manipulative and nonmanipulative social relations" (*After Virtue*, p. 23). If moral expressions are used simply to express my attitudes and to shape the attitudes of others, it is difficult to see how this distinction could be drawn. The primary indication that contemporary culture has indeed obliterated this distinction is the central role played in it by certain social roles – called by MacIntyre "characters" – that function "to morally legitimate a mode of social existence" (*After Virtue*, p. 29).[10] MacIntyre identifies the characters central to contemporary culture as the manager, the therapist, and the aesthete, and argues that those who embody those roles fail to acknowledge the distinction between manipulative and nonmanipulative behavior. As he puts it, "In our own time emotivism is a theory embodied in characters who all share the emotivist view of the distinction between rational and nonrational discourse, but who represent the embodiment of that distinction in very different social contexts" (*After Virtue*, p. 30).

The emotivist character of contemporary culture also shows itself in the concept of the self widely accepted by many prominent contemporary theorists. MacIntyre says of this self:

> The specifically modern self, the self that I have called emotivist, finds no limits set to that on which it may pass judgment for such limits could only derive from rational criteria for evaluation and, as we have seen, the emotivist self lacks any such criteria. Everything may be criticized from whatever standpoint the self has adopted, including the self's choice of standpoint to adopt. It is in this capacity of the self to evade any necessary identification with any particular contingent state of affairs that some modern philosophers, both analytical and existentialist, have seen the essence of moral agency. (*After Virtue*, p. 34)

MacIntyre argues that it can only seem plausible to take this concept of the self as the essence of moral agency if our culture is indeed emotivist.

MacIntyre's detailed historical account of modern moral philosophy is also intended to provide further support for the claim that contemporary culture is an emotivist culture. This history is primarily intended to explore two different matters – first, how we came to be in the fragmented condition in which we find ourselves, and second, why the Enlightenment theories, which were intended to address our modern difficulties, not only failed but had to fail.

In Chapters 4–6 of *After Virtue*, leading up to the hinge chapter entitled "Nietzsche or Aristotle," he gives an account of the history of modern moral philosophy in reverse order, beginning with Kierkegaard and moving backward through the Enlightenment project and its predecessors. The Enlightenment project was flawed from its inception in that it set itself a task that could not be carried out. It was asked to put back together a puzzle in which certain pieces were missing; indeed, it was a condition of any adequate solution to this puzzle that it proceed without the missing pieces.

In this historical account, he argues that both Kantian rationalism and Humean desire-based ethics – the two main instances of an Enlightenment morality – grow out of a breakdown in a classical synthesis that found a justification for moral rules in a structure that combined (in its most complete form in the Thomist synthesis) a rich teleological conception of human life together with a notion of Divine Law. The forces unleashed by the scientific revolution and the Reformation, however, made this justificatory structure untenable. Our ability to know and act in accord with the divine law was denied by the voluntarism of the Protestant reformers and their acceptance of a strong doctrine of original sin, while the teleological conception of nature at the heart of the classical conception of human life was abandoned with the acceptance of the new mechanistic science. With these classical props for the moral rules no longer available, it was inevitable that some alternative structure for justifying the moral rules should be sought, and the Humean and Kantian constructions are the fruits of this search.

MacIntyre argues that these Enlightenment responses had to fail precisely because the project of the Enlightenment with regard to the justification of moral rules was incoherent. The moral rules that the Enlightenment theories aimed to justify were crafted as corrective devices for human nature as we find it. They arose as devices for perfecting human beings whose natural state is imperfect in various ways. The perfective process (whether in Aristotle's pagan view or in Aquinas's Christian one) involved a movement toward an idealized end of human life – a movement toward the human good. It was only within a broadly teleological conception of human life that such a conception of the moral rules was coherent. In the absence of some rich notion of perfected humanity – a notion underwritten by classical teleology and the notion of divine law – the only remaining basis for grounding the moral rules are features of human nature in its unperfected state. The major Enlightenment views accordingly attempted to anchor moral rules either in the structures of our passions (an option taken by Hume and his followers) or in the structure of reason (an option taken by Kant and his followers). It is the final breakdown of these attempts – seen clearly by Kierkegaard and Nietzsche – that explains the fragmented nature of contemporary moral discourse.

MacIntyre ends his description of the moral fragmentation of contemporary culture and his historical explanation of this fragmentation with the presentation of a stark alternative for contemporary moral theorists – Aristotle or Nietzsche? This question grows out of the claims in the first half of *After Virtue* about the lessons to be learned from the careful examination of the history of modern moral philosophy. He claims to have shown that the only defensible views in moral philosophy are a return to the broadly Aristotelian conception of ethics or a Nietzchean view. Nietzsche, MacIntyre claims, saw clearly the utter failure of the ambitions of Enlightenment moralists like Kant and Hume. He also thought that their failure gave us reason to reject any attempt at a rational vindication of morality. MacIntyre describes the position of the moral philosopher in late modernity in this way:

> The defensibility of the Nietzschean position turns in the end on the answer to the question: was it right in the first place to reject Aristotle? For if Aristotle's position in ethics and politics – or something very like it – could be sustained, the whole Nietzschean enterprise would be pointless. This is because the power of Nietzsche's position depends upon the truth of one central thesis: that all rational vindications of morality manifestly fail and that belief in the tenets of morality needs to be explained in terms of a set of rationalizations which conceal the fundamentally non-rational phenomena of the will. My own argument obliges me to agree with Nietzsche that the philosophers of the Enlightenment never succeeded in providing grounds for doubting his central thesis: his epigrams are even deadlier than his extended arguments. But, if my earlier argument is correct, that failure itself was nothing other than an historical sequel to the rejection of the Aristotelian tradition. And thus the key question does indeed become: can Aristotle's ethics, or something very like it, after all be vindicated? (*After Virtue*, pp. 117–18)

In asking us to choose between Aristotle and Nietzsche, of course, MacIntyre does not intend us to focus narrowly on the writings of these two philosophers. He treats each of them as types. Aristotle "provides a central point of focus for the tradition of the virtues which held the resources of a whole tradition of acting, thinking and discourse of which Aristotle's is only a part, a tradition of which I spoke earlier as 'the classical tradition' and whose view of man I called 'the classical view of man' " (*After Virtue*, p. 119). In the same way, Nietzsche represents the tradition of emotivist and existentialist interpreters of morality. So instead of Nietzsche versus Aristotle, one could regard this choice as one between the classical tradition in moral philosophy and those forms of emotivism, existentialism, constructivism, and postmodernism that are so widely defended within contemporary moral philosophy.

The first half of *After Virtue* presents the negative pole of MacIntyre's moral theory. He develops and defends a comprehensive picture of the state of contemporary social life as it is lived out in groups dominated by the thoughts and attitudes characteristic of late modernity. He also seeks to identify and discuss in some detail the moral philosophy that he argues is embodied in this culture. Finally, he relates a complicated history of modern social life and of modern moral philosophy that aims to explain how we arrived at the thoughts and attitudes that we characteristically display. He also believes that he has demonstrated in this discussion why the two most prominent normative theories on offer in academic moral philosophy – consequentialism and Kantian rationalism – not only fail, but must fail. If he is right in all this, the stark option he leaves us with at the end of Chapter 9 is real. Either the failure of the Enlightenment normative theories make way for a Nietzschean morality of self-assertion, or we must find a way to restate in a rationally defensible way the classical Aristotelian ethics of virtue, the rejection of which in earlier centuries inspired the Enlightenment options that have, in turn, failed. He turns to this further task in the second half of *After Virtue*.

MacIntyre's Defense of the Aristotelian Alternative

The hinge chapter of *After Virtue* is followed by another historical account of the tradition of the virtues, told in a forward sequence this time and taking us from an account of the virtues in heroic society, through the development of the virtues in classical Greece and in Christian Europe, up to their emergence in slightly transformed form in modernity. We need only note here that this account of the history of the virtues demonstrates that there are enormous differences in treatments of the virtues in this tradition. Different lists of virtues are found within the tradition, but, most importantly, so are alternative accounts of what a virtue is. MacIntyre is struck especially by the deep divergence among the accounts of virtues found in heroic culture, in which virtues are those properties of human agents that allow them to discharge their social roles; the accounts in classical and Christian culture, in which virtues are properties necessary for human beings to achieve their *telos*, either natural or supernatural; and the account of the virtues of such typical moderns as Benjamin Franklin, for whom virtues are regarded as instrumental means for achieving worldly or heavenly success. The question raised for MacIntyre by this diversity is, "are we or are we not able to disentangle from these rival and various claims a unitary core concept of the virtues of which we can give a more compelling account than any of the other accounts so far?" (*After Virtue*, p. 186). Since MacIntyre has organized the second half of *After Virtue* around the project of reconstructing the core of the Aristotelian tradition of the virtues, it is essential that he demonstrate that there is a unifying core underneath this surface diversity.

MacIntyre believes that such a unifying account is possible and gives a schematic account of it in the remaining chapters. While he regards this unifying account as being expressive of the tradition of the virtues of which Aristotle was the most prominent advocate, his idealized account departs from Aristotle in a number of different ways. Most important, MacIntyre suggests that an updated account of the virtues will have to dispense with Aristotle's metaphysical biology – the metaphysical theory which provides the heart of the teleological account of nature, the loss of which is largely responsible for bringing about the crisis in the classical picture of morality. He also recognizes that he will have to reject Aristotle's commitment to the unity of the virtues and his commitment to the Greek polis as the only adequate setting for the virtues.

Macintyre's general strategy for developing a broadly Aristotelian account of the virtues is to locate the virtues in a socially constituted context now that the metaphysical basis for the traditional Aristotelian conception is no longer available. The social context is constituted by three levels of social organization – those of human practices, the narrative unity of human life, and the traditions in which our lives are embedded. Although this chapter cannot examine in detail each of these notions, it is important to notice that each situates the choices of human beings in a framework much richer than that in which the emotivist self of late modernity operates.

MacIntyre's proposal to define the virtues by locating them within these layered contexts is the key to his defense of the broadly Aristotelian alternative to Nietzschean self-assertion. Although each of these notions is discussed in great detail by MacIntyre, we can here only comment on their main features and their significance for his overall project. Practices are defined by MacIntyre in one of the most well-known – not to say notorious – sentences in *After Virtue*:

> By a practice I am going to mean any coherent and complex form of socially established cooperative human activity through which goods internal to that form of activity are realized in the course of trying to achieve those standards of excellence which are appropriate to, and partially definitive of, that form of activity, with the result that human powers to achieve excellence, and human conceptions of the ends and goods involved, are systematically extended. (*After Virtue*, p. 187)

Examples of practices given by MacIntyre are farming, physics, politics, and other similarly complicated spheres of human activity. Of first importance is MacIntyre's claim that practices make possible the achievement of goods internal to them. In contrast to what he calls "external" goods – for example, money, status, and prestige – internal goods are not objects of competition and can be recognized as goods – and realized – only by those who fully participate in practices. Virtues are required for full participation in practices in order (1) to define our relation to others within practices, (2) to define our relation to past participants, and (3) to allow us to resist the corruption of practices by institutions. At this first level, then, virtues are to be understood as those dispositions to act that allow us to participate fully in practices and to achieve the goods internal to them.

The notion of a practice, however, is not sufficient to fully define a virtue. We may need to criticize a particular practice or to understand how participation in it might contribute to the overall good of a human life. MacIntyre is particularly insistent that a good human life is not just participation in a series of arbitrarily chosen practices. These difficulties move the discussion to the second level of the social underpinning of the virtues. MacIntyre argues that contemporary culture, as well as contemporary philosophy, encourages us to think of a human life as a mere series of episodes connected by the thinnest sort of physical and psychological continuity. He suggests that we should rather regard the unity of a human life as the narrative unity of a quest. In developing this notion, MacIntyre draws on the medieval notion of a quest in which the object is not determined by a fully specified or well-defined end but is itself a quest for the good life for man. But what is this good life? MacIntyre defines it as "the life spent in seeking for the good life for man, and the virtues necessary for the seeking are those which will enable us to understand what more and what else the good life for man is" (*After Virtue*, p. 219).

Practices and the narrative unity of a life, however, are still insufficient to provide a full setting for the virtues. Both practices and the forms of narrative quest that give unity to our lives have histories, and the historical background for these features of the social setting for human lives are organized into traditions. MacIntyre defines a tradition as "an historically extended, socially embodied argument, and an argument precisely in part about the goods which constitute that tradition" (*After Virtue*, p. 222), and he argues that virtues are necessary to sustain traditions and to govern our relation to them.[11]

MacIntyre's account of the virtues, then, which he claims captures the heart of the Aristotelian tradition while eschewing Aristotle's resort to metaphysical biology, is constituted by this layered involvement of the virtues in the contents of practices, narrative unity, and tradition. He sums up this account in the following way:

> The virtues find their point and purpose not only in sustaining those relationships necessary if the variety of goods internal to practices are to be achieved and not only in sustaining the form of an individual life in which that individual may seek out his or her good as the good of his or her whole life, but also in sustaining those traditions which provide both practices and individual lives with their necessary historical context. (*After Virtue*, p. 223)

This account of the layered social world of practice, narrative unity, and tradition is not intended merely to provide a frame for the virtues. It is also intended to provide an alternative sociology to that of the emotivist culture MacIntyre had depicted in the first half of the book. In an important sense, he opposes his social world of practice, narrative unity, and tradition to the social world of the manager, the therapist, and the aesthete. But if he has now given content to the stark option that stands at the hinge of *After Virtue* – Nietzsche or Aristotle? – what are the crucial arguments for determining which option to pick? How do we determine the superior view? How can either view rationally vindicate itself?[12] There are, of course, throughout his work a number of particular arguments brought for or against particular positions implicated either in the Nietzschean position or the Aristotelian, but MacIntyre admits at the end of *After Virtue* that he lacks the resources in this book for fully defending his favored Aristotelian option. He argues that if philosophical disputes are to be settled it is necessary to stand back from the disputes and

> ask in a systematic way what the appropriate rational procedures are for settling this particular kind of dispute. It is my own view that the time has come once more when it is imperative to perform this task for moral philosophy;

but I do not pretend to have embarked upon it in this present book. My negative and positive evaluations of particular arguments do indeed presuppose a *systematic*, although here unstated, account of rationality. (*After Virtue*, p. 260)

MacIntyre takes up this task in work subsequent to *After Virtue*, especially in the final hundred pages of *Whose Justice?* He develops there a comprehensive account of what he calls tradition-based inquiry that he thinks best captures the "appropriate rational procedures" applicable to the deepest disputes in moral philosophy. This account of rationality is discussed in some detail in another chapter in this volume, but I will turn to some critical discussion of it in the final section of this chapter.

3. CRITICAL QUESTIONS

Although we have hardly done justice to the full complexity of MacIntyre's treatment of ethics (indeed, one might argue that even he has not done *full* justice to it) I would like to turn in this final section to some critical response. But first we should note how enormously successful in many respects MacIntyre's contribution to moral philosophy has been. *After Virtue* has been one of the best-selling books of academic philosophy in the last half century, and its influence, along with the additional impact of MacIntyre's more recent work, has been as considerable as the number of books sold. MacIntyre's attempt to weave his philosophical theses together with an historical account of modern ethics has surely been one of the major forces turning the attention of other moral philosophers to the history of their subject. The vigorous and high-quality scholarly work done in the history of ethics in the last two decades has been spurred to a considerable extent, I believe, by the desire either to correct what are perceived as the weaknesses in MacIntyre's account or to support his interpretations. In this respect, MacIntyre's influence on the history of ethics is much like the influence of Thomas Kuhn (1962) on the history of science. Like Kuhn, MacIntyre forced others to do careful history in order to defend their own claims against his attacks. After MacIntyre one can no longer defend a comprehensive normative theory responsibly without relating one's defense to the history of the subject.[13]

His work has also been one of the major forces in turning the attention of moral philosophers to a closer focus on the virtues and their history. In doing this, he follows the lead of others, notably Anscombe and Geach, but it was MacIntyre more than anyone else who brought the importance of the virtues to the attention of the broader culture. His work has also been enormously influential outside the narrow world of academic moral philosophy. His impact on contemporary moral theology, as well as social and political theory, has been especially important. Although he has attempted to disassociate his views from a number of popularizing movements – especially that associated with certain popular forms of communitarianism (see, for example, MacIntyre 1991b and 1995a) – his work continues to be invoked in support of a number of political, social, and religious agendas. It is difficult to name an Anglophone moral philosopher writing in the second half of the twentieth century, other than John Rawls, whose influence on the broader culture has been as great as that of MacIntyre.

Despite this influence, MacIntyre has found few disciples who follow his lead as closely as do the students of such other contemporary figures as John Rawls and Derek Parfit. It is part of his view, of course, that if he is right in his analysis of contemporary culture and the role of moral philosophers in it, one should expect his view to be widely rejected.[14] Whether or not he is right about this claim, it is certainly the case that his views in moral philosophy have been met with a wide range of criticism. While our task in this chapter is not to survey comprehensively this critical response, and certainly not to contribute to it or defend MacIntyre against it (especially since he has done such a good job of taking care of himself in these matters), a quick examination of some of the most important criticism of his view seems essential to understanding it.

Although there are many quite detailed studies of MacIntyre's account of the history of ethics[15] as well as of his account of particular matters such as the nature of practices and traditions, or the good for human beings, I will focus here on two broad responses to his overarching views in moral philosophy developed since *After Virtue*.[16] The first line of criticism is aimed at MacIntyre's negative appraisal of contemporary culture and the moral philosophy embodied in it, while the second raises questions about MacIntyre's positive defense of his alternative to emotivist and Enlightenment models of ethical theory. The first objection claims that MacIntyre's account of the character of contemporary culture and, in particular, the disordered state of moral discourse is simply wrong. This challenge can take two different forms, at odds with one another in important respects. It is sometimes argued that MacIntyre is too pessimistic about the chances of reaching agreement on moral matters in contemporary culture. In fact, the argument is sometimes made (in the spirit of Fukuyama 1992) that many of the tensions in human culture have been worked out (or soon will be) through the widespread agreement on the truisms of liberal political culture and through the mechanisms of a regulated and benign market. MacIntyre's picture of contemporary culture as constituted by a fragmented moral vocabulary, a vanishingly thin emotivist self, and interminable and incommensurable moral debates is seen on this view as simply Celtic pessimism. But others who disagree with MacIntyre's description of the state of moral discourse in contemporary culture take quite a different tack. Instead of criticizing his view for being too pessimistic, they claim that in an important respect it is too optimistic. They argue that MacIntyre goes wrong in suggesting that interminable moral disputes are a distinctive feature of late modernity, because, these critics claim, such disputes are found in many periods in the development of human culture when the particular features of breakdown and fragmentation MacIntyre finds in modernity do not hold. The first version of this criticism then holds that moral disagreement and fragmentation are not as widespread as MacIntyre claims; the second version admits that it may be as widespread in contemporary culture, but claims that interminable moral disputes have always been with us. MacIntyre can take some comfort at least that while those views are not strictly incompatible it is unlikely that both versions of this criticism will hit home.

It must be admitted that MacIntyre's claims about the character of contemporary culture and the state of contemporary moral discourse, especially as they are laid out with such sweep and with such a distinctive rhetorical note in the opening chapters of *After Virtue*, surely outrun the evidence that he presents for these claims. Indeed, it is difficult to imagine what kind of evidence would be sufficient for claims of such breadth. MacIntyre draws on a broad range of social theorists, artists, and philosophers in developing this description. Durkheim, Henry James, Goffman, Weber, William Gass, Sartre, and Kierkegaard, among others, put in appearances as witnesses for MacIntyre's view of "emotivist culture." The ambitions of his description here, of course, go far beyond those of most contemporary English-speaking philosophers. He trespasses in various ways on territory that in the neatly compartmentalized contemporary academy has been given over to disciplines other than philosophy. What can be said in defense of MacIntyre's view here, however, is considerable. First, the description he gives rings true at least in broad outline to many readers. Other philosophers such as Bernard Williams (1985) and Charles Taylor (1989), who disagree with many other features of MacIntyre's view, are in broad agreement with his claims here. Second, by placing these views on the table and depicting them in such stark terms, MacIntyre has inspired a continuing interest on the part of social theorists (for example, Bellah 1985) in confirming or disconfirming them.

But more importantly, MacIntyre has convinced many moral philosophers that, whatever the final scholarly verdict on his particular description of contemporary social structure and its ills may be, the attempt to examine carefully the social structure within which a moral philosophy will be embodied is an important part of the overall task of normative theory. However inadequate MacIntyre's particular description of contemporary culture may seem to some readers (and recall that to many of us it does not seem so inadequate), it is surely important that he at least attempts to come to terms with the character of contemporary social life. MacIntyre is right that "every moral philosophy presupposes a sociology," but if he is right about that, then it is a condition of adequacy for any moral philosophy that it attend to the sociology it presupposes – and also to the sociology presupposed by views it is opposing. This is a lesson that MacIntyre has taught all of us. It has the unfortunate consequence, of course, that philosophers must get their hands dirty in sometimes messy issues of social description,[17] but perhaps that is part of the price of developing normative theories of genuine relevance to the lives and decisions of those who hold them. MacIntyre's willingness to engage issues about the detailed social embodiment of normative theories contrasts sharply with the practice of the main proponents of neo-Kantian and consequentialist normative theories. They are content for the most part to abstract from any real engagement with detailed descriptions of contemporary social life in developing their theories. Trolley cases could as well be chariot cases if discussed by Socrates or rickshaw cases if discussed by nineteenth-century Confucians.[18] Models of idealized economic rationality or of idealized contexts of discussions in which discussants abstract from their "real" social positions may be useful in dealing with certain issues in moral philosophy, but only if care is taken to relate them by appropriate bridge principles to real conditions of the social life of those whose actions are to be guided by the normative theories under discussion. Surely one of the most important reasons for the revival of virtue theory in recent ethics is the perception (whether justified in all cases or not) that concentration on the virtues will force moral philosophers to confront the conditions of moral choice less abstractly than is frequently done.

Those critics of MacIntyre who challenge his chillingly pessimistic view of the culture of late modernity may be right then that he draws conclusions not fully warranted by the evidence he brings forward. But surely he is to be commended for attempting to discharge his responsibility, as he sees it, to discuss the disputes among contemporary normative theories in a socially realistic manner. Many of MacIntyre's philosophical opponents who are less concerned with engaging the culture purchase a certain theoretical tidiness and clarity for their views, but one suspects at the cost of irrelevance to the lives of those whose choices they hoped to influence.

The second broad response to MacIntyre's project in normative ethics calls into question his claim to be producing a normative ethical theory at all. We are reminded by these critics that he rejects the Enlightenment Project and its attempt to construct normative theories around rational principles accessible to all fully rational creatures. He also rejects (at least in *After Virtue*) any help he might get from a classical teleological metaphysical view in anchoring a justificatory normative theory. Moreover, he confesses to being a member of a culture whose moral concepts and ideas are largely fragments of dying or dead moral conceptions and that is emotivist in its use of moral language. Finally, as we saw at the end of the last section, when he does get around to producing an account of how one ethical theory might prove itself rationally superior to another, the account presupposes a view of tradition-constituted inquiry that is both historically and socially situated and that will almost certainly make use of concepts and principles that are incommensurable with those of competing traditions. In spite of this, MacIntyre continues to claim to be a moral realist whose central theoretical ambition in ethics is to achieve the truth (not just warranted assertibility) about ethics and to provide rational support for the claim that what is achieved is the truth (see MacIntyre 1994b and 1999b).

Given this puzzling combination of views it has seemed to some critics that MacIntyre would be better classified with anti-theorists like Bernard Williams. Others have thought that in spite of his protests to the contrary MacIntyre must finally be committed to some relativistic or perspectivist view in normative ethics. MacIntyre's objections to relativism and perspectivism are so strong, and have been so often repeated, however, that one can hardly suspect him of seriously holding these views, even unintentionally. The relation of his views to the sophisticated views of anti-theorists like Williams is, however, more complicated.

While MacIntyre does not regard himself as an anti-theorist, he accepts a great deal of the anti-theorist project. He wants in a way to accept their premises and reject their conclusion.[19] He accepts "the thesis that moral practice can only be understood from within and their corresponding denial that viable moral theory can find a basis for its enquiries or its conclusions independent of and external to moral practice" (MacIntyre 1994d).[20] What he rejects is "the thesis that therefore all moral theory is an illegitimate enterprise, one condemned to distortion and illusion" (MacIntyre 1994d). MacIntyre thinks he can hold these two views together by developing an ethical theory that is dependent on the local and the particular in its starting point, but worthy of being called a theory in its aspiration. He wants ethical theory to grow out of the ethical activity of communities but to aspire to make universal claims that reject any putative provenance from an impersonal or value-neutral perspective. Theory will be rooted in particular practices and the insights available only from within them, but will make claims that can conflict (and be seen to conflict) with those of alien communities. How does he flesh out this view?

MacIntyre argues that ethical theory can emerge in three stages from the ethical life of a well-ordered community. At the first stage, members of the community will need to evaluate their actions and those of others, and such evaluation may in particular cases call for a kind of justification. The need for justification will typically not arise from a general theoretical interest but rather from a particular question about a problem in action. At the second stage, MacIntyre claims that such attempts to settle questions of justification will presuppose shared standards in the community. Indeed, the intelligibility of the questions arising at the first stage presupposes such standards, and these standards will be formulated at the second stage. But there might be circumstances in which the nature of disagreement within a community is so deep that justifications for these standards themselves would be called into question. At this third stage, ethical arguments would be developed to defend alternative possible standards. In all such inquiries and at whatever degree of distance from particular problems, however, reflection begins with specific problems in the community, and MacIntyre claims that there will be particular goods and virtues connected to the project of inquiry itself. Thus, on his view, ethical theory will grow out of the normal ethical activity of communities of self-aware and reflective creatures. It will be integrated into these communities and impossible without the rootedness that comes with this kind of reflection. "The context within which theoretical moral enquiry alone has point and purpose is then that provided by the activities of some particular community" (MacIntyre 1994d).

What price does one pay in attempting to do ethical theory outside the context of a particular community? MacIntyre argues that, among other difficulties, one can have no sense of the terminus of moral debate. What brings moral reflection in a community on a particular matter to a close is the resolution of the particular dispute that gave rise to it. If theoretical inquiry is not rooted in the particularities of concrete disputes, then disagreement may be interminable. MacIntyre thinks that the anti-theorists are particularly good at recognizing the necessity for this kind of rootedness:

> In situations in which not enough is shared, theoretical argument and enquiry necessarily become practically barren. The kind of theorizing which is

> symptomatic of and generated by this condition of break-down are familiar: the setting by theorists to themselves of impossible Quixotic tasks, such as that of how to provide grounds for rationally well-grounded moral agreement and trust among individuals in Prisoner's Dilemma type situations; the genesis of interminable disagreements about the terminus of justificatory arguments; and most of all a failure to remember that especially in times of crisis theorists, like everyone else, are sustained by the continuing inarticulate, atheoretical goodness of those whose unexamined lives are well worth living. About this once again the reminders of antitheorists are often salutary. (MacIntyre 1994d)

At this point in his argument, however, MacIntyre's critics may say that he has given in to the anti-theorists altogether. What is left of the aspiration of theory for universal and objectively grounded norms on such a particularistic view? MacIntyre is clear that there need be no conflict between regarding moral norms as ultimately rooted in the particularity of community life and regarding them as aspiring to universality and genuine truth. The fact that communities typically – and perhaps necessarily – seek to combat the opposing ethical claims of distant communities suggests that they see no inconsistency. MacIntyre recognizes that, given his picture of the genesis of ethical theory from community life, these conflicts are going to be rationally problematic. In *Whose Justice?*, as we have noted, he gives an elaborate account of how rational debate among competing communities about the moral rules that govern them can be carried on without any appeal to perspectives or points of view abstracted from the concrete life of the competing communities. He also gives a good deal of practical advice about how we should conduct the details of such arguments between culturally distant communities. He thinks it is particularly important that we strive to avoid the use of power and manipulation in settling such disputes, availing ourselves of rational inquiry alone. He also suggests that we strive to separate disputes that are, at least for the present, intractable from those that give some promise of being resolvable – and that we should focus our discussions and arguments on the latter. And he suggests that we should be particularly attentive to our own failures in giving a convincing defense of our norms to others and seek rational means to make our arguments more persuasive to our interlocutors.

While giving such advice, however, and while developing his elaborate account of tradition-based inquiry, MacIntyre stops short of promising an algorithmic device that will guarantee, even ideally, a resolution of all practical conflicts across communities. But if this is what is required of moral reflection in order for it to count as genuinely theoretical, then surely hardly anyone is a theorist. MacIntyre doesn't guarantee the resolution of all conflicts, but then in this respect he is no worse off than other contemporary moral theorists.[21] Nobody is handing out guarantees.[22]

In the end it seems to me that debates about whether MacIntyre is doing normative theory or rejecting it are not very important. What is clear is that MacIntyre claims that a certain view of ethics is true, and he brings arguments in support of that view's truth. In his most recent book, *Dependent Rational Animals*, he has developed a set of concrete normative views in much more detail than in any of his previous ethical writings. His defense, in that book, of the importance of human weakness and vulnerability and the claims these features of human life make on us is developed with a clarity of conception and passion that will convince any reader of the book that MacIntyre thinks these views are *true*. For those who find his views on ethics expressed there or elsewhere implausible, their only resort is to bring arguments against those views, and then the dialogue can begin. MacIntyre's past philosophical behavior suggests that he will not hesitate to become involved in that dialogue. Indeed, his own willingness throughout his career to reformulate his views in order to make them more compelling as well as his relentless dialectical engagement with those who disagree with him are perhaps the most significant indications of his commitment to the possibility of genuine truth in ethics. There are large questions, of course, about whether he can in the end vindicate his account of tradition-based rationality, and those questions must be left aside here. There should be no doubt, however, about his commitment to the classical project of ethical theory. He makes it clear that one can criticize Enlightenment conceptions of ethical theory without abandoning the project of ethical theory altogether.

4. CONCLUSION

There seems little doubt that MacIntyre's contributions to contemporary moral philosophy will continue to be both influential and deeply controversial. His views are influential, I suspect, because they embody a critique of contemporary culture that is much more concrete than that provided by the more abstract and formal ethical theories advanced by such Kantian rationalists as Rawls and such consequentialists as Parfit. It is also a critique that rings true to many of those who feel uneasy about central features of life in late modernity – but who want to resist the excesses of postmodernism.

It is more difficult, I think, to understand why his views continue to be so controversial. At a time when most academic moral philosophers combine a deeply secular view of the world with a commitment to some form of liberal political theory, MacIntyre's orthodox Catholicism and his sharp attacks on liberalism may seem explanation enough. I suspect, however, that the reasons run deeper than this and have as much to do with his style of philosophy as with the content of his philosophical beliefs. As we have seen, he has raised far-reaching objections to the received methodologies of both metaethics and normative ethics, and has modeled in his work an alternative to these methodologies. In this respect, he is a genuine radical and stands outside the mainstream of contemporary moral philosophy. The attention paid recently by moral philosophers to the history of their subject suggests, however, that many of MacIntyre's ideas may now be entering the mainstream. What the consequences of this may be for the practice of academic moral philosophy and its role in the culture remains to be seen.

Notes

1. Most notable is J. B. Schneewind, whose *The Invention of Autonomy* (1998) brilliantly (if not always successfully) seeks to overturn MacIntyre's account of the history of modern moral philosophy from Suarez to Kant.
2. Since other papers in this volume are focusing on MacIntyre's specific engagements with the history of ethics, I will, to the extent possible, focus on MacIntyre's engagement with contemporary ethical theory. Given the nature of his view, however, it will not always be possible to keep these two contexts of thought separate.
3. This has been suggested most notoriously by A. J. Ayer in the famous fifth chapter of *Language, Truth and Logic* (1936).
4. Stevenson's most important work both expositing and defending noncognitivism is *Ethics and Language* (1944), while Ayer sends his cannon shot across the bow of cognitivist theories first in *Language, Truth and Logic* (1936).
5. This thesis has not been published. I would like to thank Professor MacIntyre for making a copy available for me to examine.
6. It is particularly penetrating in criticizing intuitionism, of which MacIntyre says, "but all intuitionist writers suffer from one difficulty: they are, on their own view, telling us only about what we all know already. That they sometimes disagree about what it is that we all know already only makes them less boring at the cost of making them even less convincing" (*Short History*, p. 254).
7. It is important not to confuse MacIntyre's indictment with that of the radical. He says of the difference:

    For the modern radical is as confident in the moral expression of his stances and consequently in the assertive uses of the rhetoric of morality as any conservative has ever been. Whatever else he denounces in our culture he is certain that it still possesses the moral resources which he requires in order to denounce it. Everything else may be, in his eyes, in disorder; but the language of morality is in order, just as it is. (*After Virtue*, 4)

8. It is significant, I think, that MacIntyre begins this book with a focus on moral disagreement and, in this, follows closely the structure of the most significant work in emotivism, Charles Stevenson's *Ethics and Language*. After this beginning, of course, there is significant divergence in their views.
9. This is yet a further development of MacIntyre's metaethical views explored in the previous section.
10. The notion of a "character" is one of the most difficult in MacIntyre's repertoire of tools of social description. He says of it:

    A character is an object of regard by the members of the culture generally or by some significant segment of it. It furnishes them with a cultural and moral ideal. Hence the demand is that in this type of case role and personality be fused. Social type and psychological type are required to coincide. The character morally legitimates a mode of social existence. (*After Virtue*, p. 29)
11. A much fuller account of MacIntyre's notion of a tradition is given in Chapter 2 of this volume.
12. Even to pose this question, of course, is to take sides in the debate, since the clash between Aristotle and Nietzsche is, in part, a clash about whether rational vindication is possible or even coherent.
13. The fact that some philosophers still attempt to do this simply testifies to how irresponsible philosophers can be.
14. Indeed, some of us who teach MacIntyre have been chastised by him for attempting to make his views more palatable than, according to him, they should be. In fact, he clearly believes that his views can only be made palatable to contemporary philosophers at the cost of making them boring. If they are to be interesting, they must be, he thinks, radical and in some sense unattractive.
15. Indeed, his treatment of Kierkegaard alone is the subject of the recent book of essays *Kierkegaard After MacIntyre* (Davenport and Rudd 2001). There also has been much critical discussion of his treatment of Aristotle, Aquinas, Hume, Kant, and Nietzsche, as well as of his interpretation of the Enlightenment.
16. I will also not comment at length on the many ad hominem remarks that he seems to attract. Moral philosophers as able as Thomas Nagel could surely do better than to snipe at MacIntyre's religious views, as Nagel does when he says in a review of *Whose Justice?* that "my sense is that MacIntyre's religion is driving his philosophy. He wants to produce an argument that does not rely on religious premises to show that only something like a religious morality is possible. This cannot be done. But to him, the conclusion of the argument is evident on other grounds" (Nagel 1995b, p. 209). I am not sure what Nagel means by "something like a religious morality" and I suspect he doesn't either. My sense is that Nagel's secularism and dislike of religion is driving his philosophy here.
17. But it is not always unpleasant. Many moral philosophers were first attracted to MacIntyre's view of moral philosophy, I suspect, because it allowed them

to spend their summers reading Trollope's novels while convincing themselves and their paymasters that they were just doing their job researching the mid-Victorian 'ought'.

18. A prominent moral philosopher recently mentioned that she forbade the mention of trolley cases in her classes – surely a policy MacIntyre would look upon favorably.
19. I am not, of course, suggesting that MacIntyre is rejecting the pressure of a valid argument, but rather that he regards the conclusions of the anti-theorists' arguments as not validly following from their premises.
20. In what follows, I am guided by MacIntyre's unpublished paper, "Moral Theory Put to the Question," presented at an American Philosophical Association symposium on anti-theory in ethics at which he appeared with Tim Scanlon and Allan Gibbard.
21. Some moral philosophers do come close to giving a guarantee. Derek Parfit seems to think that when the last residue of religious belief is wrung out of modern men and women, his austere consequentialism will carry all before it. As he says on the last page of *Reasons and Persons*:

    > Belief in God, or in many gods, prevented the free development of moral reasoning. Disbelief in God, openly admitted by a majority, is a recent event, not yet completed. Because this event is so recent, Non-Religious Ethics is at a very early stage. We cannot predict whether, as in Mathematics, we will all reach agreement. Since we cannot know how Ethics will develop, it is not irrational to have high hopes. (Parfit 1984, p. 454).

    Thomas Nagel seems to think that we have reason to hope that our primitive moral consciousness may someday find its Newton and with it a theoretical structure that will heal all wounds. His optimism is well expressed in a passage toward the end of *The View From Nowhere*:

    > In ethics, even without the benefit of many clear examples, we should be open to the possibility of progress as we are in other areas, with a consequent effect of reduced confidence in the finality of our current understanding. It is evident that we are at a primitive stage of moral development. Even the most civilized human beings have only a haphazard understanding of how to live, how to treat others, how to organize their societies. The idea that the basic principles of morality are known, and that the problems all come in their interpretation and application, is one of the most fantastic conceits to which our conceited species has been drawn. (Nagel 1986, p. 186)

22. MacIntyre's optimism about the possibility of moral agreement across communities may be one point at which his religious views do influence his moral philosophy. Mindful of the Christian injunction to avoid despair and the centrality of the virtue of hope in the Christian life, he surely has resources for expecting things to work out that are denied more secular thinkers. In this respect, it is easier for Christians to "work without a net."

6 MacIntyre's Political Philosophy

MARK C. MURPHY

In this chapter I will take up questions concerning MacIntyre's political thought as that thought has developed from *After Virtue* onward. MacIntyre's political thought is best understood in terms of its opposition to, and as an attempt to describe an alternative to, the political form that dominates modern life: the state. On MacIntyre's view, the modern state is trapped in a dilemma: it is unable to justify itself without bearing a substantive conception of the good, but the state is entirely unfit to bear a substantive conception of the good. State politics is indefensible, incoherent in theory and practice (section 1). A set of political institutions, to be rationally justifiable, will have to be able to sustain politics conceived as a practice and will have to be carried out locally within the enabling constraints set by the natural law (section 2). But there are serious questions to be raised concerning both MacIntyre's criticism of state politics and his endorsement of a politics of local community: it is unclear whether the state is as deeply flawed an institution as MacIntyre suggests and it is unclear whether the politics of local community, as MacIntyre describes it, is not itself deeply incoherent (section 3).

1. MACINTYRE'S CRITIQUE OF THE MODERN STATE

Just as MacIntyre takes the central task of moral philosophy to be that of accounting for the rational authority of morals (*After Virtue*, p. 52) – the failure of the Enlightenment project is just the failure to exhibit that authority – MacIntyre takes the central task of political philosophy to be that of accounting for the authority of political institutions. Political philosophy is centrally concerned with *political justifications*, which are

> those arguments advanced to show why we, as members of some particular political society, should or should not accept as having legitimate authority over us the commands uttered by someone claiming executive authority over

> or in that society or the laws uttered by someone or some body claiming legislative authority over or in that society (MacIntyre 1997b, p. 241).

Political institutions are law-giving and law-enforcing, and claim to have authority to give and enforce those laws. But it is a remarkable fact about contemporary political philosophy that a number of writers have, while agreeing that the central issue in political philosophy is that of political authority, denied that any satisfactory account of such authority can be provided (see, especially, Simmons 1979 and Raz 1979), and that a number of writers have, contrary to centuries of traditional political philosophy, turned their attention away from the question of political authority (whether and why political institutions have the power to give binding commands) and toward the question of political legitimacy (whether and why political institutions have the right to coerce citizens within their domains) (see, especially, Waldron 1987 and Rawls 1993, pp. 136–137). In MacIntyre's view, the failure of contemporary philosophy to provide successful solutions to the problem of political authority, and the turning of philosophical attention from political authority to legitimate use of coercion, is best explained in light of the fact that political philosophers have framed their inquiries in terms of the modern state. Again, just as MacIntyre takes the problems of moral philosophy to be, within the constraints set by the Enlightenment project, insoluble (*After Virtue*, pp. 51–61), he takes the problems of political authority to be, within the constraints set by the institution of the modern state, insoluble.

Why is the political justification of the state doomed to failure? Let us begin with a brief characterization of what exactly MacIntyre means by 'the state.' He does *not* mean "whatever political organization happens to be dominant in a particular society." He means a *particular kind* of political organization. States exhibit territorial governance. Their organization is centralized and hierarchical, and their rule over their citizens is direct and pervasive. They expect the allegiance of their citizens; indeed, they expect that allegiance to "have precedence over that formerly owed to family, clan, commune, lord, bishop, pope, or emperor" (Morris 1998, p. 45; I draw on Morris's excellent book for the salient characteristics of modern states). As is clear, the state is the form of political organization that dominates modern life: the whole political world exists as a state system. Every political philosopher, and every reader of political philosophy, carries out his or her inquiries while living under a state. Given that the state is a ubiquitous feature of modern political life, it is not hard to see why political philosophers would frame their inquiries in terms of it. But, as MacIntyre notes, the unwillingness to consider questions of political forms alternative to those that are prevailing "is always ideological in its effect" (MacIntyre 1996a, p. 62): it is to treat the present dominant forms of political life as inevitable; and to think of any form of political life as inevitable is to mask its defects, defects that can be brought out by considering what alternatives to the state could be, or might have been, realized.

MacIntyre's most thoroughly developed line of criticism of the modern state is against what we may call the "neutralist" state. A state is neutralist if it decides how to act in terms of, and bases its claims for citizens' allegiance upon, only those extremely thin conceptions of the good that are shared by all minimally rational members of that political society. MacIntyre holds that the political justifications of neutralist states inevitably fail, and thus such states receive the allegiance of their citizens only through errors on the part of those citizens. Neutralist states can expect the support of their citizens only if those citizens remain deceived.

The neutralist state, which appeals to only a thin conception of the human good, can justify allegiance to itself only by an appeal to the *public interest* – to the provision of a secure order in which individuals may pursue their own ends (MacIntyre 1997b, p. 241). In order to provide a successful account of the state's authority, the state must appeal only to those goods that are useful to all citizens in pursuit of their own ends, ends justified only in terms of each individuals' idiosyncratic conception of the good. A citizen should have allegiance to the state because it is the state that provides goods that are essential or extremely important with respect to the pursuit of that citizen's own conception of the good. But MacIntyre thinks that any account of political allegiance that appeals only to such goods is bound to fail. For one has sufficient reason to promote the public interest through one's allegiance to the state and obedience to its dictates only if this allegiance and obedience help one to promote one's individual good more successfully than would one's lack of allegiance and disobedience. This generates two problems for public-interest accounts of the state's authority (MacIntyre 1984e, pp. 225–226; see also *Whose Justice?*, p. 347; MacIntyre 1997b, p. 242).

The first problem is that of *freeriders*. One's own contribution to the public interest by obedience to the state is, in most cases, rather minimal; the vast majority of the work done in promoting the public interest is, obviously, done by others. Abstracting for a moment from the risks to one's individual good that are due to state punishment as a result of disobedience, it will be quite often true that one will do better from the point of view of one's individual good by withholding one's contribution to the enterprise of promoting the public interest rather than by contributing. And even if state punishment is figured in, the difficulty is not resolved, for the state is constructed to deal only with minor or sporadic major violations of its dictates; it is built for compliance, not noncompliance.

The second problem is that of *dangerous jobs*. No political society can survive without the existence of persons willing to do dangerous jobs – jobs whose performance is essential to the well-being of that political society, but which pose grave risks to those parties that carry them out. Police, soldiers, firefighters – even, in some areas, public high school teachers – perform jobs that are difficult to justify in terms of their contribution simply to one's individual good. So if the state's appeal for allegiance is simply what the state can do with respect to each citizen's individual good, it seems as if the state has not explained why there should be anyone willing to do the dangerous jobs essential to a state's success.

The upshot of these arguments is that if we take the public-interest account to be the story of why citizens should have allegiance to the state, then the state can survive only by having citizens that are deceived (MacIntyre 1997b, p. 242). Given the transparent inability of the public-interest argument to provide an adequate account of allegiance to the state, the explanation of the state's persistence will be a story of citizens' errors. That the state is dependent on the existence of a largely confused citizenry provides at least part of the explanation for the state's peculiar hybrid ethos:

> The modern nation-state ... present[s] itself on the one hand as a bureaucratic supplier of goods and services, which is always about, but never actually does, give its clients value for money, and on the other as a repository for sacred values, which from time to time invites one to lay down one's life on its behalf.... It is like being asked to die for the telephone company. (MacIntyre 1994f, p. 303)

Now, I take it that most defenders of the neutralist state would agree with the essentials, if not with the details, of MacIntyre's criticism of any argument for allegiance that takes as its premise merely the prospect of those benefits with respect to one's own good that can be realized instrumentally through the state. But defenders of the neutralist state are likely here to appeal to principles of justice in accounting for allegiance to the state, principles whose binding force is independent of any particular conception of the good and thus can be invoked against parties with various visions of the good life to explain why they should be reluctant to freeride and why they should do their share with respect to the performance of dangerous jobs within their states (see, for example, Hart 1955; Rawls 1964; Klosko 1992).

It may seem surprising that MacIntyre gives the criticism of the public-interest account pride of place in his attack on the neutralist state, since most philosophers defending the neutralist state would appeal to justice rather than private benefit alone in making their case (see, for example, Rawls 1971, pp. 350–355; Waldron 1993), and since the self-image of the state – if we take the writings in judicial opinions to be representative of that self-image – is often that of an institution that requires allegiance out of the demands of justice.[1] I take it that the reason that MacIntyre gives the public-interest argument pride of place, given his own views on the priority of the good to the right (MacIntyre 1990d, p. 345), is that the public-interest argument, weak as it is, is at least an argument that makes the necessary appeal to the good. The public-interest argument fails by relying on a conception of the good too thin to do the job that the state needs it to do. But it is at least the *right sort* of an argument – an argument that begins from the goods made possible by political institutions.

Why are appeals to justice as accounts of political allegiance the wrong sorts of arguments, on MacIntyre's view? The most fundamental reason is grounded in the *After Virtue* argument against the Enlightenment project. There MacIntyre argues that the task of providing an account of moral rules justifiable to rational beings in the absence of an account of the appropriate *telos* of human life is doomed to fail. I will not rehearse here that argument, which is discussed in Chapter 4, except to note that it applies as well to argument about rules that will structure not only the lives of particular people but the lives of whole communities: without some conception of the good of that community, of the form of life that is the proper end for common life, rules of justice that are rationally justifiable are not to be had.

The difficulty is not that, in the neutralist state, we can come up with no plausible candidate principles of justice. The difficulty is that we can come up with all too many, the results of different justificatory procedures, without any way of rationally deciding among them (MacIntyre 1990d, p. 348). And since these principles of justice and these procedures of deciding on principles of justice make claims to ultimacy, we seem to be stuck without any way of coming to decide rationally on such principles. (See, for an illustration of this point, MacIntyre's discussion of the Rawls/Nozick debate in *After Virtue*, pp. 244–255.) As MacIntyre notes, incommensurability between rival justificatory schemes need not mean that one of the competitors cannot emerge victorious. But we have not seen anything like progress in the debate among the various competitors – Kantianisms, utilitarianisms, intuitionisms, contractarianisms (*Whose Justice?*, p. 344).

Now, one might respond: perhaps all of this is too hasty. Perhaps MacIntyre is wrong to think that the Enlightenment project is fatally flawed: we have to allow, as MacIntyre does allow, that radical conceptual innovation is always possible, so that what is not foreseeable to us here and now might come as the result of radical invention (*Whose Justice?*, p. 346; *After Virtue*, pp. 93–95). And so even if we were to concede that it is not clear how it is even possible for rules of justice to be defended without an appeal to a substantive theory of the good, and that rival accounts of such rules are at present simply at odds with each other with no direction of progress apparent, the possibility that progress will emerge is a live one. But the allowance of the bare possibility that the rational agreement on principles of justice will emerge that provide us with justification for allegiance to the neutralist state surely does nothing to provide those living under such states, here and now, with a political justification of them (*Whose Justice?*, p. 346).

MacIntyre has two other relevant arguments against the appeal to neutralist justice to deal with the problem of political justification. The first is that further debates about appropriate principles of justice are not, within the constraints set by the neutralist state, going to be of institutional importance. The work of political philosophers in articulating conceptions of justice and arguing through them has negligible impact on the process of political decision making. We have in the modern state, MacIntyre argues, a collection of small academic circles in which inquiry takes place, and a political world in which inquiry is excluded. (It is hard to see how inquiry could play any key role in politics, given the subservience to corporations that the modern state exhibits: because the modern state is so dependent on such corporations for the revenues to fund its activities, there is little possibility of political inquiry that could effectively limit such corporations; see MacIntyre 1999d, pp. 139–140.) There are at least two important implications of this divide between rational inquiry and political processes in the state. The first is that even some success in rational inquiry into principles of justice would be of little use to someone asking about allegiance to the state, for there is little reason to think that rationally justified principles of justice would, *qua* rationally justified, ever become realized in practice. The second is that the state, through this very division, makes itself less worthy of allegiance. For it lacks the institutional settings for common inquiry that would enable the vast majority of those living under it to recognize its shortcomings. There is thus prima facie reason for suspicion of the state, that is, that it lacks the resources to bring its deficiencies to light so that they can be, so far as possible, corrected (MacIntyre 1997b, p. 239).

There is a second worry about the possibility of solving the problem of political allegiance to the modern state by an appeal to neutralist principles of justice, one to which MacIntyre calls attention in his Lindley Lecture on the virtue of patriotism. In that lecture MacIntyre considers two rival views on patriotism – that of the antipatriotic liberal, and that of the antiliberal patriot. The lecture's question, "Is Patriotism a Virtue?," is never answered; rather, he notes deep difficulties for both positions. We will consider MacIntyre's criticism of the patriot's response in the next section. But here we should note the relevance of his criticism of the liberal antipatriot's position. He understands the liberal to appeal to principles of morality that are justifiable from an impartial point of view, and those liberals that want to defend the neutralist state characteristically include as part of the impartial point of view the notion that the rules of justice are justified without appeal to one's own particular conception of the good (see Rawls 1971, p. 137; Dworkin 1978). Now, MacIntyre supposes that adherence to this sort of position will raise trouble for an argument for allegiance to some particular state. The rules of justice as articulated in this impartial framework are supposed to apply to all and to concern the treatment of all. But it is hard to see how we can pull out of justice thus understood a requirement of allegiance *to some particular state*. This difficulty has been emphasized by other theorists in the liberal tradition: John Simmons has referred to the "particularity requirement" that all accounts of political obligation must satisfy, and has argued persuasively that appeals to liberal conceptions of justice do not enable the theorist of political authority to satisfy this desideratum (Simmons 1979, pp. 30–35; see also Green 1990, pp. 232–234; for MacIntyre's clear endorsement of the particularity requirement, see MacIntyre 1983e).

But justice can be realized only in particular settings, under particular institutions. So the appeal to a neutralist conception of justice to justify allegiance to the state brings with it the same danger that we noted above with respect to a public-interest justification of the state. The public-interest argument fails, and so if the citizens see clearly the failure of that argument, the state's capacity to promote the public interest will be undercut. The argument from liberal justice must fail, and so if citizens see clearly the failure of that argument, the state's capacity to realize a conception of justice is undercut.

The neutralist state must appeal either to a conception of the good that is thin enough to be neutral among citizens with different substantive conceptions of the good or to a conception of justice that is defensible apart from an appeal to a substantive conception of the good. But in MacIntyre's view, neither of these justifications for allegiance to a neutralist state can succeed. Why is this not, then, an argument for a *nonneutralist* state, a state that is the bearer of a thick, substantive conception of the good? This is, after all, the conception of state politics that goes by the label 'communitarianism' (see Sandel 1980), a doctrine with which MacIntyre is often associated. But MacIntyre rejects communitarianism, insofar as it is understood as a recommendation for the politics of the modern state.

> Contemporary communitarians, from whom I have strongly disassociated myself whenever I have had an opportunity to do so, advance their proposals as a contribution to the politics of the nation-state. Where liberals have characteristically insisted that government within a nation-state should remain neutral between rival conceptions of the human good, contemporary communitarians have urged that such government should give expression to some shared vision of the human good, a vision defining some type of community. Where liberals have characteristically urged that it is in the activities of subordinate voluntary associations, such as those constituted by religious groups, that shared visions of the good should be articulated, communitarians have insisted that the nation itself through the institutions of the nation-state ought to be constituted to some degree as a community. . . . [F]rom my own point of view communitarians have attacked liberals on one issue on which liberals have been consistently in the right. (MacIntyre 1994f, p. 302; see also MacIntyre 1991b)

The modern state as an all-embracing community is rightly resisted by liberals, "understanding how it generates totalitarian and other evils" (MacIntyre 1994f, p. 303). Why exactly does MacIntyre take the modern state's bearing of a conception of the good to be totalitarian? What is objectionable about the state taking an official position on such matters?

I take it that the imposition of such a conception of the good is intolerable, on MacIntyre's view, both because the state's decisionmaking processes are isolated from procedures of rational inquiry into the good and because that decisionmaking proceeds hierarchically. The result of these features in tandem is that a conception of the good would be imposed from above without adequate rational inquiry into the defensibility of that conception of the good and without adequate participation in decisionmaking by those whose lives will be governed by that conception. This is objectionable from MacIntyre's point of view because of his endorsement of the Aristotelian view that the human good is realized in large part through practical reasoning, and that practical reasoning is not simply a means to achieving one's good but a major constituent of that good. Indeed, MacIntyre goes so far as to identify oppression with deprivation of the capacities and opportunities for rational inquiry (MacIntyre 1997b, p. 250). To have a way of life imposed on one by an elite – and, what's more, the sort of elite that tends to end up in decisionmaking capacities within states, elites of status and wealth – is to have opportunities to achieve one's good through practical inquiry frustrated by the exercise of pervasive state power, and thus to be oppressed.

So MacIntyre agrees with the communitarians against the liberals that the neutralist state must lack authority. And MacIntyre agrees with the liberals against the communitarians that a non-neutralist state is, in the end, intolerable. This does not imply that we should reject the possibility of political forms capable of calling for our rational allegiance; all that it implies is "that the modern state is not such a form of government" (*After Virtue*, p. 255). What sort of political organization could admit of successful justification?

2. THE POLITICS OF LOCAL COMMUNITY

Recall that while MacIntyre thinks that the argument from the public interest is grossly inadequate as an account of why citizens would owe allegiance to the neutralist state, he gives that argument pride of place in his criticism of the neutralist state because it is at least an argument of the right kind: one that proceeds from the goods made possible by political life. The notion of the public interest available within the neutralist state is simply too thin to make it rational for its members to give the state the allegiance that it calls for. In providing a sketch of an alternative form of political life and political organization, MacIntyre begins by considering what the goods of political life would have to be like in order to justify a set of political institutions. He then considers what the character of these goods tells us about how politics would have to be conceived, and what political institutions would have to be like, in order to succeed where the politics of the modern state was shown to fail.

Any successful political justification, on MacIntyre's view, will have to proceed by taking the notion of the *common good* as its central normative concept. The notion of the common good as MacIntyre understands it differs fundamentally from the notion of the public interest as MacIntyre understands it. The public interest is defined in such a way as to be logically posterior to the goods of the members of the public: it is a set of conditions that support individuals' goods. We would have to be able to provide an account of the individual's good that is independent of the notion of the public interest in order to make sense of that idea. The normative claim that the public interest has on each practical reasoner derives entirely from the instrumental relationship that holds between the realization of the public interest and the realization of his or her individual good. Even though the public interest is defined to be those conditions that are instrumentally valuable to the realization of a rational individual's concept of the good, no matter what the content of that concept, we can be sure that each individual will have an interest in the provision of that good. But because adherence to what the state calls upon an individual to do in pursuit of the public interest may further that individual's good less than the failure to adhere to the state's dictate would, the normative pull of the public interest is not sufficient to support the state's claim to allegiance. Because the individual's good is defined independently of the public interest, so that what one must do to achieve the public interest and what one must do to achieve one's individual good can pull massively apart, public interest political justifications are doomed to failure.

By contrast, the concept of a common good, as MacIntyre understands it, is one that is not subordinate to a prior notion of an individual's good. Rather, a good that is common to a number of persons is not merely instrumental to the furtherance of their individual ends; it is constitutive of and partially defining of those individuals' goods. MacIntyre's favorite example is that of a fishing crew (see, for example, MacIntyre 1994f, pp. 284–286; 1997b, p. 240). The good of each of the members of the fishing crew cannot be characterized independently of the good common to all members of the crew: that they work together properly at a high level of excellence in catching fish. The good of a member of a fishing crew is partially characterized in terms of whether the good of the whole crew is being realized, and so what it is for the fishing crew to be realizing a common good cannot itself be defined in terms of the goods of the individual members of that crew.

The space in which common goods are possible is, in MacIntyre's view, the space of practices. (For a more complete discussion of practices than that which appears here, see Chapter 5 of this volume.) A practice is

> any coherent and complex socially established cooperative human activity through which goods internal to that form of activity are realized in the course of trying to achieve those standards of excellence which are appropriate to, and partially definitive of, that form of activity, with the result that human powers to achieve excellence, and human conceptions

> of the ends and goods involved, are systematically extended. (*After Virtue*, p. 187)

That there be goods internal to that form of activity is essential to whether a form of activity constitutes a practice. Goods that are internal to a form of activity can be defined only in terms of that activity: they are not merely contingently associated with a practice, but can be had only by participating in that practice. By contrast, goods external to a form of activity can be defined independently of that activity, are only contingently associated with it, and can be had other than by participating in that activity. So while the development of skills especial to fishing, and the exhibition of those skills in common action through the excellent catching of fish, are goods internal to fishing, the financial rewards (not to mention the fish) that accrue to members of successful fishing crews are goods external to that practice.

Now, while MacIntyre's definition of internal and external goods emphasizes the necessary and contingent (respectively) connections to the practices in which these goods can be realized, he suggests that another salient contrast concerns the way that internal goods tend to be common goods and external goods private goods.

> It is a characteristic of what I have called external goods that when achieved they are always some individual's property and possession. Moreover characteristically they are such that the more someone has of them, the less there is for other people. . . . External goods are therefore characteristically objects of competition in which there must be losers as well as winners. Internal goods are indeed the outcome of competition to excel, but it is characteristic of them that their achievement is a good for the whole community who participate in that practice. (*After Virtue*, pp. 190–191)

We can thus see why MacIntyre would take to be key to providing an account of the sort of politics that admits of justification that it would include an appeal to a conception of politics as a practice, indeed as a practice that is indispensable in each human life. For it is in the province of practices that common goods – goods that are constitutive of, and partially define, individual's goods – can be realized. And it is only common goods that can provide the normative support for successful political justifications.

Does it make sense to conceive of politics as a practice? If 'politics' is understood simply as large-scale jockeying for power or wealth, then its concern is with external goods only, and it cannot constitute a practice. But there is a not-unfamiliar human activity that naturally arises within human communities that has the salient characteristics of a practice and that

MacIntyre takes to be properly political. Every human society is marked by the presence of a multiplicity of practices, and individual human lives are characteristically marked by participation in a number of practices. Each individual inevitably faces questions about how the practices in one's life are to be ordered. If I am a father and a member of a fishing crew, my good is partially defined in terms of the goods of family life and partially in terms of the goods of fishing, and I will need to determine how best to order those practices, and the goods internal to them, in my life. But we face similar questions within our communities about how the various practices within these communities are to be ordered. What places should such goods as fishing, family life, academic inquiry, aesthetic endeavor, and athletic achievement have in our common life? This is a question that members of a community face in common, and must deliberate about in common: the answers that one reaches on this question depend on the answers reached by others (MacIntyre 1997b, p. 240).

So consider the question that arises in communities of any complexity: how are the practices, and the goods internal to these practices, to be ordered in this community? This is a practical question: it is not for the sake of speculation but for action. There is a range of excellences that are necessary for answering this question well, and there is a range of capacities that are developed through successive attempts to answer these questions in common. An adequate explication of these excellences and developed capacities, and of the worthwhile activity engaged in by those attempting to answer this question, cannot be offered except in terms of the activity itself. There are goods internal to the activity of attempting to answer questions about how the practices in a community's life are to be ordered. This activity is, therefore, a practice. And it is this practice that MacIntyre understands the practice of politics to be.

Politics is, then, a second-order practice: its goods are those of deliberation about practices.[2] It is, as MacIntyre understands it, an intensely cognitive activity. All practices are to some extent cognitive. Consider football, for example. Participation in a practice such as football involves not just the playing of football – playing which includes a significant component of intelligent thought and judgment – but also the assessment of one's own and others' playing of the game, and the assessment of the standards by which playing is assessed. Politics is, however, cognitive in an even deeper way: its activity is practical reasoning, reasoning for the sake of action. Its activity is common practical reasoning about the common life.

Politics is a practice that is indispensable to the achievement of one's individual good. The notion that some particular practice would be indispensable with respect to the achievement of one's good has a strange ring to it. If one were to say that participation in the practice of architecture, or badminton, were essential to the achievement of one's good, this would seem strange indeed. But politics has a special place, on MacIntyre's view. It has a special place because it is the practice best suited to the development of one's rational powers, because of its role as a master practice organizing the various other practices (MacIntyre 1997b, p. 243). Engaging in politics involves deliberation about the whole range of goods available to humans, and thus is the most demanding and enriching of the various practices.

Suppose that MacIntyre is right about the goods internal to politics, and the central place that those goods should have in a human life. How does one proceed from these claims to the conclusion that there is some possible set of political institutions whose authority we would be reasonable to accept? While MacIntyre takes it to be a terrible mistake to confuse practices with institutions, he also thinks that institutions are indispensable for practices: "No practices can survive for any length of time unsustained by institutions" (*After Virtue*, p. 194). The institutions of governance that have a rightful claim to our obedience and allegiance are those that sustain and make possible the practice of politics. From our understanding of the practice of politics, sketchy as it is, we can see that such an institution would have to be one that made possible *effective common deliberation*.

By effective common deliberation I mean deliberation by everyone in a political community, the outcome of which is a set of common actions. When it is going well, political deliberation, on MacIntyre's view, includes all persons, for there is no one who has nothing to teach that is relevant from the point of view of how goods should be ordered within a political community's life. This is a point on which MacIntyre takes great pains to insist in his most recent work. Those whose temporary or permanent disabilities prevent their personally taking part, MacIntyre argues, should not be excluded from political deliberation. It is crucial that those who are thus disabled have proxies to speak for them, from their perspective. Only one who is a friend to such a person will be able to be his or her voice in political inquiry, for only a friend can know someone sufficiently intimately (*Dependent Rational Animals*, p. 150).

So one crucial matter is that governing institutions must preserve and foster an arena of inquiry in which rational investigation into the good can be pursued, an arena from which no one is excluded. But governing institutions must also make the outcomes of these deliberations effective. Just as individual practical reasoning, when adequately carried out, issues in individual action, political practical reasoning, when adequately carried out, issues in political action. Governing institutions make effective the decisions reached in common deliberation by members of the political community through the promulgation of directives, directives which call for the allegiance of the participants in the practice.

Invariably the practice of politics, and the institutions sustaining that practice, will have to be exemplified on a small scale. Politics, conceived and carried out as a practice, is on MacIntyre's view invariably a local matter. This view, MacIntyre emphasizes, is not based in some love of the local as such. It is simply a brute truth that the conditions under which common deliberation can take place require a small community. The very size of the typical modern state precludes state politics from being a matter of common deliberation (*Dependent Rational Animals*, p. 131). In the same vein, politics, conceived and carried out as a practice, requires a shared culture. But the value of such a political community is not constituted by its possession of a shared culture; having a shared culture is simply a condition sine qua non for the carrying out of rational inquiry in common into the good. The shared culture that is necessary is a culture of deliberation, the very sort of culture that is needed for one to pursue in common an investigation that can put one's traditions and shared culture to the question (MacIntyre 1997b, p. 241).

It is with MacIntyre's emphasis on the good of politics being a good of inquiry that we can look back to the worries that MacIntyre entertains about the virtue of patriotism. In section 1 I noted that in his Lindley Lecture MacIntyre considers the views of the patriotic antiliberal and the antipatriotic liberal and raises objections to each of their positions, objections that are never satisfactorily resolved. We have seen already that MacIntyre's worry about antipatriotic liberalism is just that the carrying out of liberal objectives may very well require the sort of particular allegiance characteristic of patriotism that liberalism seems unable to provide. By contrast, MacIntyre's worry about patriotism is simply that it involves one in a kind of blindness. To be a patriot, MacIntyre says, is to exempt from criticism one's political community, at least in some respect: MacIntyre identifies this respect with one's political community conceived as a project (MacIntyre 1984e, p. 221). The liberal critic notes that the sustenance of one's political community as a project can be contrary to the best interests of humankind impartially considered, and so patriotism presents a certain moral danger. But it seems to me that MacIntyre's present identification of the goods internal to political life with goods of inquiry blunts the liberal's criticism here. For the point is that it will only be within properly functioning political communities as

MacIntyre understands them that reasoners will have adequate resources for putting anything effectively into question at all. To put it another way: the liberal's worry is that allegiance to one's political community will make one unable to engage in rational criticism of one's political community in light of potentially competing goods. But MacIntyre's point is that a political community, when in good condition, is just that sort of community in which one *is* enabled to engage in rational criticism of one's political community in light of potentially competing goods. Making clear that the project of a justifiable political community is a project of rational inquiry enables the patriot to have allegiance to his or her political community without being subject to the criticism that patriotism involves a self-imposed moral blindness.

That the practice of politics offers a good that is common to members of a political society makes possible, on MacIntyre's view, a successful solution to the problem of political justification. But it also points the way to an account of political justice – something that the neutralist state, with its refusal to appeal to anything more than a thin conception of the public interest, seemed unable to provide. The inability of plain persons to come to agreement in matters of political justice, an inability echoed in the stalemates in debate in academic philosophy, is a result of the loss of the notion of the common good of political life, a good which can serve as the standard for matters of justice (*After Virtue*, pp. 250–251). Political justice is ultimately a matter of what members of the political community deserve. MacIntyre here is, again, deeply Aristotelian: for one to be deserving of some goods, or some bads, there must be a common enterprise, and those who are more deserving have contributed more to that good, and those who are less deserving have contributed less. Further, there must be some shared view as to how contributions to the common enterprise are to be measured and how rewards are to be ranked (*After Virtue*, pp. 150–154; *Whose Justice?*, pp. 106–107). Because this is so, questions of justice cannot even begin to be answered without the presence of those conditions under which the proper ordering of the practices within a community can be the object of deliberation. For the good, contribution to which is the ultimate standard of justice, and the scale of goods and bads that determines the deserts for members of the political community, can be known only through political deliberation. Members of the political community will deserve more or less depending on their contributions to the various practices that constitute the life of the community, but the importance of their contributions can only be assessed once some sort of ordering of these goods, albeit a provisional one, is reached.

Questions of political justice are going to be, to some extent, dependent upon the conditions that hold in a particular community: for what members of that community deserve is going to depend on the proper ordering of practices within that community, and how practices are properly ordered will depend on contingent circumstances. There is no guarantee that there is one ordering of goods that is appropriate for every political community, and thus there is no guarantee that the particular desert that attaches to contributions to specific practices will be the same for all political communities.[3] But to allow that there is some variability in political justice among political communities is not thereby to allow that there are no nontrivial standards of justice that hold in all political communities. These universal standards of justice MacIntyre identifies with the precepts of the natural law.

The precepts of the natural law, as MacIntyre understands them, are in one sense substantive: they preclude an agent from engaging in certain sorts of attack on others, thus establishing these others as immune from certain harms. But the precepts of the natural law, as MacIntyre understand them, are in another sense procedural: they are justified as those precepts that all agents must observe in order to engage in common enterprises, which are, we should keep in mind, always at least in part enterprises of common inquiry. As procedural, they are enabling rules[4] that enable persons to pursue ends in common, rather than mere side constraints on conduct.

What needs explanation is how the substantive and the procedural aspects of the natural law come together on MacIntyre's view. The idea is that it is essential to the pursuit of common ends that those pursuing them be able to expect immunity from certain sorts of harm at the hands of others. Think about it this way. Common projects are threatened by anything that disrupts, that makes impossible for a time, the communal ties of those that are participating in them. And certain kinds of harm – lies, betrayals, assaults, and so forth – invariably disrupt the communal relationships that make common inquiry and pursuit of goods possible. The natural law absolutely forbids us from performing such actions. We have reason to adhere to those precepts because adherence enables common pursuit of common goods, goods that are, as we have already seen, partially constitutive of and defining of our individual goods.

One might wonder why these precepts are absolute in form, rather than, for example: "refrain from (e.g.) assaults when refraining from assaults better promotes the pursuit of the common good than assaulting does." After all, we can conjure up cases in which it might appear that the common good of a group might be better promoted by acting contrary to allegedly absolute precepts of the natural law. MacIntyre's reply would be that it is crucial to the preservation of the communal relationships necessary for common inquiry that those involved in that inquiry not be willing to calculate whether assaulting, lying to, or betraying another member of the enterprise will better promote that enterprise. I cannot have the relationship of complete trust in a fellow inquirer into and pursuer of the good if this fellow evinces a willingness, on some occasions, to lie to, betray, or assault me. The natural law requires respect for "the preconditions of a kind of rational conversation in which no one need fear being victimized by others as the outcome of their engagement with those others." (MacIntyre 1994a, p. 184)

The natural law, on MacIntyre's view, is eminently knowable. Participants in practices come naturally to be aware of its precepts because if a particular exemplification of a practice fails to recognize them that exemplification will disintegrate. Those who participate in practices must have at least some sort of implicit awareness of the principles of the natural law, so that a basic, tacit knowledge of it can be ascribed to them; formulation of the principles of the natural law is thus an exercise in making explicit in reflection what is implicit in practice. (See MacIntyre 1997a, in which MacIntyre considers the views of Anthony Lisska [Lisska 1996], John Finnis [Finnis 1980], and himself on this issue.) It is a signal merit of MacIntyre's account of the natural law that it is subject to empirical testing in a way that other recent conceptions of natural law seem not to be.[5] Note that even within the practice of philosophical inquiry as presently carried out – which is on the whole extraordinarily hostile to natural law thinking – there seems to be a widespread, if usually implicit, agreement on the principles of the natural law as MacIntyre characterizes them. Philosophers, even though highly critical of natural law thinking, take a very dim view of false citation, betrayal of one's colleagues, and assault on one's philosophical enemies. It is not just that they reject the correctness of an argument that one might give on a particular occasion that false citation, betrayal, or assault ultimately furthers the good of philosophical inquiry. It is that they reject any appeal to a consequentialist weighing as being inappropriate. So even the activity of those that are deeply skeptical of natural law thinking gives some testimony to the truth of MacIntyre's account of the natural law (MacIntyre 1994a, pp. 173–174).

The conclusions for politics, then, are straightforward. Those institutions that support the practice of politics must recognize and adhere to the precepts of natural law if they are to be worthy of allegiance. And whether such institutions are upholding the natural law is a matter to which all persons, through the eminent knowability of the natural law, are competent to pass judgment. No political institutions are insusceptible to the critical scrutiny of those living under them, at least with respect to the most basic matters of justice (MacIntyre 1996a, p. 68).

Now, MacIntyre's recent endorsement of natural law as central to an adequate conception of politics raises a question about the extent to which MacIntyre's views have undergone a transformation since *After Virtue*. In that work MacIntyre had echoed Bentham's assessment of natural rights as nonsense on stilts and had equated belief in natural rights with belief in witches and unicorns (*After Virtue*, p. 69). In recent work, however, he is perfectly happy to talk about natural law; and natural law requires the recognition of an immunity of a rational inquirer to certain sorts of harm at the hands of others. But what is the recognition of this sort of immunity other than the recognition of a natural right?

I do not think that MacIntyre's views on this matter have altered: natural rights are still, on his view, nonsense on stilts. That there are certain ways that human beings ought not to be treated, and that the fact that they ought not to be treated thus is not due to convention but nature, is not sufficient for the existence of a natural right. What is key is the locus of justification for the immunity – what gives point and purpose to refraining from treating others in a certain way. Natural rights doctrines are characteristically individualistic in at least the following sense: each of them holds that the immunities that a human being enjoys by nature have as their locus of justification something intrinsic to that human being. Either that individual's good (the so-called Interest conception of rights; see, for example, Raz 1986, pp. 165–192), or that individual's choice about how to live his or her own life (the so-called Choice conception of rights; see, for example, Hart 1955, pp. 175–191), is supposed to ground the individual's immunity to certain sorts of treatment. But rights understood in this way, MacIntyre thinks, are unintelligible. One has no natural interest in others' receipt of some benefit, or in their choices to live a certain way. Since whatever else a natural right is supposed to be, it is supposed to provide reasons for others to act in a certain way, natural rights do not make sense.

By contrast, the immunities dictated by the natural law do not have an individualistic basis. The reason for recognizing these immunities is that their recognition is essential for the carrying out of common projects. The normative force of the immunities is borne by the common good, not some individual's private good. And insofar as the good that is common is partially constitutive of the good of all of the individuals taking part in the activity, all have reasons to adhere to the natural law and thus to preserve these immunities. There is no significant shift in MacIntyre's rejection of a natural rights perspective in ethics and politics.

3. TWO WORRIES

I want to close by considering two worries about the conception of politics that MacIntyre offers. The first has to do with whether the modern state is necessarily as dismal a creature as MacIntyre makes it out to be. The second has to do with the coherence of the notion of politics as a practice that MacIntyre offers.

As we have seen, MacIntyre's verdict on the possibility of a political justification of the modern state – a justification that would enable the state to back up its claims to authority with adequate reasons – is entirely negative. But MacIntyre is always careful to temper his condemnation of any acceptance of the state's global pretensions with endorsement of ad hoc acceptance of the state's benefits and sometime cooperation with the state's worthwhile activities. (This tempering is itself tempered with reminders of the dangers to local community present in entangling itself too thoroughly with the state.) Virtuous members of local communities "will recognize [the state] as an ineliminable feature of the contemporary landscape and they will not despise the resources that it affords. It may and on occasion does provide the only means for removing obstacles to humane goals" (*Dependent Rational Animals*, p. 133). MacIntyre's remarks suggest the following view: because the state is not going away, and because, given the existence of the state, there is often no way to achieve certain ends that practitioners of the politics of local community have reason to promote other than through cooperation with the state, there will sometimes be occasions on which practitioners of the politics of local community have reason to acquiesce with or participate in the state's initiatives. But this concession, sensible as it is, raises questions about whether practitioners of the politics of local community, if there were no state, would find it necessary, or highly desirable, to invent it. And if it is indeed the case that practitioners of the politics of local community would find it necessary, or highly desirable, to invent some set of institutions like the state in some relevant respects, this would raise questions about whether the state is, as MacIntyre describes it, a deeply, fundamentally flawed set of incoherent institutional structures, or whether it is instead an admittedly imperfect realization of a fundamentally sound political structure.

Here is an argument for the prima facie desirability, from the point of view of a politics of local community, for a statelike set of institutions. As MacIntyre notes, no practices can go unsupported by institutions, for institutions are characteristically concerned with the provision of external goods, and practices, while aiming at goods internal to them, cannot get by without external goods (*After Virtue*, p. 194). The practice of politics will be no different. In addition to those external goods necessary for carrying on the goods of common deliberation central to that practice, the fact that politics is about appropriately ordering all of the practices within a community's life will make politics a practice that is particularly demanding in its need for external goods. For to order the practices in a community's life will be, in part, to see to it that those practices more central to the life of the local community be better provided with respect to external goods, and indeed that all practices that are deserving in some way be supported in their pursuits. And so there will need to be institutions that are able to provide external goods – security, wealth, and so forth – in light of the decisions reached within political practice.

Now, there is, *ceteris paribus*, reason to pursue efficiency with respect to the provision of such goods. (I will return to ways in which the *ceteris* may not be *paribus* below.) And so there would be very good reason for several local communities to sustain in common a set of institutions that could provide external goods to them all that would be much less efficiently provided by them individually. The premier example of an external good likely to be provided more efficiently in this way would be security from external threats, and we may take this good as central to the defense of a statelike institution, a *quasi-state*, from the point of view of a politics of local community.

If several local communities saw the point of putting into place a statelike institution, it would have several key features. First, the quasi-state would self-consciously have limited resources for communal deliberation, for, being an institution that straddles several communities of deliberation, it would recognize that the possibilities of extended debate would be far more limited than can be entertained within such communities. Second, it would have to proceed from a relatively thin theory of the good, concerned only with its limited mandate to provide a particular set of external goods for a given set of local communities. And third, in demanding the support that all institutions require in order to survive, it would have to make a double appeal. It would have to appeal to the goods of the local communities themselves that are best realized with the provision of external goods. But communities as well as individuals can be freeriders, and so such institutions would have to appeal to a conception of justice, articulated initially within local communities but making demands that extend beyond their borders, to account for the reason freeriding is intolerable.

There is a prima facie case from the point of view of the politics of local community, then, for a quasi-state. Note some relevant similarities between the quasi-state and the modern state that MacIntyre criticizes. It proceeds on the basis of a thinner theory of the good than that endorsed by any of the communities that it seeks to serve, aiming to provide goods that are useful to each. It has limited aspirations with respect to public deliberation about the goods that it serves. And it calls for allegiance on the basis of the importance of the goods that it provides to the local communities that it serves and on the basis of requirements of justice in distribution. Now, admittedly, modern states often overstep their bounds, and go beyond the quasi-state. Their claims to be the final objects of allegiance are overblown, and even idolatrous. And they tend to make disastrous mistakes about the entities that they serve: they tend to understand their service to be to individuals simply as such, and to ignore the key points to which MacIntyre draws our attention – that individuals can only come to understand their good and to articulate defensible conceptions of justice in local communities and within traditions of inquiry. But it makes a great deal of difference with respect to the success of MacIntyre's criticism of the state whether it is best conceived as a distorted, defective quasi-state or as an institution presupposing a set of first principles entirely at odds with the politics of local community.

Now, MacIntyre could admit all of this while still denying that the state is ultimately cast in any better light. For I admitted in my exposition of the quasi-state that in it the opportunities for common deliberation are limited. And this may well doom the quasi-state from MacIntyre's point of view. Any institution that lacks the possibility for meaningful self-correction through deliberation should be rejected as simply too unwieldy and dangerous. Quasi-states that overstep their bounds and make serious mistakes with respect to their mission – thus becoming too much like modern states – are not sufficiently subject to correction. But this is, I think, where there remains empirical work to be done. It needs to be asked what ways there are for local communities to hold in check statelike institutions, and it needs to be asked whether, for all of the potential for overreaching by statelike institutions, local communities are not in fact more successful in their own terms within the context of states than outside of that context. This is very much in line with the sort of empirical inquiry into the conditions under which local communities flourish or languish that MacIntyre calls for in his most recent work (*Dependent Rational Animals*, pp. 142–143).

The second line of criticism that I want to press against MacIntyre's view to my mind generates far more serious difficulties for his position. Recall some of the salient features of practices as MacIntyre characterizes them. What makes an organized activity a practice is, in part, that it is an activity through which goods internal to that activity are realized (*After Virtue*, p. 187). In labeling the goods of practices "internal" goods, he means to emphasize a contrast between those goods that can be defined only in terms of the activity of a practice and those – "external" goods, such as money, power, status, etc. – that can be defined without reference to the particularities of a practice. MacIntyre also takes it to be a defining feature of goods internal to practices that one who has not been initiated into and educated within a practice is not competent as a judge of internal goods: such a person cannot appreciate them adequately, cannot understand when they have been achieved, and cannot discern greater or lesser achievement with respect to the realization of those goods (*After Virtue*, pp. 188–189). MacIntyre thus places some emphasis on the virtue of educability: "To enter into a practice is to accept the authority of those standards and the inadequacy of my own performance as judged by them. It is to subject my own attitudes, choices, preferences, and tastes to the standards which currently and partially define the practice" (*After Virtue*, p. 190). Initiation into practices is transformative: while persons often and characteristically enter practices for the sake of the external goods contingently associated with those practices, to be initiated into them is to be made able to appreciate adequately the goods internal to them (*After Virtue*, p. 188).

So far as I can tell, the notion that the goods internal to a practice cannot be adequately known by outsiders, by those that have not been initiated into that practice, is an ineliminable part of MacIntyre's account of practices. To deny it would be to deny the distinction between internal and external goods, a distinction that is crucial in MacIntyre's account of the virtues. And so if it were to turn out that the thesis that "those who lack the relevant experience are incompetent thereby as judges of internal goods" (*After Virtue*, p. 189) makes trouble for MacIntyre's conception of politics, the trouble could not be eliminated by mild revisions in his position.

But the notion that goods internal to practices cannot be adequately known by outsiders *does* make serious trouble for MacIntyre's conception of politics. For politics, as we have seen, is that practice concerned with proper deliberation about, and communal action regarding, the ordering of the practices and the goods internal to those practices within a community. But rational communal deliberation about the place of the goods of the different practices within the life of the community is bound to be a chimera. For such deliberation would have to be founded on an adequate appreciation by participants in that deliberation of the goods of the practices to be ordered, and no political deliberator could have all of the knowledge required. No one can enter sufficiently into the multifarious practices that make up the life of a community to be able adequately to appreciate the goods internal to each of those distinct practices. There are simply too many, and entering into a practice requires too much time, for adequate appreciation of the goods to be ordered in political deliberation to be a live possibility for human beings.

Now, one might respond that this objection to MacIntyre's conception of politics underestimates the resources for political deliberation that are provided by such deliberation being *common*. Political deliberation is not private, but public. And so even if it is conceded that no individual deliberator would be able to deliberate rationally in political matters on his or her own, it is a commonplace about communal deliberation that the shortcomings of individual deliberators is remedied by the strengths of their fellows. What a single person does not know can be supplied by those that do. But while it may often be true that individual deficiencies in knowledge can be compensated for in communal deliberation, it does not seem to help in this case. For the deliberation at issue concerns, essentially, *comparative* knowledge – knowledge of the relative importance of different goods, of how some goods should or should not be subordinated to others. For one person to have intimate knowledge of the goods of one practice and for another to have intimate knowledge of the goods of another practice does not help much at all in dealing with the question: how are the goods of these two practices to be *ordered* in the life of our community? A participant in one practice will not be able adequately to convey the importance of the goods of his or her practice just through talking about it; MacIntyre notes "the meagerness of our vocabulary for speaking of [internal] goods" (*After Virtue*, p. 188) in emphasizing the point that knowledge of such goods is acquired only through experience within the relevant practice. So it does not seem that the knowledge of the goods needed to make rational judgments in political matters can be supplied by one's fellow political deliberators.

If this second line of criticism of MacIntyre's political philosophy is successful, then we can go even further than the claim, defended in the first line of criticism, that perhaps MacIntyre is wrong to dismiss the potential of some statelike system of institutions. I suggested in the first line of criticism that a statelike system of institutions can be endorsed from within MacIntyre's politics of local community from a conjunction of three facts: first, that such communities practicing local politics would rationally want an efficient provision of external goods; second, that an efficient provision of external goods can be better brought about through an institution that crosses the boundaries of local communities; and third, that deliberation within such an institution would have to be far thinner than deliberation within any local community. But what this second line of criticism suggests is that if MacIntyre is committed to a conception of internal goods in which knowledge of such goods is denied to all but insiders, then rational deliberation that takes place *within* a politics of local community is going to be far more austere than originally envisaged. The question, even within local communities, cannot be: "Given the various practices that constitute the life of the community, what relative importance should we ascribe to each of these practices, so that those practices can be properly ordered in our common life?" The question will instead be something like: "Given our individual inabilities to know the goods of these practices in anything like an adequate way, and given our collective inability to overcome these individual deficiencies, how is it reasonable to respond to the various practices?" To retreat to this question is not to deny that there is a best way to order the practices within political communities; it is only to deny that knowledge of this best way is available to us, with our ineliminable human limitations.[6]

Notes

1. For an account of the sources of allegiance considered in United States Supreme Court opinions, see Hall and Klosko 1998; for an understanding of the courts as the prime example of public reason, see Rawls 1993, pp. 231–240.
2. Including the practice of politics itself: one question that will have to be answered will be about how the good of engaging in politics should be set against other goods.
3. This is not to deny that for *each* political community there will be some best way of ordering the goods in *that* community; that there is such a best way, or a limited class of best ways, is what makes politics as MacIntyre understands it a matter of seeking after truth.
4. The enabling character of the principles of the natural law is emphasized in MacIntyre 1994a, p. 177.
5. For example, Finnis 1980, pp. 33–34. Even my own is, sadly, subject to some version of this criticism; see Murphy 2001, pp. 36–40.
6. I owe thanks to Paul Weithman and Ben Lipscomb for helpful comments on drafts of this chapter. I also owe thanks to Alasdair MacIntyre, who in reading this chapter exhibited his usual just generosity in both receiving and offering criticism.

7 MacIntyre's Critique of Modernity

TERRY PINKARD

The modern period is usually dated as beginning roughly in 1789, the year not only of the French Revolution but also of the opening of the new federal government in the United States and correspondingly the securing of that country's new nationally oriented commercial society. Within a short period of time, "modernity" saw democratic revolutions, authoritarian revolutions, and the explosive growth of industrial society. There are now many who think that the modern period has run its course and is giving way to a new form of "postmodern" civilization.

Modernity, with its factories and steam engines, its mass culture and its creation of weapons of immense destruction, has long been the object of both admiration and dislike. Its admirers tend to see it as marking progress beyond what preceded it: human life has been lengthened in industrial society, many of the great masses who were formerly excluded have become empowered, wealth has increased, and freedom has become the great watchword across the globe. (Even the capitalism-critical Marxists bought into their own version of the idea of progress.) However, modernity has also been the object of intense, emotional attack, and in the late eighteenth and early nineteenth century in Germany, criticizing modernity became a genre unto itself. Even before the onset of industrialization, people like F. H. Jacobi were already expressing dismay in the emerging trust in reason to solve all our problems and were criticizing all Enlightenment thought as potentially "nihilistic" (a term Jacobi coined) – enlightened reason, so Jacobi's claim went, could tear things down, but it could not satisfactorily build anything up to replace it. Indeed, the forces of modernity simply destroyed all that was good and beautiful and replaced it with an alienated, potentially godless moral wasteland.

There are easily typified reactions to the distresses of modernity. One is to want to accelerate Enlightenment thought to its completion: the only cure for the ills inflicted by the Enlightenment, so the saying goes, is more Enlightenment. The other is to indulge in nostalgia, which in the nineteenth century was quite often coupled with an intense desire actually to turn the clock back, to restore a lost world; that desire in the twentieth century has been more typically associated with a kind of cultural despair. As a form of cultural despair, nostalgia takes the form of wishing that that we had never lost the innocence that we formerly had, and while it implicitly accepts the fact that the clock cannot be turned back, it still sees the movement forward in history as nonetheless inevitable, although altogether for the worse, and quite often is driven to the rather quietist conclusion, as Heidegger so famously put it, that "only a god can save us now" (a statement made some time after Heidegger had already suffered the ignominy of his support of a self-appointed German demigod to do the job).

Jacobi's attack on "Enlightenment" – by which he meant "modernity" – was both a cultural and a philosophical attack. If the culture of modernity was lacking, its predicament was traceable to the philosophical view in which that culture was rooted, which, for Jacobi, was the culture and philosophy based on universalizing reason. That "modern" outlook had brought forth a world of alienated people unable to be at home in their world, whose lives would therefore in some crucial sense be stunted or lacking in a kind of depth that they had earlier possessed.

MacIntyre has also been a fierce critic of modernity, and one of the key elements of his most famous book, *After Virtue*, is an attack on the failure of the "Enlightenment Project." His celebrations of the philosophical superiority of both Aristotle and, most recently, Thomas Aquinas, along with his admiring descriptions of ancient Athens and Catholic medieval Europe, along with his own closing of *After Virtue* with the lines about waiting for a new Saint Benedict to save us from modernity's barbarians (*After Virtue*, p. 263), certainly make it natural to interpret MacIntyre as some kind of slightly Romantic elegist for the past, a man confounded by the moral laxness of the present, hoping that it all will somehow just go away – maybe even wishing that we would all turn our computers off and go back to writing with quill pens on rag paper.

The charge of nostalgia quite naturally has been an underlying theme in much of the criticism of MacIntyre's work, but it is a serious misreading of his key ideas. In MacIntyre's writings one indeed finds an admiration of much of ancient Greece, but one also continuously finds in that same work more or less condemnatory judgments that it was based on slavery and the oppression of women; Aristotle, while praised, is convicted of grievous mistakes, among them his endorsement of the idea of natural slavery; and, for MacIntyre, the inequalities of the medieval world clearly disqualify it from serving as the perfect model of human development. On the other hand, what makes Aristotle, Aquinas, ancient Athens, and the medievals appealing is that they all involved a way of thinking about and living out *nonindividualist* ways of life in which the "individual" was not taken to be the ultimate, irreducible unit of political and social discourse, the "individual" was not taken to have rights prior to his relationship to others, and the status of institutions was not solely to provide "individuals" with the means for efficiently realizing their desires or for "actualizing" their "selves."

To understand MacIntyre's dissatisfaction with modernity, one therefore has to look in places other than the Romantic nostalgia for a nonexistent, unified and harmonious past in order to find the other sources of his distaste for modernity, in particular the rather politically conservative Max Weber and the non-Marxist socialist Karl Polanyi.

Polanyi's influence on MacIntyre is quite straightforward (see Polanyi 1975). In the 1940s and 1950s, Polanyi challenged the conventional wisdom that economics was a value-free science that only described and explained what all rational persons would, under very rarefied conditions, freely elect to do. Instead, he argued that modern economics only formalizes a contingent, modern sense of the cash economy and modern capitalism; for Polanyi, not only are alternative arrangements of the economy possible, but it is the case that many past and present societies have in fact presented us with such alternatives. In saying this, Polanyi was by no means inspired by nostalgia for the past; he simply wanted to undermine the notion that the modern economy and its attendant conceptions of rationality, exchange, and efficiency were natural and inevitable. Premodern economies, for example, did not presuppose such notions but were instead based on notions of reciprocity: each person in such an order produced or performed the task at which they were best, and the whole was then redistributed among the society at large. The fundamental glue holding such premodern economies together was not the desire to further one's own (narrow or broad) interests but to *establish one's standing* in society by performing well and virtuously those tasks that society required and expected of oneself. Such premodern economies thus rested on a shared but rarely explicit sense of what the "whole" *required* of them, and on a shared but rarely explicit understanding of what the whole *owed* to them. For Polanyi the individual was neither submerged nor crushed by the social wholes; both the individual and the social whole had their place, and each received its due in such an order.

Market economies, on the other hand, abolish that shared understanding. Markets operate only on price, not on orientation to the social whole.

Unfettered from social roles, the individual produces and acts not in terms of how he is contributing to the social whole, nor in terms of the impact of his actions on the social whole at large, but only in terms of whether his behavior can "clear" the market (whether the price for his labor or goods is too high). However, all economic relationships, Polanyi argued, ultimately have their basis in a certain feature of human sociality, namely in our need to appear to others in certain ways, to gain standing in their eyes. In market societies, this ultimately takes place through the acquisition of status items and simply of more money itself. In saying this, though, Polanyi never held that capitalism was only a way station to full socialism, nor did he endorse the Marxist view that individualism was only an ideology by which the bourgeoisie maintained its control over the means of production. He only wanted to argue that modern economics is not written into the nature of rationality or into the metaphysical structure of human agency. There are and have been alternatives, and understanding the sheer contingency of modern economic life can free us up to think about what our modern alternatives to capitalism might be.

Weber's well known critique of the rise of modernity also has an obvious influence on MacIntyre's thought. In Weber's telling of the story, the rise of capitalism represents the triumph of the "spirit of Protestantism," a kind of shorthand for political and moral individualism. Once such individualism is accepted, then social and political theory have to begin with the question of what rights or moral claims these individuals have *prior* to their being conceived in terms of their social relations; against such a backdrop, the only plausible scenario is some type of social contract among such individuals, and the reasoning that establishes the contract is ultimately instrumental reasoning. Following up on Polanyi's point about the historical embeddedness of economic relations, MacIntyre takes over Weber's point that prior to the rise of capitalism – of individualism, modernity – instrumental rationality was given its due share in the social order by a larger view of the whole that kept it in check, and that larger view was itself sustained by the social authority of religion. As the new form of economic, capitalist activity took over in Northern Europe, individualist models of social life quickly eroded the social bases of authority that religion has formerly claimed for itself. Religion gradually became socially powerless and was relegated to the realm of private belief and private inspiration. Where religion had been, individualist modes of reasoning and social organization stepped in, and in place of a conception of society as structured around common goods, the basis of legitimacy came to be the efficiency with which the rulers or the basic structure of society provided economic goods (and maintained the liberal political goods that were a condition of achieving the economic goods). Instead of the good and publicly fulfilling life, modernity substituted a promise only of increasing wealth and private satisfaction (provided one has the requisite skills to prosper in the marketplace).

It is not hard to see how elements of both Polanyi's and Weber's story coalesce in MacIntyre's own account. In both Polanyi's and Weber's narrations, modern individualism replaces something older and breaks apart what had been a unified, more or less harmonious social whole; however, in neither Weber's nor Polanyi's narration is that social whole romanticized, and in both cases, there is an appeal to an underlying human nature that explains why such a system came to replace what had preceded it. It is this more hard-edged (and itself much more modern), nonnostalgic sense of modernity that is behind Polanyi's, Weber's, and MacIntyre's criticism of the modern transformation. The great Romantic notion of an original, harmonious unity that has shattered into fragments and whose memory remains as a project for the future reconstitution of the original harmony is for the most part absent from MacIntyre's writings (although faint traces of it admittedly appear from time to time in them).

What seems to provoke MacIntyre's ire is the unspoken assumption that the point at which we have ended up – in the triumph of global capitalism and the widespread affirmation of the market as the only proper social institution to deal with our problems – is necessary (that we *had to* end up in this place in history), is the only proper or authentic expression of unalloyed human nature (that it is the only social system that fits human nature instead of being at war with it), or represents *progress* over the past. Like the progressive modernists who so much displease him, MacIntyre sees modernity as not simply a historical periodization or a "style" (to be found, for example, in art) but as an unprecedented rupture in human time, something that marks a new and fundamentally different beginning and presents fundamentally new options for human life. To see the present, however, as progress is essentially to endorse it as something against which it would only be irrational to complain since it represents an essential improvement on what came before it, and any attempt to undo it (especially in the name of any of the older goods and values that it claims to have superseded) could, if successful, only count as a loss. Indeed, MacIntyre's sustained attack on the notion that "the present is progress" has fueled that idea that he must be some kind of nostalgic premodern thinker, a kind of Irish-Scottish Heidegger, wishing, as it has been unkindly said, for all of us to return to some vanished Catholic world in which the cacophony of the modern condition is absent.

Any reasonably close reading of his work, however, belies such an interpretation. MacIntyre clearly endorses all kinds of very "modern" social movements (the women's movement, claims for minority rights, and so forth) that under no stretch of the imagination could be imagined to be the kinds of things that a return to some premodern condition would underwrite, and one does not find any hint that MacIntyre would like to turn back the clock on those developments. MacIntyre does not so much call for a return to the past as for a rethinking of what is actually required of a modern conception that could endorse the "progressive" social movements that have led to recognition of minority and women's rights while at the same time dispensing with the underlying conceptions that have seemed to be necessary to justify those rights.

MacIntyre's major criticism of modernity has to do with its underlying individualism, the practical failures of that form of individualism, and the social structures and modern philosophies that systematically distort our abilities to comprehend any real alternative to themselves. In *After Virtue*, he introduced this notion with his now-famous analogy of the loss of science: just as we can imagine a world in which various people try (fruitlessly) to revive vanished scientific practice (not understanding that what they were doing was completely different from the way science was actually done), we should understand our own modern world as having lost the practices of the virtues, such that modern attempts to speak of the virtues can only be falsifications, pale and failed attempts at doing something in a new context that only had its home in another, older, vanished context. This analogy seems to suggest that if retrieving the virtues was important, the only way to do that would be to turn back the clock. However, MacIntyre's proposal has never been for us even to attempt to move back to a premodern, nonindividualist society; he has instead suggested what alternative process would be necessary for a new, nonindividualist society of the future to take shape. If anything, MacIntyre's critique of modernity is better characterized as revolutionary than as reactionary. For MacIntyre, the rupture in human time that modernity represents is therefore to be understood as some kind of *error* that, while marking out fundamentally new possibilities for individual and collective life, unfortunately also diminishes human life and must itself be "overcome" in the way it overcame the premodern world it replaced.

"Individualism" in MacIntyre's sense has at least three aspects to it: (1) It holds that all the resources needed to generate correct moral judgments and to act on them exist within the individual; (2) It holds that any *shared* morality can therefore only come about in the form of some kind of basic *agreement* about choices, attitudes, and/or preferences; (3) It holds that social institutions can therefore only be understood as *means* through which individuals give expression to their preferences and aims, and through which they achieve their ends. (For a short statement of this view, see MacIntyre 1990b). What is wrong about such individualism, so MacIntyre seems to think, is not so much that it denies a metaphysical fact about human agents, but rather that it represents a kind of *practical failure* on their part. That is, he does not deny that we can be or become individualists in the relevantly misguided sense, nor does he claim that, for example, we must always transcendentally presuppose some kind of nonindividualism when conceiving of ourselves as individualist agents of the type he scorns. His argument is not analogous, for example, to Kant's argument that when deliberating and acting we simply cannot regard ourselves from the practical point of view as determined in our choices, and thus all determinism founders on a practical (even if not theoretical) impossibility.

Fundamental to MacIntyre's view is that one's status as an agent is bound up with one's capacities for practical reasoning, and those capacities cannot be understood outside of the social and biological contexts in which they are realized. To *have* a reason for action is something humans share with certain higher animals (dolphins are MacIntyre's examples of choice), since having a reason for action has to do with the *goods* to be obtained by those actions. A human or a dolphin can be said to have certain goods (given their natures, both biological and social), and one must understand much of their behavior as an *aiming* at those goods (at least in terms of the way the world *appears* to them – dolphins, like humans, can be mistaken about that world). Some higher animals aim at their good, and, so MacIntyre controversially also argues, can be said both to engage in social practices and to alter their behavior accordingly. To the extent that those conditions are met, such higher animals should, along with humans, be said to *have reasons* for actions (and, so MacIntyre also argues, although there is no need to elaborate here, thereby also to possess conceptual capacities) (*Dependent Rational Animals*, pp. 43–51). Whereas both humans and the higher animals may thus be said to *have* reasons for action, only humans have, however, the power of *reasoning*, since that requires the kind of sophisticated linguistic, and therefore social, capacities that apparently only humans possess. It also follows, so he thinks, that our capacities for reasoning should not be opposed to our animal natures but should be viewed as the realizations of certain natural powers within us, powers that have a less fully actualized form in higher animals and in ourselves as infants.

If agency is to be understood as a capacity both to have reasons and to reason in light of them, the most obvious question to ask is Kantian in spirit – "are there logical conditions under which any agent at all must reason, or are there conditions that set the boundaries or determine what counts as an instance of successful practical reasoning?" – and the usual answer has to do with something like impartiality or universality of reasoning. MacIntyre, however, not only denies that this is the proper question, he also thinks that it is a seriously misleading "modernist" answer. *Having* a reason is only intelligible in terms of there being some goods for an organism in terms of which it adapts its behavior. *Reasoning*, on the other hand, refers to the way in which humans (social creatures possessing language) go about moving from having reasons to regulating their behavior to altering their conceptions of what it even means to have a reason in the first place. To the extent that we think about *having* a reason and *reasoning* in any substantive way, our notions of both of them are bound up with whatever substantive goods we take to be the objects of those reasons. Thus, what counts for an agent will never be best understood abstractly as "the" good at which he or she is aiming; it will always be a *specific conception* of a good, which in turn will affect what will count as the appropriate reasoning about it, and it is only out of these more specific acts of reasoning about goods that we finally generate some more general notion of the "human good" per se.[1]

This is crucial for MacIntyre since he holds that when we change our determinate conceptions of the goods at issue, we also thereby change our determinate conceptions of what it means for each of us, individually and collectively, to *be* the kinds of historically specific agents that we are. Someone for whom "the good" is simply the satisfaction of one's desires will take the appropriate model of reasoning to be more or less instrumental and will have a very determinate conception of the kind of agent one is, what place one has in society, what kinds of things are rationally appropriate for one to suffer or endure, and so forth. Alternatively, someone who conceives of "the good" as the successful execution of a social role and as establishing one's standing in the eyes of the appropriate others will not take such instrumental reasoning as the appropriate model but will more likely have a more complex model of reasoning as deliberation about what will appropriately achieve the good and the best in such and such a type of situation in which one finds oneself. This agent will have, no doubt, a different conception of what is worth enduring, what is worth suffering, and for what one can reasonably hope than the former agent. (In fact, in the latter case, an agent engaging in such instrumental reasoning, seeking the most efficient means to look good, will be judged to have failed in the attempt at establishing individual standing.)

In MacIntyre's view, therefore, moral reality itself changes as conceptions of the good themselves change – there is neither one moral reality out there waiting for us to respond to it, nor a substantive constraint bound up with the formal conditions of constructing such a reality (as there might be for a Kantian). Rather, there are different moral realities relative to the different conceptions of the good at work in different substantive conceptions of practical reasoning. The issue therefore is not: "What is the one true moral reality (against which all the competitors are merely illusions or perversions) that has to be presupposed in all moral judgments?" but rather: "What is the moral reality that proves to be the best in some non-question-begging way in its encounters with alternative moral realities?" Leaving open the possibility that that there is a "best" moral reality that can emerge out of competing moral traditions leaves MacIntyre open also to endorse a historicized form of moral realism (a topic to which we shall return).

The answer for MacIntyre is to be found in a combination of a moral reality's coherence within itself and the way in which it promotes (or fails to promote) some kind of human flourishing. In particular, modern moral reality (the conception of goods at work in it and the appropriate structure of practical reasoning that accompanies it) has within itself, on MacIntyre's account, a deep incoherence that makes it actually damaging to the agents who live within it.

But why is such incoherence, if it really is there, so damaging? What is so bad about living with such incoherence? (Is fear of contradiction the hobgoblin of small minds?) For MacIntyre, what is at stake is not just any old set of contradictions (such as might be found in the "paradox of the preface" and similar conundrums) but an incoherence, if not contradiction, in the structure of agents' practical reasoning such that they find themselves pursuing certain types of goods in ways that undermine their ability ever to achieve those goods fully or to achieve them at all. The kind of incoherence at stake has to do with the basic premises of practical reasoning, and that incoherence fundamentally alienates agents from themselves, from nature, and from each other. (There is no doubt a not accidental resemblance to the young Marx's theory in play here.)

A form of practical reasoning undermines itself when the conditions for its success make it impossible for it to fully succeed. To see this is to go to the heart of MacIntyre's social-practice theory of rationality and to why he thinks that such incoherence is a feature of modernity and not just an individual failure to hold fast to the right norms. If one contrasts this with a kind of simple Kantian conception of holding oneself to norms, one can see MacIntyre's point. (I will call this a simple form of Kantianism in order to sidestep all the intricate textual and philosophical issues about whether this "really is" Kant, or whether, even if it is, there is a better reading of Kant that avoids these errors.) For the simple Kantian, the source of such incoherence could only lie in the agents themselves: One who imposes the rules for behavior on oneself can alone can be responsible for such incoherence and can remove it; for the simple Kantian, such incoherence from the social point of view at best reveals something about lacks in the structure of coordination among independent agents, or perhaps problems about freeriders and the like, and at worst simply points to some deep fact such as "radical evil" at work in human nature (the propensity to substitute self-interest for the moral law).

In MacIntyre's social-practice conception of rationality, however, there can be no such thing as the simple Kantian's self-imposition of the law. MacIntyre does not of course deny that there can be individual failure to live up to the demands of morality; he claims only that certain types of failure are not best construed as individual failings but as social breakdowns elicited by deep contradictions within that way of life. Reasoning is always carried out in terms of shared, socially established standards and in light of what he calls a "tradition" (a more or less technical term for him, meaning an inquiry directed toward a truth independent of the inquiring mind, whose normative standards are developed over time in light of the problems, anomalies, and clashes with other such traditions that appear in its history). MacIntyre's point about the social nature of rationality follow some familiar post-Hegelian, post-Wittgensteinian lines of thought: No sense can be given to the notion of a private language (of words whose meanings consist in links to private mental states known only to their possessor) or of a kind of rule following that is carried out entirely by one's own individual private apprehensions of what the rule requires since, in both cases, the distinction between really following the rule and only thinking that one was following the rule would be obliterated and with that, all notion of rule following and intelligible action itself would vanish. Instead, any adequate conception of (particularly practical) reasoning will have to be substantive and not merely formal in character.

Practical reasoning is inherently substantive since it cannot even be identified without reference to the goods it seeks to realize. The very notion of *having* a reason for action is completely dependent on the notion of there being a good that is to be realized or obtained in the action (*Dependent Rational Animals*, p. 24). *Having* a reason is thus tied up with the notion of *being* an organism (at least of a certain type) that aims at its own good as it registers it, engages in social practices, and alters its behavior in light of those practices. With humans, there are clearly goods that can only be realized in an appropriate social setting – for example, that of a satisfying career – and the modes of practical reasoning must take into account what is necessary for the realization of those goods, particularly what kinds of suppression or reeducation of desire are necessary if such goods are to be achieved. It involves MacIntyre's well-known view that a certain type of character, a possession of a certain set of *virtues*, is necessary for the realization of these goods. For MacIntyre, there cannot be any simple Kantian priority of practical reason (or a purely formal conception of practical reason) from which substantive goods are then inferred (as in fact it looks like Kant himself is doing in the *Metaphysics of Morals*, where he deduces the two obligatory ends of benevolence and self-perfection from the unconditionally binding practical law).

If certain types of goods are only possible in some forms of social relationships and not in others, then it makes all the difference as to what those relationships might be. In that connection, it is worth noting how, in all of MacIntyre's writings, the themes of dependence and independence are always present and always coupled, although they sometimes function only in the background. A key element of all of his writings has to do with the necessity of the formation and sustenance of the virtues, which requires us to acknowledge our dependence on others and on certain types of social practices and institutions to make acquisition and sustenance of the virtues possible. These types of dependency can take different forms, but they are not ultimately malleable, and it seems that some forms of social life can clearly *distort* the ways in which those dependencies are recognized and responded to – distort them in the sense that they make us blind in our practical reasoning to these dependencies or to their ineluctability.

The two lenses through which MacIntyre views these problems – a language of realism, of a *distortion* of the true way in which we should view moral reality, and a language of constructivism, as a failure to construct the rules and principles by which we live in a rational manner – points to a fundamental element, if not tension, in his thought, which links him with Kant and the other German idealists in ways he himself often downplays. His realism (moral and otherwise) is quite apparent in all his writings and is distinctly emphasized in *Whose Justice? Which Rationality?*, where he rejects all notions of truth as "warranted assertability" in favor of a more realist, Thomistic (in a reinterpreted sense) concept of truth.[2] However, as even the title of *Whose Justice? Which Rationality?* already indicates, he also subscribes to some kind of historicist view of moral reality in light of which moral reality itself changes over time. What distinguishes MacIntyre's views from what looks like the relativism implicit in such historicism is his notion of rationality, that only those moral realities that can be rationally defended are suitable and are livable. He thinks, that is, that only in a *rationally defensible* moral reality can we actually *be* the kinds of agents who flourish in the proper ways, and that, ultimately, irrational modes of social and moral reality inflict so many psychological wounds on their members that they can only be sustained both by the construction of elaborate ideologies that justify the suffering imposed as historically or socially necessary and by sustaining practices and institutions that, although inimical to the reigning social practice, are necessary for its sustenance (as soothing the wounds that are otherwise inflicted or preventing the entire social order from undermining itself by the force of its irrationality and unlivability) (see MacIntyre 1990b). To do the latter – keep alive the matters that the practice undermines but without which the practice could not survive – the ideologies in turn have to function so as to distort or even conceal what is actually going on.

MacIntyre's notion of "moral error" as brought on by insufficient social practice thus puts him disturbingly close to his bête noire, Kantianism. The Kantian position, quite generally, is that "goodness" or "value" is not found in the world but is instead legislated or constructed by human agents, and the condition under which all such legislation must fall is that of rational justifiability. Objective principles of morality – and thus a robust doctrine of moral error – are possible because and only because of this constraint. What separates MacIntyre from Kant is MacIntyre's semi-Hegelian rejection of the more specifically Kantian notion of rational justifiability in favor of the priority of a more substantive notion of reason: It is only in light of our conception of specific types of goods that we form notions of having reasons and reasoning correctly, and those conceptions of goods themselves have a history and are not simply "seen" by us or follow directly from some very general conception of formal reasoning.

Because of this, MacIntyre is led to construct his notion of "tradition" and of "tradition-constituted inquiry" to highlight just why he thinks Kantianism is not the position toward which he is pushed. That is, if moral error is to be accounted for in terms of a failure to justify one's actions, then we need a conception of reason and rational justifiability that is capable of showing that some types of practical judgments are true (or are in error), but which does not claim that there is only one possible perspective on such justification. That requires a historicized conception of rational justification, which, in MacIntyre's rendering, has to do with the way in which one tradition of inquiry can resolve anomalies found in another that the other could not in its own terms resolve.[3] That is, it has to be the case that inadequate moral realities eventually can be shown to be insufficient in light of the irrationality of the way that such moral realities make goods available and present for their participants (and the substantive modes of practical reasoning that attach to such goods) in comparison to some other way of life (and, consequently, way of reasoning). It need not be the case that inadequate and wounding ways of living *undermine themselves* and thus come to require something different from themselves (although in principle they may be so intolerable as to collapse under their own weight); rather, when confronted with an alternative "tradition" or way of life that explains to them why their agents inflict such psychological wounds on themselves and are blind to other kinds of goods, they find ultimately that the alternative being presented is superior to the way in which they had been living to that point.

For MacIntyre as much as for the Kantians, an agent is motivated by what he takes to be good *reasons* for action. The "motivational force" of the existing moral reality has to do with the kinds of reasons that are available to the agents within that set of social relationships and practices. Since modern social relationships are structured around individualist self-understandings, modern people, so MacIntyre's story goes, find that the major motivating reasons for them are either matters of bargaining for rational self-interest or matters having to do with emotional sympathies or antipathies. Yet none of these modes of reasoning (none of the powerful modern sources of motivation) can dispense with nonmodern reasons for action having to do with acknowledged and unacknowledged dependencies; the way of life in which social relationships are based either on bargaining or sympathies is itself unsustainable unless there are relationships holding the whole together, relationships which themselves are neither matters open to bargaining nor matters reducible to blind sentiments.

Yet in all this, MacIntyre's retains his acceptance of the idea that modernity represents something qualitatively different, a crucial rupture in human history, and it is thus crucial for him to show that modern liberal individualism is not necessary, that it is at best only one tradition among many, and thus can itself be defeated by a demonstration of its inherent irrationality and of the existence of a live alternative that is free from those irrationalities.

MacIntyre thus has as his target something like Hegel's conception of the "rationality of the actual," namely by showing that the motivational force of the "actual," of the existing moral reality, is fundamentally irrational, that there is no way in principle to reorder it so that it is rational, and that the traditions that it claims to have already defeated are in fact still alive.

The notion of defeated traditions is crucial for MacIntyre to make his claim, since he clearly does not claim that all of modernity is to be discarded. (He does not, as for example Heidegger sometimes seems to do, throw modern science into the same wicker as modern capitalism, and he clearly has no sympathy to those who bemoan the rise of civil rights for minorities and oppressed peoples; nor does he see all of modern culture as an expression of some kind of vague "technocracy," however much he derides the dominance of instrumental reasoning in the culture at large.) Pre-Galilean and pre-Newtonian science, for example, is clearly a defeated tradition. By virtue of having been decisively defeated by the force of better reason, it is no longer on the cultural agenda, and any attempts to revive such science are doomed. Likewise, MacIntyre would hold that all the various forms of premodern and early-modern slavery are equally off the political and cultural agenda. Even if clever scholarship can find ways to reinterpret Aristotle's thoughts on slavery so as to make some sense of them in a modern context, still there can be no sense in trying to revive slavery per se.

Yet at least two major problems remain if MacIntyre is willing to accept that what he views as "defeated traditions" are really defeated: first, there is the problem of whether the notion of a "tradition" (which is further specified as a "tradition of inquiry") is itself adequate and not too intellectualistic to provide an account of the kinds of existential breakdowns of ways of life consistent with the rest of his thought; and second, there is the question of whether he is committed to the possibility of "defeating" modernity in a way that is itself undercut by his own arguments. The second of these is the more crucial consideration. On the one hand, MacIntyre sees modern culture as the outcome of a series of social and economic forces that have resulted in a mode of practical reasoning that itself produces a deficient moral reality for the participants of modern moral life – deficient in the sense of being irrational, an irrationality that leaves in its wake profound alienation and wounded psyches. On the other hand, he wants to see the development of modernity as a completely contingent, even irrational series of events, whose justification was lacking at the time and whose adequate justification has not since appeared. On MacIntyre's account, that modern tradition – with its attendant individualism – has been defeated in the sense that all the arguments in its favor can be and have been shown to be deficient, although it is clear that, in any cultural or political sense, it not only has *not* been defeated, it is apparently even stronger than ever.

However, there are powerful arguments in MacIntyre's own work for concluding that the kind of fragmented modernity he decries simply cannot be defeated in the way that much of his work suggests it can. The very things he accepts – the rise of modern science, the rejection on grounds of justice of the exclusion of oppressed peoples from power – are the kinds of matters that underwrite the impossibility of forging the kind of authoritative consensus he often seems to advocate. MacIntyre wants to see social relationships as contingent and our own standards of reasoning as contingent; yet he also wants to understand the moral reality brought about by those relationships as necessitating some attempt at justification of them. In that context, the problem of the existence of a "natural" standard of practical reasoning – taking "natural" here in its eighteenth-century sense as embodying those standards that are "fixed" in contrast with the variable standards of "positive" law – appears just as acute for MacIntyre, who eschews appeal to pre-Galilean conceptions of nature, as it is for the Kantians who accept the same thing. It may well be that our rational capacities should be seen as the realization of natural powers and not as something so far different from them that they belong to a different order of being (or have to be seen as manifestations of a wholly different type of substance). But it still is not the case that nature sets the normative standards of practical reasoning or that practical reasoning is only a *perfection* of some latency already there in nature. (Some such argument may be implicit in the *Naturphilosophie* of metaphysical idealists such as Schelling, but that is another story.) Practical reasoning arises against the background of natural life, but its norms are not determined by that background; it is social, and therefore, in Hegel's sense, a "negation" of nature, a departure from the regularities of nature, such that it becomes in human life a "second" nature.[4]

Nor can MacIntyre accept the quasi-organic notion that competing conceptions of rationality simply "fit" their times, grow with them, and live and die with them. For him, it is crucial not to understand reasons as simply having a hold on people and "fitting" them like some evolving parasitic organism; rather, it is crucial to understand the *justifiability* of the hold that they have, the way in which agents' basic orientation is something that makes up what they are, and in his work the claim is always right under the surface that failure of rationality, failure to collectively hold ourselves to certain norms, is what undermines ways of life. If so, then the specifically *modern* issue of self-determination – the issue first explicitly raised by Kant, even if prefigured mightily in Rousseau – and the conditions under which such collective and individual self-determination is possible, are as much problems for MacIntyre as they are for Kant and all the post-Kantians. Appealing to natural goods will not help matters here, even if clarification of the centrality of our natural dependencies and our continuity with the animal world (in contrast both to classical dualism and contemporary single-minded naturalism) is brought front and center, as MacIntyre himself so effectively does. The Reformation did not happen because people failed to reason through things correctly; the emerging sense of the individual, already making its first fledgling appearances in Giotto's frescoes with their more realistic and individually realized faces, were already pointing to the way in which the hold of the medieval church – that is, its capacity to provide the binding reasons for collective life – was under pressure from the very forces that Christian culture had set in motion. The very things that MacIntyre decries – the excessive individualism of modern life and the way in which its social institutions and market society shape a moral reality centered around the satisfaction of sovereign individual desire – themselves could not take place until a Christian conception of equality before God had come to be realized as the only alternative to the collapse of the slave-owning societies of antiquity. The basic norm behind the moral reality in which rational choice theory (with its attendant freerider and prisoner's dilemma problems) really *is* one of the going options is one in which the individual agent can find no reason to subordinate his desires to some authority other than his own self-interest, and that presupposes the breakdown of the kind of hierarchical set of social relationships to which people had formerly had so much allegiance. Indeed, the Christian appeal to the equality of all before God is both an expression of and a response to the collapse of the binding power of natural mastery, of the existence of some in the world to whom others must simply submit their will because nature has decreed some to be better than others. That Christian critique of the ancient world not only made it *possible* for individuals to see themselves as being intrinsically neither master nor slave, but actually came to *require* it. Unless there is some way of resurrecting Christianity as the binding force in modern life (and thereby denying the pluralism that MacIntyre otherwise so eloquently defends), the dilemmas of rational choice theory are deeply written into modern moral reality. (It is worth noting, though, that although MacIntyre defends pluralism, he never endorses liberalism as the best account of that modern form of pluralism.[5])

Indeed, if there are no natural masters and no natural slaves, then the Kantian way of framing the issue becomes all the more compelling: Failing an appeal to nature, we can only appeal to our own reason as that to which we must subordinate our wills, but failing a metaphysical conception of reason, we must understand rationality as expressing our own spontaneity, as being an activity that in its normative dimension is underdetermined (if not fully undetermined) by nature. In that respect, both Kant and MacIntyre begin from the same point. Kant's critique of all traditional, supersensible metaphysics was supposed to put aside once and for all any appeal to natural goods via a conception of some kind of perfection of human nature (and, so it seems, MacIntyre himself seems implicitly to accept the basic premises of the Kantian critique of traditional metaphysics).

What sets MacIntyre apart from Kant is his insistence that such practical reasoning cannot begin in a vacuum but must instead begin with norms that, viewed from the standpoint of embodied reasoning agents, are not matters of *legislation* at all but instead furnish the substantive conditions of all further self-legislation. In that respect, MacIntyre is as far as he could be from Kant and his followers who insist on a fundamental independence for practical reason, an ability to step outside of all traditions and to evaluate them from a standpoint not indebted to any tradition at all. For practical reason to function as a *reason* and not as something that simply "fits" into the working of the organism, it must incorporate a set of commitments that themselves depend on a collectively shared form of life. Such a background, prereflective shared form of life is necessary to orient people; in living out one's life, one is oriented to taken-for-granted notions of the goods of that form of life – what we have called the "moral reality" of that form of life – that in turn structure one's practical reasoning as a kind of skill, a know-how in making one's way around in that life. There is and can be, however, no sense to the notion of any basic good or presupposition in a form of life being immune to criticism, and even though many things must be taken for granted in any way of life, we always simply "find" ourselves in a historical community for whom some things simply "are", at least from our point of view on them, goods.

To make that same point, Hegel cited Antigone's line about ethical norms – "Not now, nor yesterday's, they always live/and no one knows from whence they came"[6] – as expressing the experience of those basic authoritative norms as matters to which we must simply keep faith, that are not optional for us. Hegel goes on in that passage to elaborate what that experientially means: "They are. If they are supposed to be legitimated through my insight, then I have already set their unwavering being-in-itself in motion and regard them as something that, for me, perhaps might be true and perhaps might not be true." That is, they have to be binding on us even if ultimately they are not themselves immune to historical breakdown. We must adopt a stance of moral *realism* about those norms even as we insist on their *relativity* to what historically counts as a reason for us, and on their consequent revisability.

MacIntyre, like Hegel, rejects a conception of this kind of moral realism as being only an "as-if" realism, something that, while it must "appear" to us as "not now, nor yesterday's, they always live," is in fact only a contingent creation by human beings pursuing other contingent ends. Both MacIntyre and Hegel follow Kant's lead in rejecting the idea that being a moral realist in this sense either requires reducing moral norms to something more respectable to contemporary naturalists or requires positing Platonic idealities to which our statements about them correspond. To be a realist in this sense is only to claim that we can show that there are good reasons for doing one thing as opposed to another, and that requires us to work out the conception of what counts as a good reason. If we can show that there is a genuinely good reason to do something, that is enough to claim a realism about those goods. However, like Hegel, MacIntyre also is deeply suspicious that there is a single conception of reason that spans all historical periods and all civilizations that is substantive enough to do all the work of showing us what counts as a "good" reason. Practical reasons are dependent on our conceptions of substantive goods, and no generalized notion of reason detached from all social and historical context will be weighty enough to do the heavy lifting that so many modern philosophers have required of it.

There is also no sense in MacIntyre, as there is in many other critics of modernity and antimodernists, that there is simply some kind of irresolvable, tragic conflict in human nature (between, for example, the passions and intellect, or between attempts to hold fast to rules while not being able to abide by them) that blocks any *rational* answer to social problems. MacIntyre, like Hegel, seems at least to hold out for the possibility for a reconciliation – a *Versöhnung* in Hegel's rather charged theological imagery – among citizens of the modern world that is based on reason and not on something else such as tradition or revelation. Although this might seem to be at odds with MacIntyre's well-known appeal to the "authority of tradition" in *After Virtue*, nonetheless even there the "authority of tradition" is invoked in order to provide underpinnings for the social-practice account of rationality that is central to the account of the virtues in that work. If we are to avoid the difficulties (both conceptual and practical) in a conception of reason that has to claim that it starts from nowhere (as if we always had to deliberate on the principles of deliberation, ad infinitum, before we could ever reason), then we need an account of how we always start from somewhere, particularly from some historically located point, and an account of how we could ever come to be in a position whereby we could rationally revise those standards. (MacIntyre by and large avoids the over-intellectualistic bent of neo-Kantian attempts to provide some kind of general and relatively formal test for rational permissibility with his own more existential and practice-based account of why certain conceptions of practical reason turn out to be unlivable.)

Central to MacIntyre's account of practical reason, as we have seen, is the refusal to separate it into some rock-bottom distinction of "form" and "content" and to argue instead that our conceptions of what counts as good reasoning is linked to our conceptions of those substantive goods about which we are reasoning. In that light, the appeal to the "authority of tradition" is necessary since it is only in certain social relationships and by building and sustaining certain forms of character that we are able to reason well at all. However, MacIntyre does not subscribe to an account of social life that holds that "the authority of tradition" is the final, nonrevisable stopping point at which all questioning must stop and that citizens can at best reconcile themselves with each other – understand what has to be endured, hoped for, and sacrificed – only when they all submit to the "authority of tradition" even where there can be no rational account of why that tradition could or should hold their allegiance. The "authority of tradition" is itself subject to assessment by reason, even if the capacities for good reason are not capacities that can be exercised outside of some appeal to such authority.

MacIntyre's own moral *realism* therefore has to make room for the other idea implicit in his view that *moral reality* can itself come to change as social practices change and the substantive goods that are part and parcel of our practical reasoning therefore change. Thus, there are true and false judgments to be made within changeable moral realities; the judgments made within one such moral reality are incommensurable with judgments made in the other; and some moral realities can be shown to be more rational than others (and hence better as offering more sustainable lives) by virtue of the way in which they emerge for MacIntyre as answering the problems raised in some other failed tradition.

MacIntyre's own commitment to the primacy of practical reason (along with his rejection of Kantian dualisms about form and content in reasoning) puts him squarely into the post-Kantian camp, however Aristotelian and Thomistic he might otherwise wish to be, and that makes it difficult to see just how he could think that that modernity itself could be defeated in the way he apparently thinks it can. For example, he thinks that his social-practice conception of reason is not simply one option among many but has itself come to be required of us by virtue of the way in which the social realities of our time have "defeated" its immediate competitors, such as the nineteenth-century encyclopedic version of rationality discussed in *Three Rival Versions of Moral Enquiry: Encyclopaedia, Genealogy, and Tradition*. In that book, MacIntyre argued that by virtue of the Victorians understanding of their *particular* conception of rationality as universal, they necessarily put themselves in the position of being unable to treat other competing versions in their own terms, and thus were able only to redescribe their own competitors (particularly those in non-European cultures) as merely failed versions of themselves, and to understand themselves as markers of "progress" beyond the superstitions of the European past and the contemporary non-European world (*Three Rival Versions*, pp. 21–22). The breakdown of that encyclopedic project had to do with the way in which their assumption of a single, substantive rationality to which all educated persons would obviously consent fell apart under the pressure of both Nietzschean criticism and the crises brought about by the Great War, which elicited in turn a dark skepticism about the European way of life as embodying inevitable progress in comparison with all others (*Three Rival Versions*, pp. 23–24).

Against that, MacIntyre has famously argued for a Thomist understanding of the failure of modern morality (the successor to and continuation of the encyclopedic project) as being due to the fact that it is only a set of "fragmentary survivals posing problems that cannot fail to be insoluble so long as they are not restored to their places in those wholes from which they took their character as parts" (*Three Rival Versions*, p. 192). Given MacIntyre's own social-practice account of reason, for his argument against modernity to work and for Thomism to defeat modernity the social wholes that are necessary for Thomist reasoning to be successful would themselves have to be reconstituted – the medieval way of life would have to be revived – and there is simply no reason to think that is possible. For it to be possible, the kind of pluralism that gives rise to the problems of incommensurability would itself have to be overcome, and everything MacIntyre says seems to constitute an argument to the effect that it cannot, that pluralism is a necessary, even rationally required component of the modern world.[7]

The very primacy that he gives to reason and his emphasis on changeable moral reality is itself the result of the rupture in human time that he otherwise wishes to deplore, and the very conception of the primacy of practical reason itself as forming the basis by which moral reality is constituted is itself the result of the breakdown of those earlier medieval wholes; medieval agents did not so much lose an argument with the moderns as they came to discover that they simply could no longer *be* those types of people any more – indeed, for all the kinds of reasons that MacIntyre himself lays out.

MacIntyre is thus left with a conception of modernity that is definitely not encyclopedic but is nonetheless inevitably "negative" in character. Central to all of MacIntyre's arguments about the incommensurability of fundamentally different viewpoints – nicely captured in the title of his book, *Whose Justice? Which Rationality*? – is a form of what Hegelians would call modern self-consciousness, namely the very modern suspicion that what we have taken as fixed and eternal is perhaps only the posit of a contingent, even arbitrary viewpoint, or perhaps only the expression of some hidden power or interest. That view – against which the Victorian encyclopedic view is at best a holding maneuver, an attempt to affirm an industrial and colonialist self-understanding as resting on eternally fixed norms – itself provokes the kind of eternal dissatisfaction with itself that is most fundamentally characteristic of modernity, a capacity to continually undermine itself in light of the failure of its own standards of rationality to prove themselves free of contingency and interest.

MacIntyre shares with both Hegel and Wittgenstein the view that definitive of the modern standpoint is the double awareness of the historical and social *contingency* of all our points of view and the necessity to provide *justifications* of those points of view, which itself forms the basic, underlying tension in all modern life and culture. Hegel metaphorically described this as the eternal production of the opposition of subjective and objective points of view and their eternal reconciliation – the recognition of the contingency of our norms and the equal necessity to justify them – a tension which Robert Pippin has encapsulated as "unending modernity."[8] There is no reason to think that there is anything on the horizon other than what MacIntyre has described as the clash of incommensurable viewpoints and the necessity to adopt standards of justification that take that clash into consideration – and that just *is* modernity, something radical, something that cannot be overcome and that is therefore "absolute."[9]

This of course replaces a morality and politics of perfection with one of self-determination, but it cannot see this self-determination as free-floating, purely spontaneous, and able to generate its principles autonomously out of itself. Instead, it is a historically circumscribed form of self-determination. Moral and political action and reflection always begins in a particular, historical situation, and what is always "given" to us is not some set of nondefeasible norms or fixed standards of rationality but only the inherited social and historical situation in which we find ourselves. We always begin, that is, within a contingently formed point of view, and to be a responsible *modern* ethical agent requires acknowledgment of that contingency, a recognition that what we take as the exigencies of the world – "the way the world is" – might themselves be only expressions of some particular interest or serving the goals of some particular, contingent powers. What MacIntyre stresses (and what links him with the post-Kantians) is the failure of a purely individualist understanding of our agency to make sense of that historical embeddedness. His book, *Dependent Rational Animals: Why Human Beings Need the Virtues*, brings out quite clearly his emphasis on the acknowledgment of mutual dependency as opposed to the fantasy, perhaps infantile in origin, of complete and utter independence in moral reasoning. Only through a properly *structured* set of mutual *dependencies* can we even become *independent* practical reasoners at all.[10] The truly vexatious side of modern market society for MacIntyre seems to be the way in which its ideal of and celebration of the sovereign consumer and the independent citizen effectively mask the layers of dependencies that are necessary for such attempts at individualism even to get going. Modern "individualist" society thus effectively undermines itself, having to preserve the structures of mutual dependency against which it then rebels and that, from the standpoint of individualist modernism's self-understanding, can only appear as irrational (instead of being seen as what they are, the condition of independent practical reasoning itself).

MacIntyre's critique of modernity is thus a critique from within modernity itself, even though it is often clothed as a rejection of the modern world, a call for a lost medieval and Thomist past. On his own terms, modernity represents a radical break with the past, and on his own terms, it is not something to be overcome in a new epoch. A "new Saint Benedict" would be a *modern* Saint Benedict, preserving the virtues appropriate to an individualist way of life by fostering the social structures that make our proper mutual dependencies apparent and rational, which would abolish the structures of exploitation that currently pervade the falsely understood and comprehended modern world. If he in fact accomplished that task, he would do it not as a *Saint* Benedict at all but only a Mr. or Ms. Benedict, an equal citizen of a modern, constitutionalist political order. Indeed, MacIntyre's emphasis on the necessity of acknowledging contingency and the incommensurability of points of view, the necessity of preserving a notion of truth that is not reducible to "warranted assertability" (not relative, that is, to particular points of view), and the necessity of justifying ourselves to each other in order to hold ourselves mutually to norms that are livable and rational, make him a modernist per excellence – much more so than those who insist on a noncontingent, nonperspectival notion of reason and a context-free celebration of science, and much, much more so than those who vapidly insist on the relativity of everything.

Notes

1. This seems to be the point of the question asked in the title of *Whose Justice? Which Rationality?* MacIntyre makes it clear that this does not rule out any more general conception of the good. For example, in *Dependent Rational Animals* (p. 67), MacIntyre says:

   > We therefore need to distinguish between what it is that makes certain goods goods and goods to be valued for their own sake from what it is that makes it good for this particular individual or this particular society in this particular situation to make them objects of her or his or their effective practical regard. And our judgments about how it is best for an individual or a community to order the goods in their lives exemplify this third type of ascription, one whereby we judge unconditionally about what it is best for individuals or groups to be or do or have not only *qua* agents engaged in this or that form of activity in this or that role or roles, but also *qua* human being. It is these judgments that are judgments about human flourishing.

   Nonetheless, even when we begin from a premise such as "such and such is unqualifiedly the good and the best," our reasoning cannot reach its conclusion unless it is also mediated by deliberation on things like "what means will achieve the good and the best in the type of situation in which I find myself?"
2. *Whose Justice?*, pp. 356–357:

   > The mind is adequate to its objects insofar as the expectations which it frames on the basis of these activities are not liable to disappointment and the remembering which it engages in enables it to return to and recover what it had encountered previously, whether the objects themselves are still present or not . . . One of the great originating insights of tradition-constituted inquiries is that false beliefs and false judgments represent a failure of the mind, not of its objects. It is the mind which stands in need of correction. So the most primitive conception of truth is of the manifestness of the objects which present themselves to mind; and it is when mind fails to re-present that manifestness that falsity, the inadequacy of mind to its objects, appears.

   See also *Three Rival Versions*, pp. 121–122.
3. See *Three Rival Versions*:

   > The rational superiority of that tradition to rival traditions is held to reside in its capacity not only for identifying and characterizing the limitations

> and failures of that rival tradition as judged by that rival tradition's own standards, limitations and failures which that rival tradition itself lacks the resources to explain or understand, but also for explaining and understanding those limitations and failures in some tolerably precise way. Moreover it must be the case that the rival tradition lacks the capacity similarly to identify, characterize, and explain limitations and failures of the Aristotelian-Thomistic tradition. (p. 181)

4. On the one hand, since MacIntyre clearly subscribes to some version of natural law, there is a very extended sense in which he believes that nature, suitably described, does in fact set the law for us, and, as he makes it clear in *Dependent Rational Animals*, he thinks our rational capacities should be counted as realizations of a human *nature*. But even there he still qualifies those capacities as social and thus not as something to be developed out of some account merely of our *biological* nature. MacIntyre's endorsement of natural law therefore turns on how much weight is to be put on the notion of our rational, social natures as realizations of our more directly biological nature.
5. There are those who find it odd even to claim that MacIntyre *defends* pluralism, but they overlook the many passages in which he does so. For example, in the concluding chapter of *Three Rival Versions*, he argues against Allen Bloom's and William Bennett's claims for reinstituting a "great books" program since until the problem of how to *read* those books has been resolved, "such lists do not rise to the status of a concrete proposal" (p. 228). He adds that they

> often defend it as a way of restoring to us and to our students what they speak of as *our* cultural tradition; but we are in fact the inheritors . . . of a number of rival and incompatible traditions and there is no way of either selecting a list of books to be read or advancing a determinate account of how they are to be read . . . which does not involve taking a partisan stand in the conflict of traditions.

In such a pluralist society, the appropriate role of the university is to be a "place of constrained disagreement, of imposed participation in conflict, in which a central responsibility of higher education would be to initiate students into conflict." MacIntyre does believe that a unified consensus on what is good is a necessary condition of a fully flourishing social life, but he also claims in various places that *imposing* such unity on the heterogeneity of modern life would not itself be a good:

> [T]he shared public goods of the modern nation-sate are not the common goods of a genuine nation-wide community and, when the nation-state masquerades as the guardian of such a common good, the outcome is bound to be either ludicrous or disastrous or both . . . In a modern, large-scale nation-state no such collectivity is possible and the pretense that it is is always an ideological disguise for sinister realities. (*Dependent Rational Animals*, p. 132)

6. Hegel 1988, p. 286: "Sie sind. Wenn sie sich meiner Einsicht legitimieren sollen, so habe ich schon ihr unwankendes Ansichsein bewegt, und betrachte sie als etwas, das vielleicht wahr, vielleicht auch nicht wahr für mich sei."

7. There are some other important tendencies in MacIntyre's thought that seem to involve restricting Aristotelian-Thomist reasoning to being appropriate only to the way of life of small communities, such that: something like it always tends to emerge whenever a small enough community with the requisite consensus on human flourishing comes to be; the realm of "empire" therefore has been and will continue to be inimical to such "communal" Thomism; and such reasoning is a realization of our natural powers that nonetheless point us beyond ourselves toward our dependencies on a power greater than us, and that, when realized, lead us to acknowledge our own lack of self-sufficiency. However, this view (if it is indeed part of MacIntyre's view) rests on a much less historicist thesis than does much of the rest of MacIntyre's thought, since it claims in effect that Aristotelian-Thomist reasoning naturally grows out of a certain basic human reality instead of growing out of a certain very determinate historical and social practice. Thus the question is whether Thomism is tied to the practices that gave rise to it, or whether it can make a more universalistic claim to being the appropriate mode of reasoning of all those small communities that have escaped corruption by the temptations of empire.
8. See Hegel 1971b, pp. 459–460:

   > Pure thought has progressed to the opposition of the subjective and objective; and the true reconciliation is the insight that this opposition, pushed to its absolute peak, dissolves itself, that in itself, as Schelling says, the oppositions are identical, and not only in themselves but rather that eternal life is this, to eternally produce opposition and eternally to reconcile it.

   On "unending modernity," see Pippin 1991 (the phrase "unending modernity" is Pippin's).
9. In that context, it is significant that Hegel himself characterized "absolute knowing" as just the comprehension of the necessity of that fundamental, nondefeasible tension in modern life. See Hegel 1971b, p. 460: "*Absolute knowing* is knowing the opposition within the unity and the unity within the opposition; and science (*Wissenschaft*) is knowing this unity in its whole development through itself."
10. The notion of structured dependencies is also a major theme in Rousseau. See Neuhouser 1993, pp. 363–395. A brilliant elaboration of the relatedness and the ineluctability of these paired notions of dependence and independence is to be found in Pippin 2000.

Bibliography

This bibliography consists of four sections. The first section includes all books authored or edited by MacIntyre. The second section includes all of the articles by MacIntyre cited in this book as well as a number of his other more important papers. The third section is a selected bibliography of works about MacIntyre, and the fourth section includes other works cited in this volume.

All books authored or edited by MacIntyre are cited in this volume by abbreviated title; all other works are cited by the author's last name and the year of publication. Second and later editions are cited by the year of publication of the first edition; the year of publication of the cited edition is given in brackets.

1. Books Authored or Edited by MacIntyre

1951. *The Significance of Moral Judgments*. M.A. Thesis, University of Manchester. Unpublished. Cited as *Significance of Moral Judgments*.

1953. *Marxism: An Interpretation*. SCM Press. Cited as *Marxism: An Interpretation*.

1955. *New Essays in Philosophical Theology* (edited, with Antony Flew). Macmillan. Cited as *New Essays*.

1957. *Metaphysical Beliefs: Three Essays* (with Stephen Toulmin and Ronald W. Hepburn). SCM Press. Cited as *Metaphysical Beliefs*.

1958. *The Unconscious: A Conceptual Analysis*. Routledge and Kegan Paul. Cited as *Unconscious*.

1959. *Difficulties in Christian Belief*. SCM Press.

1965. *Hume's Ethical Writings* (edited). Collier.

1966. *A Short History of Ethics*. Macmillan. Cited as *Short History*.

1967. *Secularization and Moral Change*. Oxford University Press.

1968. *Marxism and Christianity*. Schocken. Cited as *Marxism and Christianity*.

1970. *Herbert Marcuse: An Exposition and a Polemic*. Viking.

1971. *Against the Self-Images of the Age*. University of Notre Dame Press. Cited as *Self-Images*.

1972. *Hegel: A Collection of Critical Essays* (edited). Anchor. Cited as *Hegel*.

1981 [1984]. *After Virtue: A Study in Moral Theory*. 2nd ed. University of Notre Dame Press. Cited as *After Virtue*.

1983. *Revisions: Changing Perspectives in Moral Philosophy* (edited with Stanley Hauerwas). University of Notre Dame Press. Cited as *Revisions*.

1988. *Whose Justice? Which Rationality?* University of Notre Dame Press. Cited as *Whose Justice?*.

1990. *First Principles, Final Ends, and Contemporary Philosophical Issues*. Marquette University Press. Cited as *First Principles*.

1990. *Three Rival Versions of Moral Enquiry: Encyclopaedia, Genealogy, and Tradition*. University of Notre Dame Press. Cited as *Three Rival Versions*.

1998. *The MacIntyre Reader*, ed. Kelvin Knight. University of Notre Dame Press. Cited as *MacIntyre Reader*.

1999. *Dependent Rational Animals: Why Human Beings Need the Virtues*. Open Court. Cited as *Dependent Rational Animals*.

2. Articles and Reviews by MacIntyre

1950. "Analogy in Metaphysics." *Downside Review* 69, pp. 45–61.

1955a. "Cause and Cure in Psychotherapy." *Proceedings of the Aristotelian Society* 29 (supplement), pp. 43–58.

1955b. "The Nature and Destiny of Man: Getting the Question Clear." *Modern Churchman* 45, pp. 171–176.

1955c. "A Note on Immortality." *Mind* 64, pp. 396–399.

1955d. "Visions." In *New Essays*, pp. 254–260.

1956. "Marxist Tracts." *Philosophical Quarterly* 6, pp. 366–370.

1957a. "Determinism." *Mind* 66, pp. 28–41.

1957b. "The Logical Status of Religious Beliefs." In *Metaphysical Beliefs*, pp. 157–201.

1957c. "What Morality Is Not." *Philosophy* 32, pp. 325–335. Cited to reprinted version in *Self-Images*, pp. 96–108.

1958. "Notes from the Moral Wilderness I." *New Reasoner* 7, pp. 90–100. Cited to reprinted version in *MacIntyre Reader*, pp. 31–40.

1959a. "Hume on 'Is' and 'Ought.'" *Philosophical Review* 68, pp. 451–468. Cited to reprinted version in *Self-Images*, pp. 109–124.

1959b. "Notes from the Moral Wilderness II." *New Reasoner* 8, pp. 89–98. Cited to reprinted version in *MacIntyre Reader*, pp. 41–49.

1960. "Purpose and Intelligent Action." *Proceedings of the Aristotelian Society* 34 (supp.), pp. 79–96.

1962. "A Note about Causality in the Social Sciences." In Laslett and Runciman 1962, pp. 48–70.

1965a. "Imperatives, Reasons for Action, and Morals." *Journal of Philosophy* 62, pp. 513–523. Cited to reprinted version in *Self-Images*, pp. 125–135.

1965b. "Pleasure as a Reason for Action." *Monist* 49, pp. 215–233. Cited to reprinted version in *Self-Images*, pp. 173–190.

1965c. "Weber at His Weakest." *Encounter* 25, pp. 27–37.

1966a. "The Antecedents of Action." In Williams and Montefiore 1966, pp. 205–225. Cited to reprinted version in *Self-Images*, pp. 191–210.

1966b. "Recent Political Philosophy." In Thompson 1966, pp. 189–200.

1967a. "The Idea of a Social Science." *Proceedings of the Aristotelian Society* 41 (supp.), pp. 95–114. Cited to reprinted version in *Self-Images*, pp. 211–229.

1967b. Review of Rudner 1966. *British Journal for the Philosophy of Science* 18, pp. 344–345.

1967c. Review of Lévi-Strauss 1966. *Philosophical Quarterly* 17, pp. 559–561.

1968. "Son of Ideology" (review of Lichtheim 1967). *New York Review of Books* 10 (9), pp. 26–28.

1969. Review of Brodbeck 1968. *British Journal for the Philosophy of Science* 20, pp. 174–175.

1970. "Is Understanding Religion Compatible with Believing?" In Wilson 1970, pp. 62–77.

1971a. "Emotion, Behavior, and Belief." In *Self-Images*, pp. 230–243.

1971b. "The End of Ideology and the End of the End of Ideology." In *Self-Images*, pp. 3–11.

1971c. "Is a Science of Comparative Politics Possible?" In *Self-Images*, pp. 260–279.

1971d. "Ought." In *Self-Images*, pp. 136–156.

1971e. "Rationality and the Explanation of Action." In *Self-Images*, pp. 244–259.

1971f. "Some More about 'Ought'." In *Self-Images*, pp. 157–172.

1972a. "Hegel on Faces and Skulls." In *Hegel*, pp. 219–236.

1972b. "Justice: A New Theory and Some Old Questions" (review of Rawls 1971). *Boston University Law Review* 52, pp. 330–334.

1972c. "Praxis and Action." (Review of Bernstein 1972.) *Review of Metaphysics* 25, pp. 737–744.

1973a. "The Essential Contestability of Some Social Concepts." *Ethics* 84, pp. 1–9.

1973b. "Ideology, Social Science, and Revolution." *Comparative Politics* 5, pp. 321–342.

1974. "Durkheim's Call to Order" (review of Lukes 1973). *New York Review of Books* 7, pp. 25–26.

1975. "Toward a Theory of Medical Fallibility" (with Samuel Gorowitz). *Hastings Center Report* 5, pp 13–23.

1976. "Causality and History." In Manninen and Tuomela 1976, pp. 137–158.

1977a. "Epistemological Crises, Dramatic Narrative, and the Philosophy of Science." *Monist* 60, pp. 453–472.

1977b. "Utilitarianism and the Presuppositions of Cost-Benefit Analysis." In Sayre 1977, pp. 217–237.

1978a. "Behaviorism: Philosophical Analysis." In Reich 1978, pp. 110–115.

1978b. "Objectivity in Morality and Objectivity in Science." In Englehardt and Callahan 1978, pp. 21–39.

1978c. "What Has Ethics to Learn from Medical Ethics?" *Annual Proceedings of the Center for Philosophic Exchange* 2, pp. 37–47.

1978d. Review of Gellner 1974. *British Journal for the Philosophy of Science* 29, pp. 105–110.

1979a. Review of Benn and Mortimore 1976. *American Journal of Sociology* 85, pp. 217–219.

1979b. Review of Berlin 1979. *New Republic* 9, pp. 113–114.

1979c. Review of Sills 1979. *New York Review of Books* 27, pp. 14–16.

1981. "The Nature of the Virtues: From Homer to Benjamin Franklin." *Hastings Center Report* 11, pp. 27–34.

1982a. "How Moral Agents Became Ghosts: Or, Why the History of Ethics Divided from That of the Philosophy of Mind." *Synthese* 53, pp. 295–312.

1982b. "Philosophy and Its History." *Analyse und Kritik* 4, pp. 102–113.

1983a. "The Indispensability of Political Theory." In Miller and Siedentop 1983, pp. 17–33.

1983b. "The Magic in the Pronoun 'My'" (review of Williams 1981). *Ethics* 94, pp. 113–125.

1983c. "Moral Philosophy: What Next?" In *Revisions*, pp. 1–15.

1983d. "Moral Rationality, Tradition, and Authority: A Response to O'Neill, Gaita, and Clark." *Inquiry* 26, pp. 447–466.

1983e. "Philosophy of Politics." In Capps 1983, pp. 131–161.

1984a. "*After Virtue* and Marxism: A Response to Wartofsky." *Inquiry* 27, pp. 251–254.

1984b. "Bernstein's Distorting Mirrors." *Soundings* 67, pp. 30–41.

1984c. "The Claims of *After Virtue*." *Analyse und Kritik* 6, pp. 498–513.

1984d. "Does Applied Ethics Rest on a Mistake?" *Monist* 67, pp. 498–513.

1984e. "Is Patriotism a Virtue?" Lindley Lecture at the University of Kansas. Cited to reprinted version in Beiner 1995, pp. 209–228.

1984f. "The Relationship of Philosophy to Its Past." In Rorty, Schneewind, and Skinner 1984, pp. 31–48.

1985. "Relativism, Power, and Philosophy." *Proceedings and Addresses of the American Philosophical Association*, pp. 5–22.

1986a. "The Intelligibility of Action." In Margolis, Krausz, and Burian 1986, pp. 63–80.

1986b. "Positivism, Sociology, and Practical Reason: Notes on Durkheim's *Suicide*." In Perovich and Wedlin 1986, pp. 87–104.

1986c. "Which God Ought We to Obey, and Why?" *Faith and Philosophy* 3, pp. 359–371.

1987a. "Can One Be Unintelligible to Oneself?" In McKnight and Stchedroff 1987, pp. 23–37.

1987b. "Practical Rationalities as Forms of Social Structure." *Irish Journal of Philosophy* 4, pp. 3–19. Cited to reprinted version in *MacIntyre Reader*, pp. 120–135.

1988a. "The Objectivity of Good." Mackay Memorial Lecture. St. Lawrence University.

1988b. "Poetry as Political Philosophy: Notes on Burke and Yeats." In Bell and Lerner 1988, pp. 145–157.

1988c. "*Sophrosune*: How a Virtue Can Become Socially Disruptive." *Midwest Studies in Philosophy* 13, pp. 1–11.

1990a. "The Form of the Good, Tradition, and Enquiry." In Gaita 1990, pp. 242–262.

1990b. "Individual and Social Morality in Japan and in the United States: Rival Conceptions of the Self." *Philosophy East and West* 40, pp. 489–497.

1990c. "Moral Dilemmas." *Philosophy and Phenomenological Research* 50 (supp.), pp. 367–382.

1990d. "The Privatization of Good."*Review of Politics* 52, pp. 344–361.

1990e. "Rejoinder to my Critics, Especially Solomon." *Review of Politics* 52, pp. 375–377.

1991a. "An Interview with Alasdair MacIntyre." *Cogito* 5, pp. 67–73. Cited to reprinted version in *MacIntyre Reader*, pp. 267–275.

1991b. "I'm not a Communitarian, But . . ." *The Responsive Community* 1, pp. 91–92.

1991c. "Incommensurability, Truth, and the Conversation between Confucians and Aristotelians about the Virtues." In Deutsch 1991, pp. 104–122.

1991d. "Nietzsche or Aristotle?" In Borradori 1994, pp. 137–152. Cited to reprinted version in *MacIntyre Reader*, pp. 255–266.

1992a. "Colors, Cultures, and Practices." *Midwest Studies in Philosophy* 17, pp. 1–23.

1992b. "Plain Persons and Moral Philosophy: Rules, Virtues, and Goods." *American Catholic Philosophical Quarterly* 66, pp. 3–19.

1992c. "What Has Not Happened in Moral Philosophy." *Yale Journal of Criticism* 5, pp. 193–199.

1994a. "How Can We Learn What *Veritatis Splendor* Has to Teach?" *Thomist* 58, pp. 171–195.

1994b. "*Kinesis* Interview with Professor Alasdair MacIntyre." *Kinesis* 20, pp. 34–47.

1994c. "Moral Relativism, Truth, and Justification." In Gormally 1994, pp. 6–24.

1994d. "Moral Theory Put to the Question." American Philosophical Association Symposium paper.

1994e. "My Station and Its Virtues." *Journal of Philosophical Research* 19, pp. 1–8.

1994f. "A Partial Response to My Critics." In Horton and Mendus 1994, pp. 283–304.

1994g. "The *Theses on Feuerbach*: A Road Not Taken." In Gould and Cohen 1994, pp. 277–290. Cited to reprinted version in *MacIntyre Reader*, pp. 223–234.

1995a. "The Spectre of Communitarianism." *Radical Philosophy* 70, pp. 34–35.

1995b. "Truthfulness, Lies, and Moral Philosophers: What Can We Learn from Mill and Kant?" In Peterson 1995, pp. 307–361.

1995c. Review of Elster 1993. *Ethics* 105, pp. 183–185.

1996a. "Natural Law as Subversive: The Case of Aquinas." *Journal of Medieval and Early Modern Studies* 26, pp. 61–83.

1997a. "Natural Law Reconsidered" (review of Lisska 1996). *International Philosophical Quarterly* 37, pp. 95–99.

1997b. "Politica, Filosofia, e Bene Commune." *Studi Perugini* 3, pp. 9–30. Cited to the English translation "Philosophy, Politics, and the Common Good" in *MacIntyre Reader*, pp. 235–252.

1998a. "Aquinas's Critique of Education: Against His Own Age, Against Ours." In Rorty 1998, pp. 95–108.

1998b. "What Can Moral Philosophers Learn from the Study of the Brain?" (review of Churchland 1995). *Philosophy and Phenomenological Research* 58, pp. 865–869.

1999a. "John Case: An Example of Aristotelianism's Self-Subversion." In O'Callaghan and Hibbs 1999, pp. 71–82.

1999b. "Moral Pluralism without Moral Relativism." In Brinkmann 1999, pp. 1–8.

1999c. "Social Structures and their Threat to Moral Agency." *Philosophy* 74, pp. 311–329.

1999c. "Toleration and the Goods of Conflict." In Mendus 1999, pp. 133–155.

2000. "Theories of Natural Law in the Cultures of Advanced Modernity." In McLean 2000, pp. 91–115.

2001. "Once More on Kierkegaard." In Davenport and Rudd 2001, pp. 339–355.

3. Works on MacIntyre

Allen, A. 1997. "MacIntyre's Traditionalism." *Journal of Value Inquiry* 31, pp. 511–525.

Almond, Brenda. 1990. "Alasdair MacIntyre: The Virtue of Tradition." *Journal of Applied Philosophy* 7, pp. 99–103.

Annas, Julia. 1989. "MacIntyre on Traditions." *Philosophy and Public Affairs* 18, pp. 388–404.

Baier, Annette C. 1991. "MacIntyre on Hume." *Philosophy and Phenomenological Research* 50, pp. 159–163.

Bakhurst, David. 2000. "Ethical Particularism in Context." In Hooker and Little 2000, pp. 157–177.

Beam, Craig Allen. 1998. "Gadamer and MacIntyre: Tradition as a Resource of Rationality." *Kinesis* 25, pp. 15–35.

Bellantoni, Lisa. 2000. *Moral Progress: A Process Critique of MacIntyre*. State University of New York Press.

Benn, S. I. 1984. "Persons and Values: Reasons in Conflict and Moral Disagreement." *Ethics* 95, pp. 20–37.

Bernstein, Richard. 1984. "Nietzsche or Aristotle?" Reflections on Alasdair MacIntyre's *After Virtue*." *Soundings* 67, pp. 6–29.

Bloechl, Jeffrey. 1997. "The Virtue of History: Alasdair MacIntyre and the Rationality of Narrative." *Philosophy and Social Criticism* 24, pp. 43–61.

Bond, E. J. 1990. "Could There Be a Rationally Grounded Morality?" *Journal of Philosophical Research* 15, pp. 15–45.

Bradley, James. 1990. "Alasdair MacIntyre on the Good Life and the 'Narrative Model.'" *Heythrop Journal* 31, pp. 324–326.

Bradley, M. C. 1959. "A Note on Mr. MacIntyre's 'Determinism.'" *Mind* 68, pp. 521–526.

Burchell, David. 1998. "Civic Personae: MacIntyre, Cicero and Moral Personality." *History of Political Thought* 19, pp. 101–118.

Chapman, Mark D. 1998. "Why the Enlightenment Project Doesn't Have to Fail." *Heythrop Journal* 39, pp. 379–393.

Clark, Stephen R. L. 1983. "Morals, Moore, and MacIntyre." *Inquiry* 26, pp. 425–445.

Cochran, Clarke E. 1988. "The Thin Theory of Community: The Communitarians and Their Critics." *Political Studies* 37, pp. 422–435.

Cohen, Andrew Jason. 1999. "In Defense of Nietzschean Genealogy." *Philosophical Forum* 30, pp. 269–288.

Cohen, Andrew Jason. 2000. "Does Communitarianism Require Individual Independence?" *Journal of Ethics* 4, pp. 283–305.

Coleman, Janet. 1994. "MacIntyre and Aquinas." In Horton and Mendus 1994, pp. 65–90.

Curthoys, Jean. 1997. "Thomas Hobbes, the Taylor Thesis and Alasdair MacIntyre." *British Journal for the History of Philosophy* 6, pp. 1–24.

Davenport, John J., and Anthony Rudd, eds. 2001. *Kierkegaard after MacIntyre: Essays on Freedom, Narrative, and Virtue*. Open Court.

Davenport, John. 2001. "Towards an Existential Virtue Ethics: Kierkegaard and MacIntyre." In Davenport and Rudd 2001, pp. 265–323.

Diamond, Cora. 1988. "Losing Your Concepts." *Ethics* 98, pp. 255–277.

Dombrowski, Daniel. 1992. "On Why Patriotism Is Not A Virtue." *International Journal of Applied Philosophy* 7, pp. 1–4.

Doody, John A. 1984. "Recent Reconstructions of Political Philosophy." *Philosophy Today* 28, pp. 215–228.

Doody, John A. 1991. "MacIntyre and Habermas on the Practical Reason." *American Catholic Philosophical Quarterly* 65, pp. 143–158.

Duffy, James. 1999. "Insights into and in the History of Philosophy." *American Catholic Philosophical Quarterly* 73 (supp.), pp. 109–124.

Dworkin, Gerald. 1981. "Ethics, Foundations, and Science: Response to Alasdair MacIntyre." In Callahan and Engelhardt 1981, pp. 21–28.

Dworkin, Gerald. 1982. "Comments on MacIntyre's 'How Moral Agents Became Ghosts.'" *Synthese* 53, pp. 313–318.

Elie, Paul. 1998. "A Rebel in Defense of Tradition: The Incommensurable Lives of Alasdair MacIntyre." *Lingua Franca* 6, pp. 55–64.

Flett, John. 1999–2000. "Alasdair MacIntyre's Tradition-Constituted Enquiry in Polanyian Perspective." *Tradition & Discovery* 26, pp. 6–20.

Flew, A. G. N. 1969. "Determinism and Rational Behaviour." *Mind* 68, pp. 377–382.

Fowl, Stephen E. 1991. "Could Horace Talk with the Hebrews? Translatability and Moral Disagreement in MacIntyre and Stout." *Journal of Religious Ethics* 19, pp. 1–20.

Frankena, William K. 1958. "MacIntyre on Defining Morality." *Philosophy* 33, pp. 158–161.

Frankfurt, Harry. 1982. "Comments on MacIntyre's 'How Moral Agents Became Ghosts.'" *Synthese* 53, pp. 319–321.

Frazer, Elizabeth, and Nicola Lacey. 1994. "MacIntyre, Feminism and the Concept of Practice." In Horton and Mendus 1994, pp. 265–282.

Gaita, Raymond. 1983. "Virtues, Human Good, and the Unity of a Life." *Inquiry* 26, pp. 407–424.

George, Robert P. 1989. "Moral Particularism, Thomism, and Traditions." *Review of Metaphysics* 42, pp. 593–605.

Gill, Emily. 1992. "MacIntyre, Rationality, and the Liberal Tradition." *Polity* 24, pp. 433–457.

Graham, Gordon. 1994. "MacIntyre's Fusion of History and Philosophy." In Horton and Mendus 1994, pp. 161–175.

Grene, Marjorie. 1978. "Response to MacIntyre." In Engelhardt and Callahan 1978, pp. 41–47.

Gutmann, Amy. 1985. "Communitarian Critics of Liberalism." *Philosophy and Public Affairs* 14, pp. 308–322.

Gutting, Gary. 1999. *Pragmatic Liberalism and the Critique of Modernity*. Cambridge University Press.

Haldane, John. 1994. "MacIntyre's Thomistic Revival: What Next?" In Horton and Mendus 1994, pp. 91–107.

Haldane, John. 2001. Review of *Dependent Rational Animals*. *Mind* 110, pp. 225–228.

Herdt, Jennifer A. 1998. "Alasdair MacIntyre's 'Rationality of Traditions' and Tradition-Transcendental Standards of Justification." *Journal of Religion* 78, pp. 524–546.

Hibbes, Thomas S. 1991. "MacIntyre, Tradition, and the Christian Philosopher." *Modern Schoolman* 68, pp. 211–223.

Hibbs, Thomas. 1993. "MacIntyre's Postmodern Thomism." *Thomist* 57, pp. 277–297.

Hill, R. Kevin. 1992. "MacIntyre's Nietzsche: A Critique." *International Studies in Philosophy* 24, pp. 3–12.

Hinchman, Lewis P. 1989. "Virtue of Autonomy: Alasdair MacIntyre's Critique of Liberal Individualism." *Polity* 21, pp. 635–654.

Hittinger, Russell. 1989. "After MacIntyre: Natural Law Theory, Virtue Ethics, and Eudaimonia." *International Philosophical Quarterly* 29, pp. 449–461.

Horton, John, and Susan Mendus, eds. 1994. *After MacIntyre: Critical Perspectives on the Work of Alasdair MacIntyre*. University of Notre Dame Press.

Irwin, T. H. 1989. "Tradition and Reason in the History of Ethics." *Social Philosophy and Policy* 7, pp. 45–68.

Jones, L. Gregory. 1987. "Alasdair MacIntyre on Narrative, Community, and the Moral Life." *Modern Theology* 4, pp. 53–69.

Kallenberg, Brad J. 1997a. "The Master Argument of MacIntyre's *After Virtue*." In Murphy, Kallenberg, and Nation 1997, pp. 7–29.

Kallenberg, Brad J. 1997b. "Positioning MacIntyre within Christian Ethics." In Murphy, Kallenberg, and Nation 1997, pp. 45–84.

Kelly, Michael. 1990. "MacIntyre, Habermas, and Philosophical Ethics." *Philosophical Forum* 21, pp. 70–93.

Kenner, Lionel. 1964. "Causality, Determinism, and Freedom of the Will." *Philosophy* 39, pp. 233–248.

Kent, Bonnie. 1994. "Moral Provincialism." *Religious Studies* 30, pp. 269–285.

Kerr, Fergus. 1995. "Moral Theology after MacIntyre: Modern Ethics, Tragedy, and Thomism." *Studies in Christian Ethics* 8, pp. 33–44.

Kitchen, Gary. 1997. "Alasdair MacIntyre: The Epitaph of Modernity." *Philosophy and Social Criticism* 23, pp. 71–98.

Knight, Kelvin. 1996. "Revolutionary Aristotelianism." In Hampsher-Monk and Stanyer 1996, pp. 885–896.

Knight, Kelvin. 1998. "Introduction." In *MacIntyre Reader*, pp. 1–27.

Lee, Seung Hwan. 1992. "Was There a Concept of Rights in Confucian Virtue-Based Morality?" *Journal of Chinese Philosophy* 19, pp. 241–261.

Lemos, John. 1997. "Virtue, Happiness, and Intelligibility." *Journal of Philosophical Research* 22, pp. 307–320.

Lemos, John. 2000. "The Problems with Emotivism: Reflections on Some MacIntyrean Arguments." *Journal of Philosophical Research* 25, pp. 285–309.

Levy, Neil. 1999. "Stepping into the Present: MacIntyre's Modernity." *Social Theory and Practice* 25, pp. 471–490.

Long, A. A. 1983. "Greek Ethics after MacIntyre and the Stoic Community of Reason." *Ancient Philosophy* 3, pp. 184–199.

Loughran, Thomas. 1994. "Freedom and Good in the Thomistic Tradition." *Faith and Philosophy* 11, pp. 414–436.

Lucas, George R. 1988. "Agency After Virtue." *International Philosophical Quarterly* 28, pp. 293–311.

MacLean, Anne. 1984. "What Morality Is." *Philosophy* 59, pp. 21–38.

MacNiven, Don. 1996. "Bradley and MacIntyre: A Comparison." In Bradley 1996, pp. 349–365.

Madigan, Arthur. 1983. "Plato, Aristotle, and Professor MacIntyre." *Ancient Philosophy* 3, pp. 171–183.

Margolis, Joseph. 1965. "Moral Utterances and Imperatives." *Journal of Philosophy* 62, pp. 525–527.

Markham, Ian. 1991. "Faith and Reason: Reflections on MacIntyre's 'Tradition-Constituted Enquiry.'" *Religious Studies* 27, pp. 259–267.

Martin, Michael. 1964. "The Explanatory Value of the Unconscious." *Philosophy of Science* 31, pp. 122–132.

Mason, Andrew. 1994. "MacIntyre on Liberalism and Its Critics: Tradition, Incommensurability and Disagreement." In Horton and Mendus 1994, pp. 225–244.

Mason, Andrew. 1996. "MacIntyre on Modernity and How It Has Marginalized the Virtues." In Crisp 1996, pp. 191–209.

McMylor, Peter. 1994. *Alasdair MacIntyre: Critic of Modernity*. Routledge.

McMylor, Peter. 2001. "Classical Thinking for a Postmodern World: Alasdair MacIntyre and the Moral Critique of the Present." In Flanagan and Jupp 2001, pp. 21–34.

Meagher, Sharon. 1990. "Histories, Herstories, and Moral Traditions." *Social Theory and Practice* 16, pp. 61–84.

Meilaender, Gilbert. 1999. "Still Waiting for Benedict." *First Things* 96, pp. 48–55.

Miller, David. 1990. "In What Sense Must Socialism Be Communitarian?" *Social Philosophy and Policy* 6, pp. 51–73.

Miller, David. 1994. "Virtues, Practices and Justice." In Horton and Mendus 1994, pp. 245–264.

Morrison, Paul G. 1972. "Do Social Events Defy Scientific Prediction?" *Philosophic Exchange* 1, pp. 23–31.

Mouw, Richard J. 1985. "Alasdair MacIntyre on Reformation Ethics." *Journal of Religious Ethics* 13, pp. 243–257.

Mulhall, Stephen, and Adam Swift. 1992. *Liberals and Communitarians*. Blackwell.

Mulhall, Stephen. 1994. "Liberalism, Morality and Rationality: MacIntyre, Rawls and Cavell." In Horton and Mendus 1994, pp. 205–224.

Murphy, James Bernard. 1997. "Virtue and the Good of Friendship." *American Catholic Philosophical Quarterly* 71 (supplement), pp. 189–201.

Murphy, Nancey C., Brad J. Kallenberg, and Mark Thiessen Nation, eds. 1997. *Virtues and Practices in the Christian Tradition: Christian Ethics After MacIntyre*. Trinity Press International.

Murphy, Nancey. 1995. "Postmodern Non-Relativism: Imre Lakatos, Theo Meyering, and Alasdair MacIntyre." *Philosophical Forum* 27, pp. 37–53.

Nagel, Thomas. 1995b. "MacIntyre versus the Enlightenment." In Nagel 1995a, pp. 203–209.

Nathanson, Stephen. 1989. "In Defense of 'Moderate Patriotism.'" *Ethics* 99, pp. 535–552.

Nino, Carlos S. 1989. "Communitarian Challenges to Liberal Rights." *Law and Philosophy* 8, pp. 37–52.

Nowell-Smith, P. H. 1960. "Purpose and Intelligent Action II." *Proceedings of the Aristotelian Society* 34 (supp.), pp. 97–112.

Nussbaum, Martha. 1989. "Recoiling from Reason." *New York Review of Books* 36 (19), pp. 36–42.

O'Neill, Onora. 1983. "Kant After Virtue." *Inquiry* 26, pp. 387–405.

Paul, Jeffrey, and Fred D. Miller, Jr. 1990. "Communitarian and Liberal Theories of the Good." *Review of Metaphysics* 43, pp. 803–830.

Pence, Gregory E. 1984. "Recent Work on the Virtues." *American Philosophical Quarterly* 21, pp. 281–298.

Pettit, Philip. 1994. "Liberal/Communitarian: MacIntyre's Mesmeric Dichotomy." In Horton and Mendus 1994, pp. 176–204.

Porter, Jean. 1993. "Openness and Constraint: Moral Reflection as Tradition-Guided Inquiry in Alasdair MacIntyre's Recent Works." *Journal of Religion* 73, pp. 514–536.

Quinn, Philip L. 1997. "Religious Ethics after *Ethics after Babel*: MacIntyre's Tradition versus Stout's Bricolage." In Davis 1997, pp. 151–172.

Reames, Kent. 1998. "Metaphysics, History, and Moral Philosophy: The Centrality of the 1990 Aquinas Lecture to MacIntyre's Argument for Thomism." *Thomist* 62, pp. 419–443.

Rice, Eugene. 2001. "Combatting Ethical Relativism: MacIntyre's Use of Coherence and Progress." *American Catholic Philosophical Quarterly* 75, pp. 61–82.

Roque, Alicia Juarrero. 1992. "Language Competence and Tradition-Constituted Rationality." *Philosophy and Phenomenological Research* 51, pp. 611–617.

Rudd, Anthony. 2001. "Reason in Ethics: MacIntyre and Kierkegaard." In Davenport and Rudd 2001, pp. 131–150.

Schneewind, J. B. 1982. "Virtue, Narrative, and Community." *Journal of Philosophy* 79, pp. 653–663.

Schneewind, J. B. 1983. "Moral Crisis and the History of Ethics." *Midwest Studies in Philosophy* 8, pp. 525–542.

Schneewind, J. B. 1991. "MacIntyre and the Indispensability of Tradition." *Philosophy and Phenomenological Research* 50, pp. 165–168.

Schwayder, D. S. 1965. "The Moral Inconsequence of Injunction." *Journal of Philosophy* 62, pp. 524–525.

Shanley, Brian. 1999. "Aquinas on Pagan Virtue." *Thomist* 63, pp. 553–577.

Shrader-Frechette, Kristin. 2001. "MacIntyre on Human Rights." *Modern Schoolman* 79, pp. 1–22.

Simmons, Lance. 1997. "On Not Destroying the Health of One's Patients." In Oderberg 1997, pp. 144–160.

Solomon, W. David. 1990. "Comment on MacIntyre." *Review of Politics* 52, pp. 369–374.

Stackhouse, Max L. 1992. "Alasdair MacIntyre: An Overview and Evaluation." *Religious Studies Review* 18, pp. 203–208.

Starrett, Shari N. 1992. "Nietzsche and MacIntyre: Against Individualism." *International Studies in Philosophy* 24, pp. 13–20.

Stern, Robert. 1994. "MacIntyre and Historicism." In Horton and Mendus 1994, pp. 146–160.

Stout, Jeffrey. 1986. "Liberal Society and the Languages of Morals." *Soundings* 69, pp. 32–59.

Stout, Jeffrey. 1988. *Ethics After Babel: The Languages of Morals and Their Discontents*. Beacon.

Taylor, Charles. 1972. "A Response to MacIntyre's 'Predictability and Explanation in the Social Sciences.'" *Philosophic Exchange* 1, pp. 15–20.

Taylor, Charles. 1994. "Justice After Virtue." In Horton and Mendus 1994, pp. 16–43.

Thomas, Alan. n.d. "Alasdair MacIntyre." *Routledge Encyclopedia of Philosophy*. ⟨www.rep.routledge.com/philosophy⟩

Thompson, Christopher J. 1995. "Benedict, Thomas, or Augustine? The Character of MacIntyre's Narrative." *Thomist* 59, pp. 379–407.

Wallace, Deborah. "Jacques Maritain and Alasdair MacIntyre: The Person, the Common Good and Human Rights." In Sweetman 1999, pp. 127–140.

Wallach, John R. 1987. "Liberals, Communitarians, and the Tasks of Political Theory." *Political Theory* 15, pp. 581–611.

Wartofsky, Marx. 1984. "Virtue Lost or Understanding MacIntyre." *Inquiry* 27, pp. 235–250.

Winch, Peter. 1964. "Understanding a Primitive Society." *American Philosophical Quarterly* 1, pp. 307–324.

Winch, Peter. 1992. Review of *Whose Justice? Which Rationality? Philosophical Investigations* 15, pp. 285–290.

Wokler, Robert. 1994. "Projecting the Enlightenment." In Horton and Mendus 1994, pp. 108–126.

Yolton, John. 1985. "Some Remarks on the Historiography of Philosophy." *Journal of the History of Philosophy* 23, pp. 571–578.

4. Other Works Cited

Adams, Robert M. 1999. *Finite and Infinite Goods*. Oxford University Press.

Anscombe, G. E. M. 1957 [2000]. *Intention*. Harvard University Press.

Anscombe, G. E. M. 1958. "Modern Moral Philosophy." *Philosophy* 33, pp. 1–19.

Ayer, A. J. 1936. *Language, Truth, and Logic*. V. Gollancz.

Beiner, Ronald, ed. 1995. *Theorizing Citizenship*. State University of New York Press.

Bell, Vereen, and Laurence Lerner, eds. 1988. *On Modern Poetry: Essays Presented to Donald Davie*. Vanderbilt University Press.

Bellah, Robert, et al. 1985. *Habits of the Heart: Individualism and Commitment in American Life*. University of California Press.

Benn, S. I. and G. W. Mortimore. 1976. *Rationality and the Social Sciences: Contributions to the Philosophy and Methodology of the Social Sciences*. Routledge and Kegan Paul.

Berlin, Isaiah. 1979. *Concepts and Categories*, ed. Henry Hardy. Viking.

Bernstein, Eduard. 1899 [1993]. *The Preconditions of Socialism*, trans. Henry Tudor. Cambridge University Press.

Bernstein, Richard. 1972. *Praxis and Action*. Duckworth.

Borradori, Giovanna, ed. 1994. *The American Philosopher: Conversations with Quine, Davidson, Putnam, Nozick, Danto, Cavell, MacIntyre, and Kuhn*. University of Chicago Press.

Bradley, James, ed. 1996. *Philosophy after F. H. Bradley*. Thoemmes.

Brinkmann, Klaus, ed. 1999. *Proceedings of the Twentieth World Congress of Philosophy*. Vol. 1. Philosophy Documentation Center.

Brodbeck, May, ed. 1968. *Readings in the Philosophy of the Social Sciences*. MacMillan.

Burns, J. H., ed. 1988.*Cambridge History of Medieval Political Thought: c. 350–c. 1450*. Cambridge University Press.

Burrell, David. 2000. *Friendship and the Ways to Truth*. University of Notre Dame Press.

Caenegem, R. C. van. 1988. "Government, Law, and Society." In Burns 1988, pp. 174–210.

Callahan, Daniel, and H. Tristram Engelhardt, Jr., eds. 1981. *The Roots of Ethics: Science, Religion, and Values*. Plenum Press.

Capps, J. L., ed. 1983. *Philosophy and Human Enterprise*. United States Military Academy.

Chun, Lin. 1993. *The British New Left*. Edinburgh University Press.

Churchland, Paul. 1995. *The Engine of Reason, the Seat of the Soul: A Philosophical Journey into the Brain*. MIT Press.

Clanchy, M. T. 1997. *Abelard: A Medieval Life*. Blackwell.

Collingwood, R. G. 1939. *An Autobiography*. Oxford University Press.

Congar, Yves. 1982. "A Brief History of the Forms of the Magisterium and Its Relations with Scholars." In Curran and McCormick 1982, pp. 314–331.

Constable, Giles. 1996. *The Reformation of the Twelfth Century*. Cambridge University Press.

Cowling, Maurice. 1980. *Religion and Public Doctrine in Modern England*. Cambridge University Press.

Crisp, Roger, ed. 1996. *How Should One Live? Essays on the Virtues*. Oxford University Press.

Curran, Charles, and Richard McCormick, eds. 1982. *Readings in Moral Theology No. 3: The Magisterium and Morality*. Paulist Press.

Davidson, Donald. 1974. "On the Very Idea of a Conceptual Scheme." *Proceedings and Addresses of the American Philosophical Association*. Reprinted in Davidson 1984, pp. 183–198.

Davidson, Donald. 1984. *Inquiries into Truth and Interpretation*. Oxford University Press.

Davis, Stephen L., ed. 1997. *Philosophy and Theological Discourse*. MacMillan.

Dawson, Christopher. 1932 [1952]. *The Making of Europe: An Introduction to the History of European Unity*. Sheed and Ward.

Deutsch, Eliot, ed. 1991. *Culture and Modernity: East-West Perspectives*. University of Hawaii Press.

Douglas, Mary. 1966. *Purity and Danger: An Analysis of Concepts of Pollution and Taboo*. Praeger.

Dworkin, Ronald. 1978. "Liberalism." In Hampshire 1978, pp. 113–143.

Eliot, T. S. 1949. *Christianity and Culture: The Idea of a Christian Society and Notes toward the Definition of Culture*. Harcourt Brace.

Elster, John. 1993. *Political Psychology*. Cambridge University Press.

Englehardt, Tristram, and Daniel Callahan, eds. 1978. *Morals, Science, and Society*. Hastings Center.

Evans-Pritchard, E. E. 1937. *Witchcraft, Oracles, and Magic among the Azande*. Oxford University Press.

Feigl, Herbert, and Grover Maxwell, eds. 1962. *Scientific Explanation, Space, and Time*. Minnesota Studies in the Philosophy of Science 3. University of Minnesota Press.

Feyerabend, Paul. 1962. "Explanation, Reduction, and Empiricism." In Feigl and Maxwell 1962, pp. 28–97.

Finnis, John. 1980. *Natural Law and Natural Rights*. Oxford University Press.

Flanagan, Kieran, and Peter C. Jupp. 2001. *Virtue Ethics and Sociology: Issues of Modernity and Religion*. Palgrave.

Foucault, Michel. 1973. *The Order of Things*. Vintage Books.

Fukuyama, Francis. 1992. *The End of History and the Last Man*. Free Press.

Fuller, Steve. 2000. *Thomas Kuhn: A Philosophical History for Our Times*. University of Chicago Press.

Gaita, Raymond, ed. 1990. *Value and Understanding: Essays for Peter Winch*. Routledge.

Garcia, J. L. A. 1997. "Interpersonal Virtues: Whose Good Do They Serve?" *American Catholic Philosophical Quarterly* 71, pp. 31–60.

Gellner, Ernest. 1974. *The Legitimation of Belief*. Cambridge University Press.

Gormally, Luke, ed. 1994. *Moral Truth and Moral Tradition: Essays in Honour of Peter Geach and Elizabeth Anscombe*. Four Courts.

Gould, Carol C., and Robert S. Cohen, eds. 1994. *Artifacts, Representation, and Social Practice*. Kluwer.

Green, Leslie. 1990. *The Authority of the State*. Oxford University Press.

Grisez, Germain. 2001. "Natural Law, God, Religion, and Human Fulfillment." *American Journal of Jurisprudence* 46, pp. 3–36.

Hacking, Ian. 1999. *The Social Construction of What?* Harvard University Press.

Hall, Mark, and George Klosko. 1998. "Political Obligation and the United States Supreme Court." *Journal of Politics* 60, pp. 462–480.

Hampsher-Monk, I., and J. Stanyer, eds. 1996. *Contemporary Political Studies 1996*. Vol. 2. Political Studies Association of the United Kingdom.

Hampshire, Stuart. 1978. *Public and Private Morality*. Cambridge University Press.

Hart, H. L. A., 1955. "Are There Any Natural Rights?" *Philosophical Review* 64, pp. 175–191.

Hart, H. L. A., and A. M. Honoré. 1959. *Causation in the Law*. Oxford University Press.

Hegel, G. W. F. 1952. *The Philosophy of Right*. Trans. T. M. Knox. Oxford University Press.

Hegel, G. W. F. 1971a. *Werke in zwanzig Bänden*. Ed. Eva Moldenhauer and Karl Markus Michel. Suhrkamp Verlag.

Hegel, G. W. F. 1971b. *Vorlesungen über die Geschichte der Philosophie*. In Hegel 1971a, vol. 20.

Hegel, G. W. F. 1988. *Phänomenologie des Geistes*. Ed. Han Friedrich Wessels and Heinrich Clairmont. Felix Meiner Verlag.

Hook, Sidney, ed. 1964. *Law and Philosophy*. New York University Press.

Hooker, Brad, and Margaret Little, eds. 2000. *Moral Particularism*. Oxford University Press.

Hudelson, Richard. 1990. *Marxism and Philosophy in the Twentieth Century*. Praeger.

Jung, C. G. 1928. *Contributions to Analytical Psychology*. Trans. H. G. and C. F. Baynes. Harcourt, Brace.

Kautsky, Karl. 1906 [1914]. *Ethics and the Materialist Conception of History*. Trans. John Askew. Charles Kerr.

Kenny, Anthony. 1978. *Free Will and Responsibility*. Routledge and Kegan Paul.

Kent, Bonnie. 1995. *Virtues of the Will: The Transformation of Ethics in the Late Thirteenth Century*. Catholic University of America Press.

Klosko, George. 1992. *The Principle of Fairness and Political Obligation*. Rowman and Littlefield.

Kolakowski, Leszek. 1995. *God Owes Us Nothing: A Brief Remark on Pascal's Religion and on the Spirit of Jansenism*. University of Chicago Press.

Kovesi, Julius. 1967. *Moral Notions*. Routledge and Kegan Paul.

Kuhn, Thomas. 1959. "Measurement in Modern Physical Science." In Woolf 1959, pp. 31–63.

Kuhn, Thomas. 1962 [1996]. *The Structure of Scientific Revolutions*, 3rd ed. University of Chicago Press.

Laslett, Peter, and W. G. Runciman, eds. 1962. *Philosophy, Politics, and Society*. Blackwell.

Lawrence, C. H. 1994. *The Friars: The Impact of the Early Mendicant Movement on Western Society*. Longman.

Lévi-Strauss, Claude. 1966. *The Savage Mind*. University of Chicago Press.

Lichtheim, George. 1967. *The Concept of Ideology and Other Essays*. Vintage Books.

Lilla, Mark. 1998. "The Politics of Jacques Derrida." *New York Review of Books* 45 (11), pp. 36–41.

Lisska, Anthony. 1996. *Aquinas's Natural Law Theory: An Analytic Reconstruction*. Oxford University Press.

Little, Lester K. 1978. *Religious Poverty and the Profit Economy in Medieval Europe*. Cornell University Press.

Lukes, Steven. 1973. *Emile Durkheim, His Life and Work: A Historical and Critical Study*. Allen Lane.

Lukes, Steven. 2000. "Different Cultures, Different Rationalities?" *History of the Human Sciences* 13, pp. 3–18.

Manninen, Juha, and Raimo Tuomela. 1976. *Essays on Explanation and Understanding*. Reidel.

Marenbon, John. 1997. *The Philosophy of Peter Abelard*. Cambridge University Press.

Margolis, J., M. Krausz, and R. M. Burian. 1986. *Rationality, Relativism, and the Human Sciences*. Nijhoff.

Marx, Karl, and Friedrich Engels. 1968. *Selected Works in One Volume*. Lawrence and Wisheart.

McElroy, George C., Robert Vivarelli, and Alan Ryan. 2002. "Letters: 'Economic Sentiments.'" *New York Review of Books* 49 (3), pp. 86–87.

McKnight, Christopher, and Marcel Stchedroff. 1987. *Philosophy in Its Variety: Essays in Memory of Francois Bordet*. Queen's University of Belfast.

McLean, Edward B., ed. 2000. *Common Truths: New Perspectives on Natural Law*. ISI Press.

Mendus, Susan, ed. 1999. *The Politics of Toleration: Tolerance and Intolerance in Modern Life*. Edinburgh University Press.

Miller, David, and L. A. Siedentop, eds. 1983. *The Nature of Political Theory*. Oxford University Press.

Morris, Christopher S. 1998. *An Essay on the Modern State*. Cambridge University Press.

Murphy, Mark C. 2001. *Natural Law and Practical Rationality*. Cambridge University Press.

Nagel, Thomas. 1986. *The View from Nowhere*. Oxford University Press.

Nagel, Thomas. 1995a. *Other Minds*. Oxford University Press.

Nederman, Cary. 1991. "Aristotelianism and the Origins of 'Political Science' in the Twelfth Century." *Journal of the History of Ideas* 52, pp. 179–194.

Neuhouser, Frederick. 1993. "Freedom, Dependence, and the General Will." *Philosophical Review* 102, pp. 363–395.

Nozick, Robert. 1981. *Philosophical Explanations*. Harvard University Press.

O'Callaghan, John, and Thomas Hibbs. 1999. *Recovering Nature: Essays in Natural Philosophy, Ethics, and Metaphysics in Honor of Ralph McInerny*. University of Notre Dame Press.

Oakeshott, Michael. 1948. "Rationalism in Politics." Cited to reprinted version in Oakeshott 1962, pp. 1–36.

Oakeshott, Michael. 1962. *Rationalism in Politics, and Other Essays*. Basic Books.

Oderberg, David, ed. 1997. *Human Lives: Critical Essays on Consequentialist Bioethics*. MacMillan.

Olson, Charles. 1987a. *Collected Poems*. University of California Press.

Olson, Charles. 1987b. "These Days." In Olson 1987a, p. 106.

Otto, Rudolf. 1958. *Idea of the Holy: An Inquiry into the Non-Rational Factor in the Idea of the Divine and Its Relation to the Rational*. Galaxy.

Parfit, Derek. 1984. *Reasons and Persons*. Oxford University Press.

Perovich, Anthony N., and Michael V. Wedlin, eds. 1986. *Human Nature and Natural Knowledge: Essays Presented to Marjorie Grene on the Occasion of her Seventy-Fifth Birthday*. Reidel.

Peterson, Grethe, ed. 1995. *Tanner Lectures on Human Values*. Vol. 16. University of Utah Press.

Pippin, Robert. 1991. *Modernism as a Philosophical Problem: On the Dissatisfactions of European High Culture*. Blackwell.

Pippin, Robert. 2000. *Henry James and Modern Moral Life*. Cambridge University Press.

Polanyi, Michael. 1946 [1964]. *Science, Faith, and Society*. University of Chicago Press.

Polanyi, Michael. 1958. *Personal Knowledge: Towards a Post-Critical Philosophy*. University of Chicago Press.

Polanyi, Michael. 1975. *The Great Transformation*. Octagon.

Popper, Karl. 1949 [1965]. "Towards a Rational Theory of Tradition." In Popper 1965, pp. 120–135.

Popper, Karl. 1965. *Conjectures and Refutations*. Basic Books.

Quine, Willard van Orman. 1960. *Word and Object*. MIT Press.

Rawls, John. 1964. "Legal Obligation and the Duty of Fair Play." In Hook 1964, pp. 3–18.

Rawls, John. 1971. *A Theory of Justice*. Harvard University Press.

Rawls, John. 1993. *Political Liberalism*. Columbia University Press.

Raz, Joseph. 1979. *The Authority of Law*. Oxford University Press.

Raz, Joseph. 1986. *The Morality of Freedom*. Oxford University Press.

Reich, Warren T. 1978. *Encyclopedia of Bioethics*. Macmillan.

Rist, John M. 1994. *Augustine: Ancient Thought Baptized*. Cambridge University Press.

Rorty, Amelie Oksenberg, ed. 1998. *Philosophers on Education: Historical Perspectives*. Routledge.

Rorty, Richard, J. B. Schneewind, and Quentin Skinner. 1984. *Philosophy in History*. Cambridge University Press.

Rudner, Richard. 1966. *Philosophy of Social Science*. Prentice-Hall.

Ryle, Gilbert. 1949 [1993]. *Aspects of Mind*. Ed. René Meyer. Blackwell.

Sandel, Michael. 1980. *Liberalism and the Limits of Justice*. Cambridge University Press.

Sayre, Kenneth, ed. 1977. *Values in the Electric Power Industry*. University of Notre Dame Press.

Schneewind, J. B. 1998. *The Invention of Autonomy*. Cambridge University Press.

Searle, John R. 1995. *The Construction of Social Reality*. Free Press.

Sills, David, ed. 1979. *International Encyclopaedia of the Social Sciences*. Macmillan.

Simmons, A. John. 1979. *Moral Principles and Political Obligations*. Princeton University Press.

Southern, R. W. 1995. *Scholastic Humanism and the Unification of Europe*. Vol. I, *Foundations*. Blackwell.

Spruyt, Hendrik. 1994. *The Soverign State and Its Competitors*. Princeton University Press.

Steiner, Franz. 1956 [1967]. *Taboo*. Penguin.

Steiner, Franz. 1999. *Selected Writings*. Ed. Jeremy Adler and Richard Fardon. Berghahn Books.

Stevenson, Charles L. 1944. *Ethics and Language*. Yale University Press.

Sweetman, Brendan, ed. 1999. *The Failure of Modernism: The Cartesian Legacy and Contemporary Pluralism*. Catholic University of America Press.

Taylor, Charles. 1964. *The Explanation of Behavior*. Humanities Press.

Taylor, Charles. 1989. *Sources of the Self*. Harvard University Press.

Taylor, Charles. 1995a. *Philosophical Arguments*. Harvard University Press.

Taylor, Charles. 1995b. "Explanation and Practical Reason." In Taylor 1995a, pp. 34–60.

Thompson, David, ed. 1966. *Political Ideas*. Basic Books.

Thomson, Judith J. 2001. *Goodness and Advice*. Princeton University Press.

Turner, Stephen P., and Regis Factor. 1994. *Max Weber: The Lawyer as Social Thinker*. Routledge.

Waldron, Jeremy. 1987. "Theoretical Foundations of Liberalism." *Philosophical Quarterly* 37, pp. 127–150.

Waldron, Jeremy. 1993. "Special Ties and Natural Duties." *Philosophy and Public Affairs* 22, pp. 3–30.

Weber, Max. 1963. *The Sociology of Religion*. Trans. Ephraim Fischoff. Beacon Press.

Weber, Max. 1968 [1978]. *Economy and Society*. Vol. I. Ed. Gunther Roth and Claus Wittich. University of California Press.

Williams, Bernard, and Alan Montefiore, eds. 1966. *British Analytic Philosophy*. Routledge and Kegan Paul.

Williams, Bernard. 1981. *Moral Luck: Philosophical Papers 1973–1980*. Cambridge University Press.

Williams, Bernard. 1985. *Ethics and the Limits of Philosophy*. Harvard University Press.

Wilson, Bryan R., ed. 1970. *Rationality*. Harper and Row.

Winch, Peter. 1958. *The Idea of a Social Science and Its Relation to Philosophy*. Routledge and Kegan Paul.

Winch, Peter. 1964 [1970]. *Understanding a Primitive Society*. In Wilson 1970, pp. 78–111.

Winch, Peter. 1972. *Ethics and Action*. Routledge and Kegan Paul.

Woolf, Harry. 1959. *Quantification: A History of the Meaning of Measurement in the Natural and Social Sciences*. Bobbs-Merrill.

Yearly, Lee. 1990. *Mencius and Aquinas: Theories of Virtue and Conceptions of Courage*. State University of New York Press.

Index

Abelard, Peter, 63–66
Adams, Robert M., 108
After Virtue project, *see* MacIntyre, Alasdair, *After Virtue* project of
Annas, Julia, 67n2
Anscombe, G. E. M., 74, 94–95, 97, 111n4, 141
anti-theory
  MacIntyre's response to, 145–147
  as a view in normative ethics, 145
Aquinas, Thomas, 51, 57–59, 102–103, 109–110, 135, 177; *see also* Thomism
Aristotelian science, 50–52
  as related to tradition-grounded inquiry, 51
Aristotelianism, 30, 38, 44–45, 116, 138
Aristotle, 39–40, 41–42, 59, 74, 87, 135–136, 177; *see also* Aristotelianism
Augustinianism, 58–59
Austin, J. L., 108
Ayer, A. J., 117, 149n3, 149n4
Azande, 82–84
  beliefs of, as a closed system, 79–80

Barth, Karl, 76
Bellah, Robert, 143
Bernard of Clairvaux, 65–66
Bernstein, Eduard, 3–4, 5
Bernstein, Richard, 54
Blackstone, William, 25–26, 28
Broad, C. D., 94
Burke, Edmund, 112

Caenegem, R. C. van, 68–69n21
"character," MacIntyre's concept of, 150n10
Christianity, 2, 85–86, 113n12; *see also* MacIntyre, Alasdair, and Christianity
Clerke, Agnes Mary, 58
Collingwood, R. G., 10–11, 17
common good, 160–161
  contrasted with public interest, 161
communitarianism, 142, 159
Constable, Giles, 68–69n21
Cooley, Charles Horton, 91

Davidson, Donald, 49
Dawson, Christopher, 89
Descartes, Rene, 47, 111n3
Durkheim, Emile, 90

Eliot, T. S., 89–90
emotivism, 5, 15–16, 39, 132, 133–134
Engels, Friedrich, 17
Enlightenment, 43, 176–177
  project of justifying morality, 34, 96–97, 135–136, 152, 156, 177
epistemological crisis, 47–48, 87–88, 104
ethics, *see* moral philosophy
Evans-Pritchard, E. E., 83–84, 86

fact/value distinction, 99–100, 107
Feyerabend, Paul, 87–88
Finnis, John, 168, 175n5
Flett, John, 90
Flew, Antony, 9n6
Foot, Philippa, 118, 124
Foucault, Michel, 112n6
fragmentation, as feature of modern morality, 100, 107
Freud, Sigmund, 72–73
Fukuyama, Francis, 142

Gadamer, Hans-Georg, 115
Garcia, J. L. A., 107
Geach, Peter, 118, 141
Goffman, Erving, 15
Green, Leslie, 158
Grisez, Germain, 107
Gutting, Gary, 113n11, 113n13, 113n16

Haldane, John, 33–34, 98
Hall, Mark, 175n1
Hare, R. M., 118, 122, 124, 127
Hart, H. L. A., 92n5, 156, 169
Hegel, G. W. F., 24, 29, 34–35, 47, 192–193, 196, 200n8, 200n9

Heidegger, Martin, 177, 189
history of philosophy, and its relation to philosophy
  Collingwood on, 10–11
  MacIntyre on, 7, 11–37
  Marx and Engels on, 17
  Oakeshott on, 17–18
Honoré, A. M., 92n5
Hudelson, Richard, 3
Hume, David, 20, 24, 26, 28, 99, 111n5
Humeanism, 135
Husserl, Edmund, 115
Hutcheson, Francis, 20, 24

"identifications"
  as a defective form of argument, 91
  as a kind of social scientific argument, 70–71, 79
ideology, 2–3, 17, 82
  and tradition, 8n2
individualism, 14–15, 100, 107, 169–170, 181–182, 188
institutions
  political, 164
  and practices, 164
intelligibility, 41, 78, 86
intuitionism, 120, 149n6

Jacobi, F. H., 176, 177
Jung, Carl, 97
justice, 43–44, 98, 102–103, 156–158, 166–167

Kant, Immanuel, 185, 186, 190, 192; *see also* Kantianism
Kantianism, 5, 135
Kautsky, Karl, 3–4
Kenny, Anthony, 71
Kent, Bonnie, 68n19
Khruschev, Nikolai, 3, 8n3
Kierkegaard, Søren, 136, 150n15
Klosko, George, 156, 175n1
Knight, Kelvin, 2
Kolakowski, Leszek, 92n3
Kovesi, Julius, 68n16
Kuhn, Thomas, 80, 81–82, 87–88, 104, 141

Lawrence, C. H., 68–69n21
Leo XIII, 58
Lévi-Strauss, Claude, 112n6
liberalism, 43, 101–102, 114, 159
Lisska, Anthony, 168
Little, Lester K., 68–69n21
Locke, John, 15

MacIntyre, Alasdair
  After Virtue project of, 1, 7–8
  and Christianity, 102, 110, 114, 151n22
  and Marxism, 2, 3–6, 8–9n6, 101, 102
  narrative of scholarly work of, 1
Maritain, Jacques, 115
Marx, Karl, 17, 111; *see also* Marxism
Marxism, 2–7, 11n12, 79; *see also* MacIntyre, Alasdair, and Marxism
  humanistic, 3–5, 6
  scientific, 3–5, 6
McLaurin, Colin, 22
McMylor, Peter, 4
Mead, G. H., 91
Meilaender, Gilbert, 107
metaethics, 117–128
  Hare's and MacIntyre's criticisms of, 122–124
  and historical investigation, 121–122, 126–127
  MacIntyre's criticisms of contemporary, 120–128
  in MacIntyre's master's thesis, 118–120
  naturalistic, MacIntyre's criticisms of, 127
  prescriptivist, MacIntyre's criticisms of, 122–124, 127–128
  in the twentieth century, 117–118
metaphysical biology, 38, 40, 43, 138
modernity, 176
  MacIntyre's critique of, 144–145, 177–198
Moore, G. E., 95, 117
moral philosophy
  metaethical, *see* metaethics
  modern, MacIntyre's criticisms of, 96–106
  normative, *see* normative ethics
morality, as socially and historically embedded, 6–7, 11–12, 13–16, 37, 86–87, 133–134
Morris, Christopher S., 153
Murphy, Mark C., 175n5

Nagel, Thomas, 150n16, 151n21
narrative unity of a life, as related to virtues, 41–42, 139
natural law, 167–170
  and absolute precepts, 167–168
  how known, 168
  and natural rights, 169–170
  as procedural, 167
  as substantive, 167–168
natural rights, 39, 169–170
naturalism, in metaethics, *see* metaethics, naturalistic
Nederman, Cary, 56
Neuhouser, Frederick, 200n10
New Reasoner, 5, 8n4
Nietzsche, Friedrich, 27, 57, 96, 136, 137
nihilism, 176

normative ethics
anti-theory in, *see* anti-theory
MacIntyre's Aristotelianism in, 137–141
MacIntyre's contribution to, 116
MacIntyre's nonstandard views in, 130–131
standard categories in, 130
nostalgia, charge of, against MacIntyre's work, 177–178, 180–181
Nozick, Robert, 112n8, 156
Nussbaum, Martha, 112n8

Oakeshott, Michael, 17–18, 89
Olson, Charles, 110
'ought' judgments, 98–99, 123–128

paradigms, 81–82
Pareto, Wilfredo, 73
Parfit, Derek, 129, 151n21
particularity requirement, 158
patriotism, 158, 165–166
perspectivism, 45–46
Pippin, Robert, 200n8, 200n10
Polanyi, Michael, 79, 88–89, 178–179, 180
as influence on MacIntyre, 178–179
political justifications, 152–153
politics, 152–175
of local community, 160–165, 170–175
and natural law, 167–170
as a practice, 162–165
and shared culture, 165
state, 152
Popper, Karl, 81, 90
practical rationality, 182–183, 184–186, 188
practical syllogisms, 74–75
practices, 29, 90, 98, 161–164, 173–175
defined, 40–41
goods external to, 41, 162
goods internal to, 41, 161–162, 173–175
and institutions, 164
and politics, 162–164
as related to virtues, 40–41, 138–139
prescriptivism, 5, 122–128
Prichard, Henry, 95, 117, 127
proxies, 164
psychoanalysis, 2, 72–73; *see also* Freud, Sigmund
public interest, 154
account of political authority, 154–155
contrasted with common good, 161

quasi-state, 171–172

rationality, *see also* practical rationality
Enlightenment ideal of, 44
traditional ideal of, 44
Rawls, John, 35, 142, 153, 156, 175n1
Raz, Joseph, 153, 169
reasons explanation of actions, 74–75, 81–82, 84–85
and causal explanation, 71–72, 77, 92n2, 92n5
Reid, Thomas, 20
relativism, 7, 33–34, 45–46, 84, 98, 103–105, 107–108, 198
religion, philosophy of, MacIntyre's work in, 8–9n6
responsibilities, as basis for 'ought' judgments, 98, 99
rights, *see* natural rights
Rorty, Richard, 105
Ross, W. D., 95, 117
Rousseau, Jean-Jacques, 191, 200n10

Sandel, Michael, 159
Sartre, Jean Paul, 15, 121
Schelling, F. W. J., 190
Schneewind, J. B., 149n1
Scottish Enlightenment, 19–27
and role of philosophy in social order, 21–22
Searle, John R., 68n16
Simmons, A. John, 153, 158
Singer, Peter, 129
Smith, Adam, 20
social sciences, 70–91
Southern, R. W., 68–69n21
Spruyt, Hendrik, 68–69n21
Stair, Viscount, 21, 25–26
Stalinism, 3–6, 90
beliefs of, as a closed system, 79–80
state, 3
ad hoc cooperation with, 170
modern, 152–158
neutralist, 154–158
nonneutralist, 159–160
as potentially justifiable, 171–172
quasi-state, 171–172
Stein, Edith, 115
Steiner, Franz, 70, 86–87, 93n6
Stevenson, Charles, 117, 118, 127, 149n3, 150n8
Strawson, P. F., 120

taboo, 8n5, 86–87, 95
Taylor, Charles, 108, 143
teleology, 41, 103, 107, 138
Thomism, 34, 51, 57–59
Thompson, E. P., 8n4
Thomson, Judith, 113n13
Toulmin, Stephen, 118

tradition, 187–188, 193–194; *see also* tradition-grounded inquiry
and MacIntyre's theory of virtue, 39–43, 140
tradition-grounded inquiry, 24–25, 27–35, 38–69, 88–91, 189–190, 192
and Aristotelian science, 51
and authoritative practitioners, 60–66
and crafts, 60
and the encyclopaedic method, 27–28, 57
and the genealogical method, 27–28, 57, 105
and incommensurability, 53–55, 56
and moral rationality, 53–56
and perspectivism, 45–46
and relativism, 33–34, 45–46
and scientific reasoning, 88–90
and Thomism, 33–34
and truth, 46–47, 50

unconscious
Freud's characterization of the, 72
MacIntyre's characterization of the, 72–73

Vico, Giambattista, 54
virtue ethics, 40, 130–131
virtues
nature of, 40–43, 138–141
as related to narrative unity of a life, 41–42, 139
as related to practices, 40–41, 138–139
as related to tradition, 42, 140
Voltaire, 19

Waldron, Jeremy, 153, 156
Weber, Max, 74, 75–78, 92n5, 179–180
as influence on MacIntyre, 179–180
MacIntyre's criticisms of, 75–77, 92n4, 92n5
Williams, Bernard, 68n16, 111n4, 143, 145
Winch, Peter, 73–74, 79, 82–86, 88
on the idea of a social science, 73–74
Wittgenstein, Ludwig, 196
Wokler, Robert, 12, 19–20, 25